Palgrave Macmillan Studies in Banking and Financial Institutions

Series Editor: **Professor Philip Molyneux**

The Palgrave Macmillan Studies in Banking and Financial Institutions are international in orientation and include studies of banking within particular countries or regions, and studies of particular themes such as Corporate Banking, Risk Management, Mergers and Acquisitions, etc. The books' focus is on research and practice, and they include up-to-date and innovative studies on contemporary topics in banking that will have global impact and influence.

Titles include:

Yener Altunbaş, Blaise Gadanecz and Alper Kara
SYNDICATED LOANS
A Hybrid of Relationship Lending and Publicly Traded Debt

Yener Altunbaş, Alper Kara and Öslem Olgu
TURKISH BANKING
Banking under Political Instability and Chronic High Inflation

Elena Beccalli
IT AND EUROPEAN BANK PERFORMANCE

Paola Bongini, Stefano Chiarlone and Giovanni Ferri (*editors*)
EMERGING BANKING SYSTEMS

Vittorio Boscia, Alessandro Carretta and Paola Schwizer
COOPERATIVE BANKING: INNOVATIONS AND DEVELOPMENTS

Vittorio Boscia, Alessandro Carretta and Paola Schwizer
COOPERATIVE BANKING IN EUROPE: CASE STUDIES

Roberto Bottiglia, Elisabetta Gualandri and Gian Nereo Mazzocco (*editors*)
CONSOLIDATION IN THE EUROPEAN FINANCIAL INDUSTRY

Alessandro Carretta, Franco Fiordelisi and Gianluca Mattarocci (*editors*)
NEW DRIVERS OF PERFORMANCE IN A CHANGING FINANCIAL WORLD

Dimitris N. Chorafas
CAPITALISM WITHOUT CAPITAL

Dimitris N. Chorafas
FINANCIAL BOOM AND GLOOM
The Credit and Banking Crisis of 2007–2009 and Beyond

Violaine Cousin
BANKING IN CHINA

Vincenzo D'Apice and Giovanni Ferri
FINANCIAL INSTABILITY
Toolkit for Interpreting Boom and Bust Cycles

Peter Falush and Robert L. Carter OBE
THE BRITISH INSURANCE INDUSTRY SINCE 1900
The Era of Transformation

Franco Fiordelisi
MERGERS AND ACQUISITIONS IN EUROPEAN BANKING

Franco Fiordelisi and Philip Molyneux
SHAREHOLDER VALUE IN BANKING

Hans Genberg and Cho-Hoi Hui
THE BANKING CENTRE IN HONG KONG
Competition, Efficiency, Performance and Risk

Carlo Gola and Alessandro Roselli
THE UK BANKING SYSTEM AND ITS REGULATORY AND SUPERVISORY FRAMEWORK

Elisabetta Gualandri and Valeria Venturelli (*editors*)
BRIDGING THE EQUITY GAP FOR INNOVATIVE SMEs

Kim Hawtrey
AFFORDABLE HOUSING FINANCE

Otto Hieronymi (*editor*)
GLOBALIZATION AND THE REFORM OF THE INTERNATIONAL BANKING AND MONETARY SYSTEM

Munawar Iqbal and Philip Molyneux
THIRTY YEARS OF ISLAMIC BANKING
History, Performance and Prospects

Sven Janssen
BRITISH AND GERMAN BANKING STRATEGIES

Kimio Kase and Tanguy Jacopin
CEOs AS LEADERS AND STRATEGY DESIGNERS
Explaining the Success of Spanish Banks

M. Mansoor Khan and M. Ishaq Bhatti
DEVELOPMENTS IN ISLAMIC BANKING
The Case of Pakistan

Mario La Torre and Gianfranco A. Vento
MICROFINANCE

Philip Molyneux and Eleuterio Vallelado (*editors*)
FRONTIERS OF BANKS IN A GLOBAL WORLD

Anastasia Nesvetailova
FRAGILE FINANCE
Debt, Speculation and Crisis in the Age of Global Credit

Anders Ögren (*editor*)
THE SWEDISH FINANCIAL REVOLUTION

Dominique Rambure and Alec Nacamuli
PAYMENT SYSTEMS
From the Salt Mines to the Board Room

Catherine Schenk (*editor*)
HONG KONG SAR's MONETARY AND EXCHANGE RATE CHALLENGES
Historical Perspectives

Noël K. Tshiani
BUILDING CREDIBLE CENTRAL BANKS
Policy Lessons for Emerging Economies

The full list of titles available is on the website:
www.palgrave.com/finance/sbfi.asp

Palgrave Macmillan Studies in Banking and Financial Institutions
Series Standing Order ISBN 978–1–4039–4872–4

You can receive future titles in this series as they are published by placing a standing order. Please contact your bookseller or, in case of difficulty, write to us at the address below with your name and address, the title of the series and the ISBN quoted above.

Customer Services Department, Macmillan Distribution Ltd, Houndmills, Basingstoke, Hampshire RG21 6XS, England

---

Financial Instability

Toolkit for Interpreting Boom and Bust Cycles

Vincenzo D'Apice
Italian Banking Association

Giovanni Ferri
University of Bari, Italy

palgrave
macmillan

The views expressed in the book are those of the authors and do not necessarily reflect those of the Italian Banking Association.

First published 2010 by
PALGRAVE MACMILLAN

Palgrave Macmillan in the UK is an imprint of Macmillan Publishers Limited, registered in England, company number 785998, of Houndmills, Basingstoke, Hampshire RG21 6XS.

Palgrave Macmillan in the US is a division of St Martin's Press LLC, 175 Fifth Avenue, New York, NY 10010.

Palgrave Macmillan is the global academic imprint of the above companies and has companies and representatives throughout the world.

Palgrave® and Macmillan® are registered trademarks in the United States, the United Kingdom, Europe and other countries.

ISBN 978–0–230–24811–3 hardback

This book is printed on paper suitable for recycling and made from fully managed and sustained forest sources. Logging, pulping and manufacturing processes are expected to conform to the environmental regulations of the country of origin.

A catalogue record for this book is available from the British Library.

A catalog record for this book is available from the Library of Congress.

10 9 8 7 6 5 4 3 2 1
19 18 17 16 15 14 13 12 11 10

Printed and bound in Great Britain by
CPI Antony Rowe, Chippenham and Eastbourne

Life can only be understood backwards; but it must be lived forwards.

– Søren Kierkegaard (1813–55)

Contents

List of Figures ix
List of Tables xii
List of Boxes xiii
Foreword by Franklin Allen xv
Acknowledgements xix
Glossary xx

Introduction 1

Part I Understanding the Financial Crises 7

1 Theories of Financial Crises 9
  1.1 The Minsky model 9
  1.2 Management and prevention of crises 14

2 Macro Models of Financial Crises 17
  2.1 The first-generation models 17
  2.2 The second-generation models 21
  2.3 The third-generation models 22

3 Micro Models of Financial Crises 25
  3.1 Adverse selection and moral hazard 25
  3.2 The role of the banking system 26
  3.3 Asymmetric information and financial crises 27

4 Transmission Channels of Financial Crises 29
  4.1. Money view 29
  4.2 Credit view 29
  4.3 The credit rating agencies 31

5 The International Monetary Fund 34

Part II Liberalization, Crises and Mega-Corporate Bankruptcies 37

6 The Great Depression of the 1930s 39
  6.1 The debate on the causes of the Great Depression 42

7 From Bretton Woods to Financial Globalization 45

8 Recent Financial Crises 48
8.1 The Latin American crisis of the 1980s 49
8.2 The Savings & Loan crisis 51
8.3 The Scandinavian crisis 57
8.4 The Mexican crisis of 1994–95 64
8.5 The East Asian crisis of 1997–98 69
8.6 The Russian crisis and the collapse of LTCM 79
8.7 The crises of Turkey and Argentina 89
8.8 The Japanese depression 102

9 The Mega-Bankruptcies of the Early 2000s 110
9.1 Enron 111
9.2 Parmalat 113
9.3 Similarities and differences between Enron and Parmalat 115
9.4 Untrustworthy auditing 116

Part III The Great Crisis of 2007–09 119

10 The Great Crisis of 2007–09 121
10.1 The chronology of the crisis 121
10.2 From liquidity crisis to financial crisis: amplification mechanisms 137
10.3 Transmission of the US subprime crisis to emerging markets 144
10.4 Origin of the crisis: macro elements 146
10.5 Origin of the crisis: micro elements 158

11 Crisis in Academic Economics 170
11.1 Questionable risk-pricing models derived from the finance theory 171
11.2 Fallacious evolutionary view subordinating banks to financial markets 175
11.3 Improvident monetary policy conduct by the Fed 181

12 Conclusions and Perspectives 184

Appendix: Some Useful Definitions 201

Notes 204

References 207

Index 215

List of Figures

0.1	The political-economy cycle of finance	4
1.1	The Minsky model: expansion	10
1.2	The Minsky model: contraction	12
7.1	Crisis frequency in industrial countries	46
7.2	Crisis frequency in emerging countries	46
8.1	Sweden stock market index	58
8.2	Sweden real estate index	58
8.3	Banks' claims on private sector (Sweden)	59
8.4	Unemployment 1985–96 (Sweden)	59
8.5	Current account balance (Sweden)	60
8.6	Policy rate and inflation (Sweden)	61
8.7	Krona to US$ (Sweden)	62
8.8	Consumer Price Index annual inflation rate (Mexico)	64
8.9	Net public debt (Mexico)	65
8.10	Bank credit to private enterprises (Mexico)	66
8.11	International reserves (Mexico)	68
8.12	Mexican pesos to US$	68
8.13	Stock market (Mexico)	69
8.14	Current account (Asia)	70
8.15	Leverage for six East Asian countries, Germany and the USA	71
8.16	Short-term debt share for six East Asian countries, Germany and the USA	71
8.17	Distribution of debt in six East Asian countries	72
8.18	Government deficit (Asia)	72
8.19	Inflation rate (Asia)	73
8.20	GDP growth (Asia)	74
8.21	GKO yield (Russia)	80

8.22	Distribution of GKO/OFZ holdings (Russia)	81
8.23	CPI annual inflation rate (Russia)	81
8.24	Roubles to US$	82
8.25	Equity index (Russia)	82
8.26	Federal budget deficit to GDP (Russia)	83
8.27	International reserves (Russia)	83
8.28	Interest-rate spread: Turkey vs USA	91
8.29	Inflation, interest rate and exchange rate: Turkey vs USA	91
8.30	Inflation rate (Turkey and Argentina)	93
8.31	GDP growth (Turkey and Argentina)	94
8.32	Interest-rate spread: Argentina vs USA	94
8.33	Current account balance (Turkey and Argentina)	99
8.34	Japan double bubble	103
8.35	Liquidity trap	106
10.1	Delinquency rates	122
10.2	The five stages of the crisis	128
10.3	US commercial paper discount rates	128
10.4	US commercial paper outstandings	129
10.5	Euribor vs ECB policy rate	129
10.6	US Libor vs Fed policy rate	130
10.7	Real GDP growth	140
10.8	General government public debt	141
10.9	US current account	147
10.10	US household debt and saving rate	148
10.11	US home price index	148
10.12	1994–95 Tightening	149
10.13	2004–06 Tightening	149
10.14	Federal funds, inflation (core) and unemployment rates in the USA	152
10.15	Actual and theoretical interest rates	153
10.16	Excess monetary policy easing	153

10.17 Balance-sheet and lending channel at work 155
10.18 Banking business models 158
10.19 Structured finance 162
10.20 Global CDO market issuance 167

List of Tables

8.1 Summary of bank behaviour in the countries affected by the crisis 77

8.2 The magnitude of non-performing loans 109

10.1 Forms of Federal Reserve lending 131

12.1 Links among the various policy dimensions of the proposed financial reforms 197

List of Boxes

2.1	Currency crises, banking crises and debt crises	18
2.2	The determinants of exchange rates	19
8.1	The Krueger doctrine	97
10.1	Timeline of key events	124
10.2	The output losses and fiscal costs of the financial crisis (by Gianluigi Ferrucci)	138
10.3	Monetary policy in the USA before the crisis (by Fabrizio Venditti)	151
10.4	The origins of financial regulation	166
11.1	Value-at-Risk (by Giovanni Tinella)	172
11.2	Efficient market hypothesis (by Giovanni Walter Puopolo)	176
12.1	The prospective financial reforms	186

Foreword

Franklin Allen

The events that started as a US financial crisis in August 2007 and mushroomed into a global crisis are changing economic structures all over the world. But, first, the crisis calls for a reassessment of the policies that allowed the build-up of the fragilities behind the crisis, namely the excessive degree of indebtedness, particularly concentrated in the US household sector and in the financial sector.

While household saving rates dropped to historical lows, the USA experienced a real estate bubble, partly due to the increasing supply of mortgages to households with low credit scores – the so-called subprime customers. When the real estate bubble burst, in 2006, default rates on subprime mortgages soared, endangering the stability of the US shadow banking system and, eventually, triggered an unparalleled liquidity crisis. In spite of the massive interventions by the Fed and other central banks to provide liquidity to it, the US financial system became increasingly feeble, and structured finance segments froze one by one, forcing deleveraging at most banks and financial institutions. Then, the liquidity crisis unfolded into a fully fledged financial crisis with the most exposed investment banks first teetering and then collapsing. By mid-September 2008, Lehman Brothers' bankruptcy had opened Pandora's Box. The three-month Ted spread – the spread between the Libor and the T-bill yield – skyrocketed to never-seen heights, revealing a dramatic rise in interbank counterparty risk.

Contagion spread intense financial turmoil from America on a global scale. Everywhere, listed financial institutions suffered heavy losses, dragging down stock indices. Equity prices were also battered by the prospect of a deep and prolonged global recession, made worse by the expectation that weakened banks would tighten lending standards, generating a credit crunch.

The genesis of the disproportionate indebtedness in the USA is related to various underlying factors in a variety of ways: for example, the poor incentives provided in a context of intense financial innovation accompanied by regulatory loopholes, an exceedingly lenient monetary policy overlooking the perils of inflation in asset prices and corporate profits, and an inadequate set-up for the governance of globalization. While the stream of structured products was rapidly swelling, much of it hinged on poorly regulated investment banks. Rating agencies were also part of the problem in several respects. The multilayered set-up of regulation and supervision made the environment less conducive to rein in excessive risk-taking at financial institutions.

For its part, the Fed seemed at length overly hesitant to take action against the build-up of unsustainable US indebtedness. In truth, the Fed was comforted by mainstream academia, which mostly suggested that central banks should worry just about CPI inflation, rather than financial imbalances and asset-price booms. Nevertheless, it is clear by now that keeping short-term rates very low for so long helped increase maturity mismatches: for example, before the crisis investment banks raised some 40 per cent of their funding at below three-month maturities – featuring lower rates – while holding assets with much longer maturities – granting much higher returns – on their asset side.

Clearly, a factor closely associated with the rise of household indebtedness was the sustained large imbalance of the USA vis-à-vis the rest of the world. The extent of this phenomenon was unprecedented and the indications of its adjustment were either lacking or too feeble for several years, in spite of the noticeable depreciation on the part of the dollar.

This book by Vincenzo D'Apice and Giovanni Ferri – *Financial Instability: Toolkit for Interpreting Boom and Bust Cycles* – nicely fills a gap. It calls for an in-depth analysis to understand the recent crisis as well as putting it in perspective.

The toolkit part of the book gives the reader the basic instruments to gauge how financial fragility builds up and to comprehend the channels of transmission of the financial crisis. At the same time, the other component of the book presents the recent crisis as the epilogue of the prolonged phase of financial instability the world experienced since the 1980s, calling for some re-regulation of the financial system as was done in the 1930s. This latter part encompasses financial crises within the intrinsic instability of capitalism and depicts how the tension towards free markets and financial innovation leads to inconsistent regulation/supervision. In turn, instability aggravates over time at the periphery of the financial system, and when the final critical financial crisis hits the centre only radical re-regulation – restoring consistent regulation/supervision – can be the solution, completing the political economy cycle of finance.

Both the toolkit and the perspective approach are fundamental to understanding how financial markets endangered stability in recent years. Financial markets should manage risk and allocate capital. They should do this together with banks. But, in the past 15 years, buoyant markets – with a sense of omnipotence also boosted by (now questionable) regulation – dominated the financial landscape contributing to a major increase in systemic risk.

As D'Apice and Ferri point out, this is not the first time that has happened. Even without going back to the 1930s, financial instability became increasingly widespread during the past 25 years in the form of various bailouts: the S&L crisis, the Mexican crisis, the Asian crisis and many others. All these crises question that the financial system has allocated capital efficiently while the high returns earned by the financial intermediaries would have presumed the opposite.

Looking forward, I concur with the authors that we have to regulate finance much more carefully. We now know that too large a part of the wave of financial innovation of the 1990s and early 2000s was motivated by regulatory arbitrage. While fine-tuning the regulation of financial intermediaries and markets is an extremely difficult task, what needs to be done is to design the regulation of the financial system based on sound theoretical footing.

Beside the impact of conflicts of interest, the distortions in finance that led to the crisis were compounded by some theoretical mistakes. D'Apice and Ferri emphasize three. First, risk pricing rests on shaky foundations as the basic models make strong unrealistic assumptions. For example, the standard Capital Asset Pricing Model (CAPM) is derived assuming that private risks and sovereign risks are uncorrelated. This was falsified by the crisis when states had to intervene to salvage banks and the credit default swaps (CDS) shrank for the banks while concurrently they grew for the sovereign issuers.

Second, the theory of asset pricing, based on the efficient market hypothesis, and the theory of banking intermediaries, based instead on the hypothesis of asymmetric information, have moved apart. To be sure, we lack an encompassing theory, and the move of bank regulation and practice along approaches quite different to asset pricing theories has been part of the problem leading to the crisis. The key example here is the metamorphosis of the banking model – from the traditional 'originate to hold' (OTH) to the 'originate to distribute' (OTD) via securitization – that allowed poorly aligned incentives. This paved the way to excess indebtedness and – by transforming private-information bilateral assets (loans on bank balance sheets) into public-information market assets (loan-based securities) – led the financial system to allocations based on poor information and incentives.

Third, easy monetary policy systematically ignored the enormous global imbalances that were accumulating. While well-known economists held the improbable view that the world was at risk because of a saving glut – due to excessive Asian frugality – the main counterpart of that external imbalance was the accumulating US household indebtedness – rising, as a ratio to GDP, from 71 per cent in 2000 to 100 per cent in 2007 – chiefly to buy real estate, betting on a continuous house-price increase. Clearly, monetary policy's focus has to be enlarged. The central banks should not care about consumption inflation only while imbalances are growing. In turn, the great moderation of inflation in the past 15 years may well have been more the result of globalization taking production to lower-cost countries than of the credibility of central banks and the firmness of their monetary policies. It is instructive recalling that during the first globalization of the 1800s developed countries experienced a drop in price levels and not only a moderation of inflation. At that time, the international monetary system, based on the gold standard, ruled out discretionary monetary policy. These considerations lead one to doubt that discretionary monetary policy by the main central banks will be important to rein in inflation in the next decades. Indeed, in intervening to salvage the hedge fund Long-Term Capital Management (LTCM) in 1998 and decidedly lowering interest rates after the burst of the new economy stock bubble, the Fed increased financial intermediaries' moral hazard, to the point that the word spread of the 'Greenspan put', that is, an option whereby if things went well they would keep the profits while when things went awry the Fed would help them out by lowering interest rates.

Much work appears to be needed to restore monetary and financial stability. This regards the role of central banks where we need to find ways to couple the responsibility of keeping inflation down with that of taming the economy's exposure to systemic risk. Coordinating the work of central banks is essential to bestowing stability at the international level. In turn, such coordination demands that the IMF is entrusted with more funds and more responsibilities. To make this evolution consistent with equilibrium among the various regions of the world, I believe a larger involvement of Asia in the governance of the IMF is required. Thus, Europe and the USA should consider moving in this direction, something that would certainly make governing the adjustment of the global imbalances somewhat easier.

This book deals with all of these aspects and, what's more, uses simple language and is just a few hundred pages long.

Acknowledgements

We are grateful to Gianluigi Ferrucci, Giovanni Walter Puopolo, Giovanni Tinella and Fabrizio Venditti for their contributions. Moreover, we are deeply obliged to many friends and colleagues for ideas, support and advice received while thinking about and writing this volume. It is impossible to cite all of them but we cannot refrain from a few special mentions. First of all, we wish to thank Gianluca Mori: his suggestion to go back from the subprime crisis to the previous financial crises and link them was the keystone to developing the concept of the political-economy cycle of finance (whether they like it or not we leave to the readers but it is a new concept). Franklin Allen (beside accepting to write the foreword to this book), Marcello de Cecco and Joseph Stiglitz were constant reference points to understand financial instability. We are indebted to Riccardo Benincampi, Paola Bongini, Gerry Caprio, Stefano Chiarlone, Vincenzo Chiorazzo, Stijn Claessens, Giuseppe Coco, Panicos Demetriades, Daniele Di Giulio, Ilker Domac, Patrick Honohan, Tae Soo Kang, Masahiro Kawai, Li-Gang Liu, Carlo Milani, Marco Pagano, Claudia Pasquini, Hyun Song Shin, Gianfranco Torriero and Giuseppe Zadra for very insightful comments and helpful discussions.

Nicola Forti and Aida Maisano provided important support to our project.

We would like to thank also Paola Casagrande, Agostino Di Fiore, Luca Luciani and Paola Pomi for the fantastic technical assistance.

Finally, a special thanks goes to Alessandro D'Apice, Andrea Ciuccoli and Maria Luisa Giachetti for their strong encouragement to write this book.

Obviously any errors and omissions rest with us, the authors.

Glossary

Algorithm: a trading system that utilizes statistical and mathematical models to buy and sell financial assets.

Arbitrage: the simultaneous purchase and sale of an asset at two different prices in two different markets in order to make a riskless profit.

Asset: an item which has a monetary value.

Asset-backed commercial paper: *see* commercial paper

Bank run: a situation in which a large number of bank depositors try to withdraw their bank deposits almost simultaneously and the bank's reserves are not sufficient to cover the withdrawals.

Basel Accords: banking supervision rules, including minimum capital requirements, issued by the Basel Committee on Bank Supervision (BCBS).

Basel Committee: *see* Basel Accords

Basel I: the first Basel Accord which established that banks with international presence are required to hold capital equal to 8 per cent of the risk-weighted assets. Basel I (issued in 1988) focused primarily on credit risk, and in order to compute the risk-weights, the assets are classified into five risk categories.

Basel II: the second Basel Accord, issued in 2004 but not yet fully implemented, unlike the first accord, focuses on credit risk, operational risk and market risk. Basel II is based on three pillars: a) regulatory capital; b) supervisory review; c) market disclosure. Under Pillar I, the credit risk component can be calculated in three different ways: Standardized Approach (SA), Foundation Internal Rating-Based Approach (FIRB) and Advanced Internal Rating-Based Approach (AIRB). Also operational risk can be calculated in three different ways: Basic Indicator Approach (BIA), Standardized Approach (TSA) and the Internal Measurement Approach (IMA). For market risk the suggested approach is VaR. Pillar II represents the supervisory review process and is based on a series of guiding principles pointing to the need for supervisory review of banks' assessments of their capital needs. Pillar III encourages market discipline through the development of a set of disclosure requirements of key information about banks' risk profiles and levels of capitalization.

Benchmark: the performance of a standard set of assets used for comparison purposes.

Bond insurers (monolines): financial firms that guarantee the timely repayment of bond cash flows if the issuer defaults. As a consequence, the bond's rating is raised to the insurer's rating which usually has a top-level rating. However, if the insurer is downgraded, the bond insured is downgraded as well.

Collateral: property or assets pledged by a borrower to secure a loan.

Commercial paper: short-term debt instrument either unsecured or backed by assets such as loans or mortgages (ABCP – asset-backed commercial paper) issued by industrial or financial firms.

Conduit: financial firm operating in the shadow banking system. It issues short-term debts to invest in long-term assets. It is supported by credit lines from a bank but it is not always listed on the bank's balance sheet.

Credit crunch: a situation in which the supply of credit is restricted below the range usually identified with prevailing market interest rates and the profitability of investment projects.

Credit default swap (CDS): a swap designed to transfer credit risk of fixed-income products. The buyer of the swap makes periodic payments to the seller and, in exchange, receives a pay-off if the credit instrument goes into default.

Credit risk: the risk of loss due to a borrower's inability to pay a loan (the principal and/or interest).

Credit score: a statistical technique that combines several financial characteristics to synthesize the creditworthiness of the customer. In the USA the most widely known type of credit score is the FICO, developed by the Fair Isaac Corporation. The FICO credit score ranges between 300 and 850.

Default: the failure to pay a debt on time (interest or principal) that has fallen due.

Deregulation: the reduction or elimination of government control in a particular industry, normally to boost competition. *See also* liberalization.

Downgrade: a negative change in a bond's rating.

Ecofin: The Economic and Financial Affairs Council consisting of the Economics and Finance Ministers of the 27 European Union member states which covers a number of EU policy areas, such as economic policy coordination, economic surveillance, monitoring of member states' budgetary policy and public finances, financial markets and capital movements.

Euribor: the rate at which euro interbank term deposits are offered.

Eurodollar market: deposit denominated in US dollars at banks outside the United States.

Fed (Federal Reserve): US central bank.

Fed funds rate: interest rate set by the Fed.

Flight to quality: the tendency of investors to move towards safer investments (often government bonds) during periods of high economic uncertainty.

Fundamental value: discounted value of future cash flows accruing to the assets.

Futures contract: an agreement to buy or sell a stated amount of a security, currency or commodity at a specific future date and at a pre-agreed price.

Gold exchange standard: a monetary system in which the US dollar is pegged to gold, and other countries' currencies are pegged to the US dollar.

Gold standard: a monetary system in which a country's government allows its currency to be converted into fixed amounts of gold and vice versa.

Irrational exuberance: a term often used to describe a heightened state of speculative fervour.

Leverage ratio: the ratio of total assets to equity of a firm. It signals the amount of debt a company has in proportion to its equity capital.

Liberalization: policy measures (such as removal of legislative constraints, privatization and lowering of trade barriers) aimed at opening up a market or industry to full competition. *See also* deregulation.

Libor (London interbank offered rate): interest rate at which banks can borrow funds from other banks in the London interbank market.

Mark-to-market: accounting technique according to which the value of a financial instrument is based on the current market price. Whereas in Mark-to-model, the value of a financial instrument is based on internal assumptions or financial models.

New economy: a term coined in the late 1990s to suggest that globalization and advanced technology had changed the world economy. Speculations included changes in productivity, the inflation–unemployment trade-off, the business cycle and the valuation of firms.

Option: a financial contract that offers to the buyer the right, but not the obligation, to buy (call) or sell (put) a particular asset (the underlying asset) at an agreed price (the strike price) during a certain period of time or on a specific date (exercise date).

Ponzi scheme: fraudulent investment in which money from new investors is used to pay off earlier investors until the whole scheme collapses.

Primary market: a market where new securities are issued.

Rating: a credit quality evaluation of a corporate or government bond.

Repo: (also called **repurchase agreement**) a contract in which the seller of securities agrees to buy them back at a specified price and time. They are usually used to raise short-term capital.

Reset option: specific feature of a mortgage loan that allows the mortgagor to pay a very low interest rate for the first few years of the contract. Subsequently, the mortgage is readjusted and reset with a higher interest rate.

Secondary market: the market in which securities are traded after having initially been sold.

Securities Exchange Commission (SEC): a US federal agency, created by Congress, to regulate the securities markets and protect investors.

Securitization: the process of converting non-marketable loans, such as mortgages, into marketable securities backed by the income generated by the loans.

Shadow banking system: financial system composed of firms that operate in the shadow of financial regulation such as SPV, SPE and conduits. The peculiar characteristic is that these firms borrow money in the short term to invest in long-term assets.

SIV (structured investment vehicle): a financial firm that works like a conduit but does not have full credit support from a bank.

Sovereign wealth fund (SWF): government-run funds created by the world's leading exporters, especially China and the major oil producers, for investment purposes that will benefit the country's economy.

Spread: the difference between the rates of return on two different investments.

SPV (special-purpose vehicle): a financial firm that works like an SIV.

Stock option: *see* option

Subprime borrower: a borrower with one or more of the following characteristics: a) two or more 30-day delinquencies in the last 12 months, or one or more 60-day; b) delinquencies in the last 24 months; c) judgment, foreclosure, repossession, or charge-off in the prior 24 months; d) bankruptcy in the last five years; e) relatively high default probability as evidenced by, for example, a FICO score of 660 or below; f) debt-service-to-income ratio of 50 per cent or greater.

Systemic risk: the risk of collapse of an entire financial system.

Introduction

Why have financial crises become increasingly frequent and serious in the past 30 years? How can financial crises be prevented? Or, if they occur, how can we mitigate their impact? What role do governments and international institutions play in this respect?

After illustrating the key elements of the economic theory essential to understanding financial crises, we use them in describing the events that since the 1980s have triggered a high level of instability, possibly culminating in the Great Crisis of 2007–09.

In our view, capitalism alternates phases in which free markets expand (e.g. globalization) and deepen (e.g. the emergence of new sectors as a result of innovation) with phases characterized by more regulated markets when rules and/or state intervention in the economy tend to be more pervasive. Over the decades, this alternation may be represented as a political-economy cycle of finance. In this book, we will repeatedly use this allegory to read the events of finance between the 1930s and the present day.

Indeed, financial instability tends to intensify with the extent of the unfettered free market economy. By and large, freer markets sooner or later build imbalances and inefficiencies in price setting mechanisms and, consequently, in the allocation of resources. This occurs when excessively optimistic expectations about future developments evolve and the financial system fuels such misplaced assumptions, leading to excessive indebtedness in the economy. As a result, a speculative bubble – that is usually identified as such in retrospect – is formed. Eventually, this triggers an epochal systemic crisis, which marks a turning point to change direction towards stricter regulation of the marketplace. In our interpretation, this represents the end of one cycle and the start of a new one.

In fact, solving the crisis requires, in general, two types of actions. The first one consists in the intervention by the state that – fully or partly – takes on itself the losses suffered by the financial institutions in a way to rebuild the trust in them by individual investors and savers and to restore the functionality of the financial system. This action may even require (some) nationalization of the banks. The second action entails stiffening regulation and supervision of finance, assembling a framework consistent with pursuing the stability of the financial system. At the international level, the new set-up for financial stability may be crowned by the emergence of a new monetary order centred on the economic power that has come out in hegemonic position from the crisis, whose currency will become thereafter the reference for international exchanges. More generally, solving the crisis implies imposing limits on the free market, beyond the financial system, thereby often swinging the balance from the global to the national dimension of economic processes. This scenario is similar to what is usually known as de-globalization.

However, over the long run (it may take decades), the regulatory framework tends to lose its consistency and the economic system begins to operate again in an uncontrolled financial environment. Three main factors push in this direction. First, the financial system on its own tends to breed innovations. Alas, the financial innovations – though generally beneficial – short-circuit the logic and the substance of the stability controls set up with re-regulation and may undermine the functioning of the international monetary order. Second, the process of market extension – to exploit the international opportunities – and of market deepening – with the start of new business segments, often linked to innovations – needs the support of finance in new forms, different with respect to those consistent with the extant regulatory/supervisory framework securing stability. This further promotes the spread of financial innovations. Third, there is a swing in ideology, whereby free market visions tend to dominate and become increasingly entrenched. Then, economic theory and the policy debate excessively lean towards stressing the negative consequences of the failure by public intervention in the economy while advocating the benefits of letting the markets free (Leijonhufvud, 2009). This calls for **deregulation** and **liberalization** of the financial system.

The mix of these three factors leads once more to the formation of overly optimistic expectations – as Hyman Minsky (1975) reminded us – and this triggers excess indebtedness, misallocation of resources and the build-up of a new speculative bubble. At this point, it is only a matter of time and a new major systemic crisis will arrive thus completing this political-economy cycle of finance that, as we described, embraces the path from one structural-breaking systemic financial crisis to the next one. To be sure, such a systemic crisis drawing the political-economy cycle of finance to a close is not a single, stand-alone episode, but rather it is the epilogue of a series of specific crises whose frequency and gravity tend to aggravate as we move on along the sequence. In fact, when the economic system is already operating within a generalized speculative bubble, even the well-meant interventions to stabilize the financial system after the initial instability events are likely, quite paradoxically, to have destabilizing effects (Vercelli, 2001). This happens because, in some way, the interventions to salvage the imperilled financial intermediaries cover their speculative losses and – unless a new consistent regulatory framework is quickly put in place – this strengthens speculation as the expectation becomes more widespread that also in the future new interventions to cover speculative losses will be offered. Accordingly, stabilizations turn out to be destabilizing because, in solving the instability of individual financial intermediaries, it amplifies **systemic risk.** Otherwise stated, in line with Charles P. Kindleberger (1978), if the Lending of Last Resort (LOLR) is heavily used to bail out financial institutions in a systemic crisis, this will backfire in terms of augmenting exponentially the moral hazard of the financial intermediaries and building the foundations of a new bigger crisis down the line.

In a sense, financial liberalization is a driver for economic growth but over time the perils of instability may outweigh those benefits. The history of financial capitalism takes the form of various repeated political-economy cycles. Though summarizing the Great Depression of the 1930s, this book focuses specifically on the financial crises of the recent decades, which possibly conclude this political-economy cycle of finance originated by the return to stricter regulation of the marketplace as a remedy to the major instability of the 1930s (see Figure 0.1). Already in the mid-1930s, countries had developed a consistent regulatory framework to achieve domestic financial stability. Only after World War II was the framework finalized at the international level, with the definition of a new monetary order centred on the US dollar. However, after the abandonment of the **gold exchange standard** (in August 1971), financial innovation, deregulation and globalization have progressively generated inconsistencies in the original regulatory framework, providing the background factor of previous crises as well as of the most recent one. By and large, as already stressed, the stabilization interventions to cope with the crises may themselves turn destabilizing when the financial system is operating under an inconsistent regulatory/supervisory framework. A case in point, as the book will specify, was the rescue in

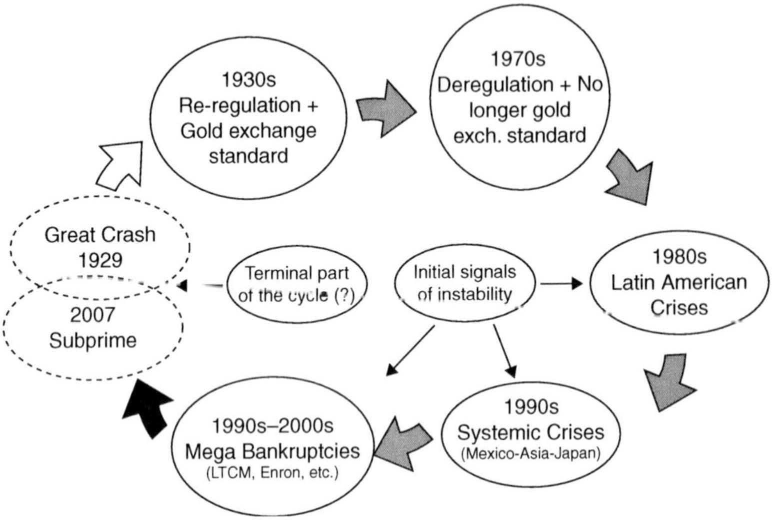

Figure 0.1 The political-economy cycle of finance

1998 of the speculative hedge fund Long-Term Capital Management (and also the abrupt drop of the **Fed** funds rate after the dotcom bubble burst in 2000–01) that, in the absence of re-regulation, was a keystone laid for the Great Crisis that started ten years later in 2007.

The triumph of excessively one-sided ideology-driven free market views contributed to build exaggerated trust in the markets and in their ability to self-regulate, motivating policy choices. On the contrary, the progress made by other economics schools – such as Joseph E. Stiglitz and several other scientists moving on that track – in terms of the analysis of the failures of the market was largely disregarded.

The epochal crisis ignited in 2007 by the turmoil in the subprime mortgage market could suggest this political-economy cycle of finance is ready to come to a close. Indeed, this crisis implies an escalation in terms of its depth and geographical extension and also of the fact that it started at the centre of the financial system and not at its peripheries, as had happened with the previous systemic financial crises of the 1990s and the beginning of the new millennium. The authorities' call for stricter regulation might mark the start of a new cycle. However, by the time we wrote this introduction (November 2009), the ongoing recovery of the financial markets and of the large financial intermediaries might strike the balance and, indeed, re-regulation appears to be losing momentum. In fact, if the pronouncements by the leaders of the G20 in their London meeting of spring 2009 were bold about re-regulation, their statements at the following Pittsburgh meeting in the autumn of the same year had become much more timid. At the same time, parliamentary actions on both sides of the Atlantic did not seem to move ahead as fast as earlier announced.

Will this mean an even bigger crisis is waiting for us in the near future? This would be a terrible event also in view of the fact that the public finances of many advanced countries have been exhausted by the interventions to salvage finance from its latest instability.

Whatever the answer, it is useful to understand the reasons for recent financial crises and possibly learn from this how to avoid making the same mistakes. Thus, this book may be helpful to scholars and practitioners working in the fields of international economics, emerging markets, financial markets and regulatory issues.

The book is divided into three parts. The first part gives the reader the interpretative instruments to understand financial crises. Even though we strove to use plain language, this part is somewhat technical and the uninterested reader is encouraged to move directly on to the second part. In fact, even though it employs those instruments introduced before, it is possible to read the second part on a more narrative level without using those technical tools. Indeed, the second part of the book presents in a reader-friendly layout the chief international financial crises since the Great Depression of the 1930s and, in more detail, since these crises intensified starting with the 1980s and 1990s. The third part of the book – also featuring both a technical and a narrative level – deals with the Great Crisis that started in 2007, triggered by the turmoil in the (relatively tiny) subprime segment of the US mortgage market. The book ends with considerations devoted to the chief mistakes made because of theory misconceptions as well as trying to lay out possible scenarios for the future.

Part I
Understanding the Financial Crises

Part I describes the 'toolkit' necessary to understanding financial crises. Specifically, Chapter 1 illustrates the prototype of financial crisis using the Minsky model. Chapters 2 and 3 look at the macro and micro models of financial crises. Chapter 4 explains the transmission channels of financial crises. Chapter 5 provides a brief description of the International Monetary Fund as the most important institution in charge of preventing and managing financial crises. The interpretative tools introduced here will be referred to whenever appropriate in the rest of the book.

1
Theories of Financial Crises

A remarkable increase in financial instability has characterized the past three decades. All the main continents have been affected by crises, with very severe effects on the real economy. In the 1980s, the instability shocked many nations in Latin America and eventually impacted on Japan, East Asia and Russia in the 1990s. A great financial crisis recently hit the United States and soon moved to Europe, Asia and the rest of the world. The depth of the latest crisis and the number of involved countries have revived interest, which indeed has never disappeared, in the causes of the financial instability and in prevention policies. In this first chapter we outline the theories of financial crises.

1.1 The Minsky model

Although there are many schools of thought about the causes of financial crises,[1] Hyman Minsky's financial instability hypothesis, developed in the 1970s (Minsky, 1975), offers us a handy *fil rouge* to understanding the arguments illustrated in this book.

Indeed, Minsky's theory is very useful in describing the dynamics of a financial crisis as well as the causes of instability, especially in situations that are characterized by speculative bubbles. The main idea is that, in periods of relative stability, the behaviour of people contains the seeds of instability. This is because, in a favourable macroeconomic context, households and businesses are encouraged to increase their borrowing level (a process called leveraging). The longer this period lasts, the higher the risks. Eventually, when the borrowing level becomes very high, even small changes in the interest rates can trigger a financial crisis because the economy is operating under high leverage (where leverage is defined as the ratio of **assets** to own capital).

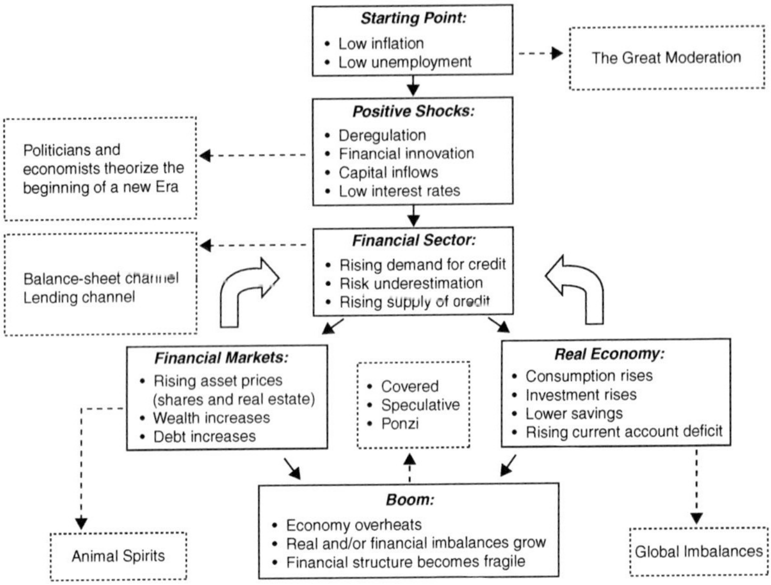

Figure 1.1 The Minsky model: expansion

Moving from this idea, we can build a logical scheme to describe the typical financial crisis. For the sake of simplicity, the scheme can be divided into two distinct phases: the expansion and the contraction (see Figure 1.1).

The starting point of the expansion phase can be a macroeconomic scenario characterized by a low inflation rate and a low unemployment rate, such as, for example, the 'Great Moderation' observed before the outbreak of the Great Crisis of 2007–09 (see Bernanke, 2004).

A favourable macroeconomic context encourages economic deregulation and financial innovation that attract capital inflows searching for high rates of return. In this phase the politicians and economists often refer to the beginning of a new 'Era', such as, for example, the **new economy**.

Abundant liquidity as well as low interest rates encourage the demand for credit and, although the actual risk of many operations is definitely underestimated, the credit supply increases too. Thus, two circular mechanisms are triggered: one in the financial markets and the other in the real economy.

With regard to the financial markets, the increase in the credit supply pushes asset prices upwards and the resulting growth in the value of **collaterals** has a twofold effect. On the one hand, more credit is obtained (e.g. growing house prices allowed subprime households to refinance their mortgages); on the other hand, more funds are collected by the intermediaries, who can loosen the credit standards even more. As a consequence, the borrowing level in the system increases significantly, while the underlying quality of the borrowers decreases dangerously. In this phase, the agents no longer take rational decisions, but Keynes' animal spirits push them to participate in the hunt for the asset-price increases.[2]

As to the real economy, the increase in the financial wealth (often temporary) increases consumption and stimulates investment, while the saving ratio drops and the current account deficit with the other countries widens (an example of the latter is the emergence of global imbalances; see Bernanke, 2007).

These two circular mechanisms amplify the increase in the asset prices and consumption, until the economy gets overheated and the economic boom hides the financial fragility caused by excessive borrowing. According to this interpretation, often referred to by economist Nouriel Roubini after the outbreak of the Asian and Great Crisis of 2007–09, the process eventually leading to the financial crash starts with the prolonged acceleration of the borrowing of three categories of borrowers: a) the hedge units, that is, 'covered' borrowers who can pay the interest and capital on their borrowing; b) the speculative units who can only pay the interest on the loan and need to rely on well-liquid and functional financial markets to be able to roll-over their debt as they would be unable to satisfy the repayment of capital; c) Ponzi units, who can pay back neither the interest nor the capital on the incurred debt and need – beside relying on well-liquid and functional financial markets – the continuous appreciation of the assets used as collateral to get new loans and remain solvent. Financial innovation and liberalization often lead to the replacement of the first type with second- and third-type borrowers, thereby heightening the financial fragility of the economy.

When, following rumours on **default**, capital controls or exchange devaluation, the interest rates increase and/or the agents' expectations on the assets value appreciation change, the capital rapidly leaves the sectors gripped by the speculative fervour or, as Shiller would say, by the **irrational exuberance** (Shiller, 2000) (see Figure 1.2). At this juncture, the heavily indebted borrowers (the Ponzi units or the subprime households in the latest crisis) can no longer roll-over their loans and default. As a consequence, the creditors try to sell the collaterals to get the loan amount back. But if the insolvencies are widespread and the

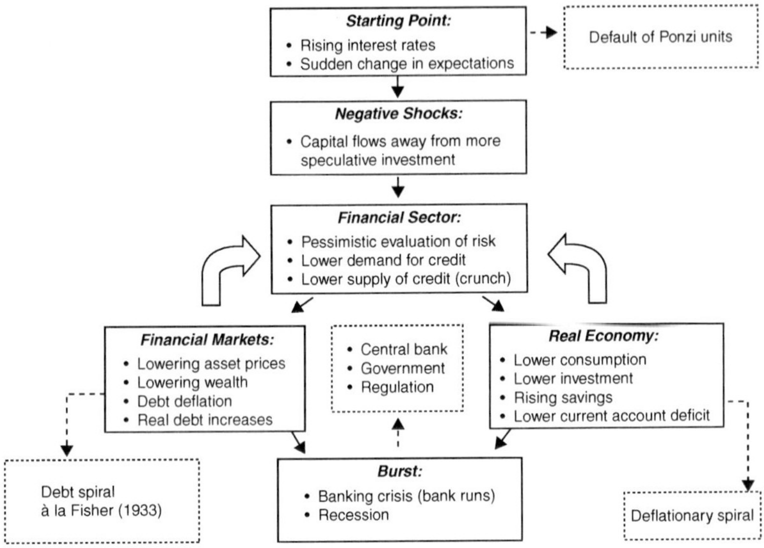

Figure 1.2 The Minsky model: contraction

market is in a speculative mode, these transactions further reduce the value of the collaterals and increase the losses for creditors. Hence, as the risk estimate shifts from very optimistic to very pessimistic, the system reaches the Minsky moment (or **credit crunch**): a phase in which getting a loan becomes extremely difficult also for the speculative and hedge units. The credit reduction triggers a liquidity crisis which forces many agents to sell their assets to repay the debts that they cannot roll-over (a process called deleveraging). As a result, the crisis spreads to more and more market segments, asset prices drop, financial wealth disappears and consumption slows down.

Now, the above-mentioned circular mechanisms start turning in the opposite direction and the economy moves slowly towards depression. This tailspin is based on four deflationary spirals (De Grauwe, 2009): a) Fisher's debt deflation; b) the bank credit deflation (or credit crunch); c) the Keynesian savings paradox; d) the cost-cutting deflation. These spirals occur because many agents carry out the same (market depressing) action at the same time, with significant effects on the macroeconomic aggregates, something which would not happen in the case of isolated actions.

More specifically, with regard to the first spiral (Fisher's debt deflation), the need to reduce the borrowing level leads borrowers to sell part of their assets. However, as the generalized asset sales reduce the market price, even more sales are needed to reduce the burden of debt. Hence, the asset value reduction triggering Fisher's debt-deflation spiral that jeopardizes the solvency of households and businesses. As regards the second spiral (the bank credit crunch), the need to reduce the risk in their portfolios leads banks to cut the supply of credit. However, the generalized reduction in the supply of credit triggers the bank credit deflation spiral that increases the risk of bank loan portfolios. This happens mainly for two reasons: first, the reduction of the bank credit supply might lead to reduced funding for another bank, thus causing a liquidity crisis; second, the reduced credit availability jeopardizes businesses that purchase goods and services from other enterprises, which as a consequence might find themselves in trouble. As regards the third spiral (the Keynesian savings paradox), the reduction in financial wealth leads individuals to increase their savings level. However, a significant and widespread reduction in consumption triggers the Keynesian savings paradox in which, if everyone tries to save more, then the total savings will be lower. Lastly, as regards the fourth spiral (the cost-cutting deflation), as consumption slows down, the companies, to keep their profit unchanged, cut their costs by reducing wages and employment. However, a generalized wage reduction triggers the cost-cutting deflation spiral that leads to a widespread drop in consumption and in business profits.

In the industrialized countries, deflation may jeopardize the stability of the whole economic system and eventually degenerate in the Minsky meltdown, in which a prolonged reduction in prices hinders investment, which in turn further reduces the rate of employment and leads to a long and deep recession (e.g. Japan in the 1990s).

In the emerging countries, the financial difficulties cause a significant outflow of international capital, which jeopardizes the exchange rate (see section 1.2 below). As the significant domestic currency depreciation opposes the deflationary spirals, the outcome may differ. In most cases, a sudden increase in the inflation rate and interest rates worsens the real impact of the crisis, but simultaneously, the renewed competitiveness of exports may pave the way to economic recovery if the crisis is geographically limited and does not depress world demand (e.g. Sweden 1991, Mexico 1994, Asia 1997).

The conclusion to this interpretative approach is that the fluctuations of the economic cycle do not depend on the external shocks affecting the economic system, but on the mechanisms of the capitalist economy which, although providing better allocations than those of a centralized economy, if not effectively regulated may lead to financial instability and deep recessions.

1.2 Management and prevention of crises

1.2.1 The management of crises

The measures available to the authorities to fight against financial crises are dependent on the degree of economic development.

In the industrialized countries, most of the time, an effective monetary policy turns out very helpful (though the Japan depression of the 1990s is an evident exception). Because the debt is principally denominated in the local currency and mostly at long term, inflation-fighting credibility enables central banks to react to the financial crisis by adopting an expansive monetary policy, aimed at reducing the debt burden in real terms. Moreover, expansion stimulates the recovery of the stock and real estate markets that positively impacts on aggregate demand.

Specifically, in the first phase, when problems take the form of a liquidity crisis, the central bank can follow the indications provided long ago by Bagehot (1873): lending at a penalty rate to every distressed institution that would be able to put up reasonable collaterals in normal times. In the second phase, if problems shift from illiquidity to the insolvency of intermediaries, the central bank can cut interest rates to reduce the cost of debt on banks, enterprises and households. In the third phase, if crisis pathologies are further aggravated, the authorities can increase their own demand of risky assets, which are sold by intermediaries that need to reduce their indebtedness, so as to mitigate the drop in financial prices and stop asset deflation. The last instrument available, which has been used in many crises, as illustrated in this book, is public intervention in the mechanisms of the free market through temporary nationalization of banks to avoid the collapse of the financial system and stymie the deep recession that would originate from it. These solutions, for example, have been adopted by many countries during the Great Depression of the 1930s, in Japan during the 1990s, and in the USA and the EU since 2007.

On the other hand, the use of an expansionary monetary policy to tackle a financial crisis is not always possible in emerging countries. This depends on the fact that most of the debt is at short term and is also denominated in foreign currency. In this context, an expansionary monetary policy would provoke a significant increase of inflation expectations, which would accentuate currency devaluation. As a consequence, the real burden of debt would increase and so also would interest rates, with the result of further depressing spending and aggravating the recession. In these countries a possible way out is the intervention of international financial institutions, whose liquidity injections do not have the undesired effects just illustrated. In fact, this is one of the most frequent solutions in the crises affecting emerging countries, and the role of coordinating aid to countries in difficult situations usually belongs to the International Monetary Fund (IMF).

1.2.2 The prevention of crises

After the crisis, reviewing financial regulation and macroeconomic policies becomes necessary to ensure the excesses that caused the crisis will not be repeated in the future.

Although they keep specific features, financial crises often present common causes (Summers, 2000):

1 Fragile banking systems;
2 Massive inflows of capital that, at the first sign of trouble, leave the countries hit by the crisis;
3 Expansive monetary policies in the case of a fixed exchange rate;
4 Weak macroeconomic fundamentals, like high inflation rate, current account and government budget deficit (twin deficits);
5 High levels of indebtedness at short term by the government and/or the private sector.

Therefore, some indications on prevention policies may be obtained from these recurrences:

1 The solidity of the banking system is the first weapon against financial crises (Mishkin, 1999). Adequate levels of capitalization and banking supervision, together with an efficient regulatory framework, are essential to financial stability. Special attention must be paid to avoid that the banking system is exposed to excessive risks, especially after liberalization and/or financial innovation processes or during economic booms. To achieve these objectives, it is crucial that: a) supervisors have the required resources, in terms of both human and financial capital, to fulfil their tasks; b) financial transparency, in terms of accounting standards and disclosure requirements, as appropriate to the development level of financial markets. Finally, also the legal context must be appropriate in terms of property rights and enforcement, especially as concerns collateral guarantees and bankruptcy procedures.

2 The liberalization processes should be managed appropriately, otherwise they might generate disastrous effects. In the presence of a fragile financial system, liberalization provokes the undertaking of excessive risks, which cause the accumulation of low-quality loans up to causing high fragility of the banking system. This does not mean that financial liberalization is always negative. On the contrary, especially in emerging economies where investments have very high returns, the inflows of capital from abroad can be a key element of economic growth. However, it is essential that capital flows are intermediated by solid banking systems operating in efficient legal contexts.
3 The adoption of a fixed exchange rate can be a very effective tool to credibly reduce inflation, but it might become very risky in contexts characterized by fragile banking systems, debts mostly denominated in foreign currency and at short term, and expansive monetary policies.
4 Solid macroeconomic environments, characterized by low inflation-rate levels and by limited current account and government budget deficit, significantly contribute to reducing the probability of crises.
5 Appropriate currency reserve levels, as compared with liabilities of the public and/or private sector, allow avoiding liquidity crises, which may generate strong tensions on financial markets.

2
Macro Models of Financial Crises

Although there have been several episodes of financial crises during the past decades (and especially in the past 15 years), only the most important international financial crises will be analysed in this book, that is, the crises that had considerable international repercussions in both real and financial terms.

The impossibility of using canonical international economics models to interpret currency crises (e.g. the well-known Mundell-Fleming model) has stimulated intense research efforts that originated three generations of models to interpret currency crises. First-generation models show the inconsistency between expansive macroeconomic policies and fixed exchange rate as a cause of currency crises (see section 2.1 below). Second-generation models feature the interaction between investor expectations and countercyclical economic policies (see section 2.2 below). Third-generation models show the role of the banking sector in generating a currency crisis or in amplifying the negative effects when the crisis occurs (see section 2.3 below). (See Boxes 2.1 and 2.2.)

2.1 The first-generation models

In the first-generation models, currency crises are caused by the inconsistency between expansive economic policies and the fixed exchange rate (Krugman, 1979; Flood and Garber, 1984). The starting hypothesis of these models is the presence of a persistent public deficit financed by the central bank through money creation. Thus, continuous monetary expansion generates inflation, depreciation expectations and capital outflows. If the central bank does not want to devalue the exchange rate, it will sell part of its currency reserves to absorb the excess of domestic currency in the exchange market. However, with a limited

Box 2.1 Currency crises, banking crises and debt crises

This Box provides some useful definitions of crises.

The financial crises are situations in which there is a sharp drop in the value of assets (e.g. exchange rate, shares, bonds, real estate), an increase in the real interest rate and a massive capital outflow. The origins of financial instability may be a currency crisis, a banking crisis or a debt crisis, or a combination thereof. In a currency crisis, a speculative attack forces a country to devalue its own currency. On the other hand, in a banking crisis, a widespread situation of **bank runs** creates difficulties for many banks, which are forced into bankruptcy, subsidized mergers or nationalization. Finally, in a crisis of the public debt, the government declares its impossibility to pay the interest rates and capital payback at the deadlines established through the contract.

Specifically, in the case of currency crisis, the speculation attack confirms the fears of investors about the possibility that the government will use seignorage (money creation) to finance public deficit or devalue its currency to reduce the burden of domestic debt. In these circumstances, on the exchange rate market there is an excess of domestic currency supply that can be absorbed by the central bank – to avoid devaluing the exchange rate – selling part of its reserves in foreign currency. However, if the pressure continues and the central bank depletes its reserves, eventually devaluation is the only possible outcome. A currency crisis is often combined with a banking crisis, as the devaluation of the domestic currency provokes an increase in the value of liabilities denominated in foreign currency (on which unhedged debt was taken), which undermine the banking system. The reduction of credit generates a significant drop of GDP and the devaluation leads to an increase in the inflation rate. However, through devaluation, domestic goods and services become less expensive as compared with foreign goods and services and, through export upswing, they may open the road to economic recovery.

amount of reserves, in the long run, the central bank will no longer be able to defend the exchange-rate parity. Thus, a very important outcome of the first-generation models is that the reduction of reserves will not be gradual, but after they touch a level below a certain minimum threshold, the reserves will immediately go down to zero. This is due

Box 2.2 The determinants of exchange rates

This Box illustrates the three main theories on the determination of the exchange rate.[a]

1 *Purchasing Power Parity (PPP)*. In its absolute form, the PPP approach establishes that the balanced exchange rate between two countries is determined by the relation between the relative price levels. In its relative form, the PPP approach establishes that the percentage variation of the balanced exchange rate between any two countries is determined by the difference between the relative inflation rates (Rosenberg, 1996). Therefore, for example, the depreciation of a currency is the result of a domestic inflation rate higher than the foreign inflation rate, and vice versa in the case of appreciation.[b] With regard to the relationship between inflation and the exchange rate, it is noteworthy that, especially in the case of emerging economies, inflation is often a political choice determined by excessive public debt. In fact, if the government is not able to reduce its public deficit, it is possible to ask the central bank to coin money for financing it. Otherwise, if the public debt denominated in local currency becomes excessive, the increase in money supply is used to generate inflation, which reduces the real burden of debt. Recently, also, the significant increase of US public debt – as a result of the crisis that originated from subprime mortgages – is weakening the US dollar, possibly through an increase of the expected inflation rate.

2 *Balance of payment*. According to this approach, the balanced exchange rate is determined when net inflow of foreign currency from transactions in the current account[c] equals the net outflow of foreign currency coming from transactions in the capital account. For example, if a country imports more than it exports, the current account deficit being originated from that must be financed by an equivalent inflow in capital account. If private capital inflows are not sufficient to cover the current account deficit, the difference will be covered by a reduction of currency reserves held by the central bank. This situation, as we will see shortly, can put pressure on the exchange rate. Indeed, in emerging economies very often inflation puts pressure on the exchange rate, as it reduces exports (which become less competitive because of higher inflation) and worsens the current account which, in turn, reduces currency

(*continued*)

Box 2.2 Continued

reserves of the central bank, in the case of no appropriate capital inflows from abroad, and undermines the exchange rate stability.

3 *Asset market approach*. This approach focuses on the willingness by investors to hold a given currency and uses the 'uncovered interest parity' to determine the exchange rate. Based on this relation, the exchange rate on domestic assets must be equal to the exchange rate on foreign assets of similar type plus (less) the expected appreciation (depreciation) rate of the domestic currency.

Notes

[a] In the Appendix, some fundamental definitions relevant for international economics are provided.

[b] The empirical evidence supports the PPP approach in the long term, but not in the short term.

[c] A current account deficit may be considered as equivalent to the amount of funds that a country must borrow from foreign countries as its imports exceed its exports.

to the fact that speculators can buy the residual reserves from the central bank, wait until the exchange rate is devalued and resell them at a higher price, which will allow them to obtain profits.

To determine the moment when the speculation attack is launched, it is necessary to introduce the concept of the 'shadow exchange rate', which is the exchange rate the investors expect to prevail on the currency market after the central bank has abandoned the fixed exchange rate and has shifted to a flexible exchange rate. When the shadow exchange rate becomes higher (the exchange rate is generally defined as the units of domestic currency to buy a unit of the foreign currency, thus a higher exchange rate means depreciation and vice versa) than the fixed exchange rate, the actual rate is overvalued and the traders can launch their speculative attack. More specifically, supposing a perfectly competitive currency market (i.e. excluding the possibility of obtaining riskless profits), every agent, in an attempt to forestall other traders, will be ready to launch a speculative attack at a shadow exchange rate increasingly closer to the fixed exchange rate, so that the attack is launched when the two rates coincide and the possibility of obtaining profits disappears. It is important to notice that the behaviour of speculators accelerates the turn of events, but it does not alter their outcome, as this is strictly dependent on the incompatibility of policies implemented by the government. The first-generation models provide an effective analytical tool to interpret the currency crises that occurred in Mexico (1973–82) and in Argentina (1978–81), both provoked by excessively expansive economic policies.[1]

2.2 The second-generation models

Unlike the models just described, in the second-generation models speculators can cause the currency crisis as their expectations directly influence the decisions on economic issues that the government has to face (Obstfeld, 1996).

The starting hypothesis of these models is a situation in which monetary authorities declare they want to adopt a fixed exchange rate; however, in the case of extraordinary events, such as a severe recession, they are expected to be ready to shift to a flexible exchange rate. This ambiguity creates multiple equilibria. In the bad equilibrium, investors expect a currency devaluation and request higher interest rates on funding, so they depress economic activity and the employment level. In this situation, monetary authorities face a difficult choice: on the one hand, defend an exchange rate that has become too overvalued as compared with investors' expectations and accept a lower employment level; on the other hand, realign the exchange rate with investors' expectations through devaluation and reduce the unemployment rate. If this latter alternative is the optimum response of the government, investors' expectations will be confirmed and the currency crisis will take on the characteristics of a self-fulfilling crisis. On the contrary, in the good equilibrium, as investors judge the fixed exchange rate credible, they do not increase the interest rate, thus the domestic economy keeps operating at the initial employment level. There are also intermediate equilibria, where market expectations are not univocal about the quality of the country's economic fundamentals (e.g. GDP, public debt, inflation). In this case, the currency crisis will only occur if a significant number of investors judge the economic fundamentals of the country as too fragile. Here, financial instability can be considered as a sudden variation of market expectations on the capacity of the country's monetary authorities to defend the exchange-rate parity, independently from the economic policies implemented by the government. However, this does not exclude the case that investors are influenced by the economic policies of the country, which – in the case where they are incompatible with maintaining the fixed exchange rate – puts these models in the interpretation scheme of the first-generation models. The second-generation models are used to explain the Mexican crisis of 1994, when the domestic currency was attacked by speculators, despite good economic fundamentals, which forced the monetary authorities to abandon the fixed exchange rate.[2]

2.3 The third-generation models

The third-generation models highlight the role of the banking sector in causing currency crises or in amplifying the negative effects when the crisis occurs.

One of the most cited papers on this issue is that by Kaminsky and Reinhart (1999). The authors studied the relation between 26 banking crises and 76 currency crises in 20 countries between 1970 and 1995 and showed that banking and currency difficulties often occur at short distance from each other, creating a mutual-propelling perverse spiral which, in the end, causes a situation of 'twin crises'. On the one hand, a banking crisis may provoke a currency crisis as very often its costs are paid through public funds, which significantly increase the burden of the government deficit and trigger the mechanisms described in the previous models. On the other hand, a currency crisis may provoke a banking crisis when hurried financial liberalization processes boost investments and consumption. Most of the time, the boom is financed through an excessive expansion of credit from banks, which in turn finance themselves at short term and in foreign currency. Eventually, the credit expansion provokes a speculative bubble on the markets which progressively weakens the current account. When the deficit reaches an unsustainable level, the investors launch the speculative attack on the currency. Hence, capital flows change direction, markets collapse and the banking system falls into a crisis. Another case in which a currency crisis can provoke a banking crisis occurs when the central bank, to defend the exchange rate from speculative attacks, increases the interest rate to such levels that undermine the stability of the banking system.

This stream of literature has many other contributors. Obstfeld (1998) highlights the role of currency mismatching in the banking sector as a cause of instability. In this model, if bank balance sheets mainly consist of assets denominated in domestic currency and liabilities are instead denominated in foreign currency, a currency crisis, increasing the value of liabilities, can trigger the banking crisis.

Krugman (1998) and Corsetti et al. (1999) highlight the role of moral hazard in private investment activities as a cause of instability. In these models, the presence of moral hazard leads to an excessive level of investment because, in the case of positive results, enterprises obtain high profits; whereas in the case of negative results, costs are charged to the government. On their part, international investors, relying on the support of public guarantees, which are more or less explicit, keep financing the borrowing country's enterprises. But, when indebtedness reaches very high levels, as soon as the first problems arise the hot money leaves the country putting severe strain on the banking system and the exchange rate.

Chang and Velasco (1998) and Calvo (1998) highlight the role of liquidity as a cause of financial crises. The hypothesis of these models is that local banks accept deposits denominated in both domestic currency and foreign currency, and use them to finance long-term projects. In such a framework, if depositors fear a banking crisis and try to withdraw the funds they have deposited, to convert them into foreign currency, they force banks to liquidate their investments before maturity. As long-term investments can only be liquidated early at a much lower price than their nominal value, even solvent banks may rapidly run out of funds and become insolvent. The bankruptcy of a bank can also cause difficulties for the other banks and subsequent capital flight can originate in a currency crisis.

Another important strand of research focuses on contagion. This effect, defined as the case in which the crisis of a country causes also an increase in the probability that neighbouring countries will suffer crises too, can have various origins:

- International interest rates. In the case of interest-rate increase, the countries that are more exposed to indebtedness in foreign currency can be simultaneously hit by a crisis.
- Trade relations. The exchange-rate devaluation of a country reduces the international competitiveness of neighbouring countries, which may fall in the crisis, if they are highly dependent on exports (Nurkse, 1944; Gerlach and Smets, 1996).
- Information asymmetries. The high cost of gathering large quantities of data on the specific risk of the countries being part of emerging markets may lead investors to neglect the specific characteristics of each country and consider all emerging countries as a substantially homogeneous region. Events affecting one country, such as a devaluation, could be interpreted as a weakness signal of all countries in the area, with the result of provoking an uncontrolled capital flight (Goldstein, 1998). Information collection costs may also induce investors to only focus on a limited number of countries, thereby

producing herding behaviour: as less informed investors copy trading strategies implemented by specialists, both optimism and pessimism waves are accentuated.

Third-generation models provide a useful interpretation key to understand the Asian crisis that burst during the second half of 1997 and extended into 1998. Due to the good economic fundamentals of these countries, second-generation models are not so appropriate to interpret the crisis, which is better explained by models focusing more on the financial solidity of businesses and banks.

3
Micro Models of Financial Crises

We now analyse the microeconomic causes of financial crises, focusing on capital markets.

The main function of capital markets is to direct investments towards the most productive uses. One of the chief obstacles in achieving this objective, which is essential for a solid and long-lasting economic growth, is the presence of information asymmetries (see section 3.1 below). This particular problem, appearing in the financial markets when some people have more accurate information than others, may cause limits in the access to credit for some kinds of businesses, usually smaller-sized enterprises. Although banks can be a good solution for this friction (see section 3.2 below), during financial crises the reduction of available information on the quality of borrowers significantly complicates their activity (see section 3.3 below).

3.1 Adverse selection and moral hazard

Information asymmetries in financial markets cause two different problems: adverse selection and moral hazard.

Adverse selection, which arises before a contract is signed, refers to a situation in which potentially less desirable borrowers from the point of view of creditors are also those who will have more chances to be selected to obtain a loan (Greenwald et al., 1984). If the risk of adverse selection becomes particularly high, creditors may decide not to grant loans even if there are good-quality businesses on the market. The mechanism leading to credit rationing is based on the assumption that, in a context of information asymmetries, creditors cannot observe the specific quality of each borrowing enterprise. So they decide to offer funds at an interest rate corresponding to the average quality of enterprises in the market. But, good-quality businesses consider this rate as being too high and decide to exit the market, where only low-quality enterprises remain. Hence, as creditors realize that increasing the interest rate further reduces the quality of the businesses looking for loans, instead of raising their lending interest rate they will choose to keep the lending rate stable and reduce the supply of credit. Accordingly, excess demand affects a share of potentially productive investments which are not financed, with clear negative consequences on economic activity. To minimize adverse selection risks, creditors must be particularly able in identifying good-quality businesses to finance (an activity called screening).

Moral hazard, which arises after a contract has been signed, refers to a situation in which creditors are exposed to the risk that borrowers undertake bad (or opportunistic) behaviour, jeopardizing loan payback. At the base of the moral hazard problems there is a misalignment of the objectives between creditors and borrowers, in a context in which the former cannot fully observe the actions undertaken by the latter. A typical moral hazard situation occurs when borrowers have incentives to invest in a particularly risky project in which, if the outcome is positive, they obtain high profits; whereas, if the outcome is negative, the creditor will bear almost the entire losses. When moral hazard risks are particularly high, creditors may reduce the supply of funds and, thus, contribute to slowing down economic activity. To minimize the problems identified in this form of information asymmetry, debt contracts usually include provisions which limit the actions of the debtor, in order to protect the creditor against the risks of potential opportunist behaviour. To ensure these provisions are effective, lenders must closely monitor borrowers, so as to be able to exercise their rights should there be an infringement of the contract terms. An additional avenue to curb opportunistic behaviour is for the creditors to require the borrowers to post some form of (real) collateral guarantee supporting their indebtedness.

Screening and monitoring activities, as we will see below, are very important for banks' solvency, but they become extremely difficult to perform during financial crises, aggravating the initial effects of the shock.

3.2 The role of the banking system

In many countries, financial markets are not the most important source of external financing for businesses because of information asymmetries. The presence of this friction prevents good-quality firms which are not able to inform the market about their true quality from operating with a level of external funding below the optimum.

A possible solution to this problem is the collection of information by private subjects on the specific quality of each enterprise. Unfortunately, this solution is not always feasible, due to another problem: free-riding. For example, suppose that it is possible to identify underpriced shares through the collection of information. Once they have been identified, the cost of collection would be rewarded by the difference between the market value and the **fundamental value** of the shares. However, if the non-informed traders can copy the trading strategies of the informed ones, the profits of the informed traders disappear and so also do their incentives to collect private information.

As financial intermediaries also specialize in collecting private information that is proprietary in nature, they are not as subject to the free-riding problem as the financial markets. Thus, the intermediaries can effectively reduce the problems of information asymmetries. In fact, by carefully and thoroughly selecting and monitoring firms, banks can collect information on the specific quality of enterprises which allows them to grant private and customized loans. Considering that this loan cannot be negotiated on the markets, unless **securitization** operations are performed (see section 10.5.1.1 below), other agents cannot free-ride on information collected by banks.

3.3 Asymmetric information and financial crises

When the risks of adverse selection and moral hazard reach very high levels, they can trigger financial crises. The literature on information asymmetries (Mishkin, 1999) identifies three key variables at the origin of a crisis: interest rate, value of collateral and bank runs.

Interest-rate increases, which often precede a financial crisis, raise the risk of adverse selection as they displace good-quality borrowers out of the credit market. Hence, the risk of financing low-quality businesses increases and creditors may decide to reduce the supply of funds, despite the increase of the interest rates the borrowers would be willing to pay.

As the collaterals are used in the financial markets to deal with information asymmetries, a sharp reduction in their value can trigger a financial crisis. In fact, if a debtor goes into default, the creditor may seize the collateral, sell it and recover part of the loan. When there is a significant reduction in the value of collateral assets, maybe as a result of a drop in the share market or of the devaluation of the exchange rate, creditors become more cautious in granting loans because, in the case of default, the share of funds they can recover is reduced.

Finally, bank runs may cause a financial crisis. In fact, if on the one hand banks solve the problem of information asymmetries between creditors and borrowers, on the other hand banks suffer an analogous problem of information asymmetry vis-à-vis depositors that do not have sufficient information to assess the quality of a bank's assets. Eventually, the lack of information may trigger bank runs. For example, suppose the economy is hit by a shock and 5 per cent of the banks go bankrupt within a few months. In the case of asymmetric information, depositors are not able to tell whether their bank is one of that 5 per cent of banks going bankrupt, and both depositors of solvent banks and depositors of insolvent banks will try to withdraw their funds immediately. As banks will refund depositors in accordance with their order of arrival at the bank branch, every depositor will have the incentive to be the first to arrive at their bank. Since the bank has to return funds to its clients, it may run out of funds, as its assets cannot be easily liquidated at short term and the forced sales can determine extensive losses. If the government does not act to re-establish the trust of the savers, with special guarantees on deposits, even solvent banks may become illiquid and go bankrupt triggering a dangerous domino effect that could transform a liquidity crisis into a serious financial crisis.

4
Transmission Channels of Financial Crises

As described above, the evolution of the interest rate plays a primary role in financial crises. It is, therefore, useful to focus on the monetary policy transmission channels to clarify how interest-rate variations influence economic activities. To do this, we illustrate two different views: the money view (section 4.1) and the credit view (section 4.2). We also provide details on the credit view, analysing the balance-sheet channel (section 4.2.1) and the bank-lending channel (section 4.2.2).

4.1 Money view

The money view, which places great emphasis on the monetary variables, considers the interest rate as the main transmission channel of monetary policy. Accordingly, an increase in the interest rate, achieved through a reduction in the supply of money by the central bank, slows down the economy and causes five relevant effects from a real economy standpoint: a) it reduces disposable income through the increase of the cost of debt; b) it generally depresses the financial wealth through a change of security prices; c) it reduces consumption due to an increased incentive to save as well as to an increase in the cost of borrowing; d) it reduces investment, as it raises the cost of funding; e) it impinges negatively on exports and positively on imports, as it amplifies capital inflows, which induce an appreciation of the exchange rate.

Vice versa, a reduction of the interest rate stimulates economic activity, producing effects that are opposite to those just described.

4.2 Credit view

Empirical studies have shown that interest-rate variations are not enough to explain the width of the economic fluctuations. For this reason, the credit view (Bernanke and Gertler, 1995) has developed a framework featuring an additional transmission mechanism of monetary policy. As this channel acknowledges the existence of frictions in the credit market, like information asymmetries, it focuses more on financial variables assigning a special importance to the role of banks. Specifically, this additional mechanism is based on the external finance premium, which is the difference between the cost of external funding and the 'opportunity cost' of using internal funds. Most of the time, the cost of obtaining funds externally is higher because of the just described risks of adverse selection and moral hazard that banks (and the other investors) have to face. Therefore, as the external finance premium goes up and down following the policy rate set by the central bank, monetary policy not only influences the general level of interest rates, but also the width of this differential, amplifying its effects on the real economy.

In particular, the credit view identifies two distinct transmission subchannels of monetary policy: the balance-sheet channel and the bank-lending channel.

4.2.1 The balance-sheet channel

The balance-sheet channel, which is induced by possible borrowing constraints, connects the width of the external finance to the borrower's financial soundness. Specifically, the higher the latter's net worth, the smaller the external finance premium. This is because, as described above, there is a low probability of conflicts of interest between the high net-worth borrowers and the lenders, due to the fact that a larger portion of the loan is backed by collateral. Monetary policy, via this channel, through a change in interest rates, not only modifies the cost of credit, but also the borrower's financial soundness, thus creating an additional propagation effect. For example, an increase in interest rates negatively affects the financial soundness of firms and their ability to borrow money, both through direct mechanisms – such as higher cost of debt at variable rate or reduction of value of collateral securities – and through indirect mechanisms – such as the reduction of household consumption levels – which in turn reduce business profits.

4.2.2 The bank-lending channel

The bank-lending channel, instead, focuses on the possible deterioration in the capacity of intermediaries to provide credit. For example, an interest-rate increase may lead savers to shift their funds from deposits to other more remunerative investments. If banks are not able to compensate this outflow of resources with other liabilities, their capacity to grant loans is considerably reduced and this may slow down economic activities. The most affected subjects are businesses using almost exclusively bank credit, which must reduce their investment level. If, on the other hand, banks can offset the deposit outflow with other kinds of liabilities, the volume of funds they raise does not change, but its cost increases, as alternative deposit funds are usually more expensive. The higher cost for funding is then translated into a further interest-rate increase for the borrowing businesses, which also in this case will have to reduce investment. Finally, when banks undergo a marked reduction of their capital, for example as a result of significant losses on loans granted at the peak of a strongly expansive credit cycle, they have two alternatives to re-establish the appropriate ratio between assets and net worth: collecting new capital or reducing the supply of credit. When losses occur in the middle of a financial crisis, raising new capital becomes extremely difficult and, as a consequence, banks usually react by reducing their supply of credit.

4.3 The credit rating agencies

A market solution for information asymmetries is, in theory, offered by the rating agencies. During the past two decades, the rating agencies have greatly expanded their business and have become a crucial pillar of the international financial system. A significant contribution to their development was given by the financial innovation and economic liberalization processes experienced by many countries. As new markets or products are often characterized by the lack of financial supervision and low information quality, rating agencies are essential references to help the investors solve the problem of information asymmetries, thanks to their specialization in assessing the quality of an issuer or a specific bond negotiated on financial markets. There are more than 100 rating agencies in the world, but only three of them work on a global scale: Moody's, Standard & Poor's and Fitch. Their **ratings**, which consist of labels from maximum AAA to minimum D, are used by most investors to estimate the underlying risk of securities: financial instruments with high ratings have a low default probability and vice versa. Since the interest rate can be seen as the cost of issuing bonds and as it is inversely proportional to the risk of default, it is much lower for investment grade securities (i.e. those securities rated BBB or higher in the S&P's rating scale) than for speculative grade securities (i.e. securities rated lower than BBB).

Investors often decide to delegate the risk-level analysis of a security to rating agencies as, at least in theory, the agencies have access to a much larger and more detailed mass of information than the information available to individuals. In fact, during the rating assignment process, the rating agencies have direct and multiple interactions with the management of the firm, which give them the opportunity to obtain confidential information.

However, the most important element in the success of the rating agencies is certainly due to the use of the ratings in financial regulations by leading institutions, such as the **SEC** and **Basel Committee**, defining the regulation of the financial intermediaries. Just a few examples are enough to understand the significance of this aspect: in the USA, investment funds are only allowed to buy financial instruments with at least investment grade rating and brokers/dealers can set aside a smaller amount of capital if their assets have high ratings. Moreover, at the international level, both **Basel I** and **II** use the external ratings as a way to estimate the risk of banks' assets to determine the minimum capital requirements.

Most regulators specify a list of recognized agencies whose ratings can be used to satisfy ratings requirements. In the USA, such agencies are referred to as Nationally Recognized Statistical Rating Organizations (NRSROs), a term coined by the SEC in 1975. This recognition is very important for the rating agencies, as it allows them to rapidly extend the range of their potential clients. Up to 2003, just the three queens of the market (Moody's, Standard & Poor's and Fitch) had the NRSRO status. Since this created considerable barriers to the entry of other rating agencies, many defined the rating industry as an oligopolistic market. In fact, any subject was forced to refer to one of the three agencies to be able to successfully issue bonds on international financial markets. Although there are now ten NRSRO rating agencies, the market is still strongly concentrated on the three main agencies.

Another critical element of the rating sector concerns the business model. Until the 1970s, the investors bought the ratings, but this procedure has now been abandoned, as the information given to an investor could be easily shared with other investors (through photocopies, fax, e-mail, etc.), to the detriment of profits for the agencies. This is why now, in general, it is for the issuers to buy the ratings, while the investors use them free of charge.

However, this model raises many doubts on potential conflicts of interest. Several times, it has been observed that businesses can do rating shopping across the various agencies until they find an agency that assigns a higher rating to attract the client. This creates situations of 'race to the bottom' in which rating agencies compete between each other to offer ratings which better meet the customer's needs. As a result, investors are neglected, and, more importantly, distortions are created in the implementation of the financial guidelines based on the ratings. Furthermore, the additional services often provided by the rating agencies to their customers might entail other types of conflicts of interest. For example, rating agencies could hesitate before reducing the rating of businesses that had requested their advice on how to manage **credit risk**, or which had purchased credit risk management software from them.

The response by the rating agencies, aware of potential conflicts of interest, is based on two compliances. First, the offices in charge of evaluating the creditworthiness of the business are totally independent from those in charge of negotiating the fees. Second, analysts are strongly motivated to comply with solid moral and ethical standards to reduce the seriousness of potential conflicts of interest as much as possible.

Certainly, the mistakes made during the Asian crisis at the end of the 1990s showed that the rating agencies still had a lot to learn in their evaluation of sovereign and business issuers operating in emerging markets. Moreover, the mistakes made in evaluating the risk of many securities, resulting from the securitization of subprime mortgages, have also recently led to questions about the role of the credit rating agencies in the USA. Although these objections are largely supported, when rating efficiency is evaluated one should take into account that the rating agencies cannot produce, in the new markets, the same economic benefits produced in the US corporate market, where they have been operating for more than a century. In relatively new and poorly developed markets, the rating should be considered as one of the various instruments available to evaluate the financial soundness of a business or a sovereign issuer, not the only one.

5
The International Monetary Fund

Worldwide, the International Monetary Fund (IMF) plays a role that is somehow similar to the role played by central banks at the national level. According to the Bretton Woods agreements signed in 1944, which set the rules for commercial and financial relations among the main industrialized countries, the IMF was established one year later – initially with 25 member countries, now with 185 members – with the following main objectives: a) facilitate international monetary cooperation and avoid imbalances in international trade; b) help the countries with difficulties in the balance of payments (BOP), by way of granting them assistance funds; c) support the order in international payments by favouring the stability of exchange rates.

Evidently, being a Bretton Woods' creature, the IMF had to change after fixed exchange rates centred on the gold exchange standard were abandoned in 1971. Since then, the IMF has mainly turned its attention to preventing and managing financial crises at either local/single country or global level. Usually, the credits granted by the IMF are assigned under the condition that the countries hit by the crisis commit themselves to implementing a specified set of reforms. Most of the time the package supplied by the IMF followed the Washington Consensus, whose satisfactory implementation was the condition for the payment of instalments following the initial payment. The Washington Consensus – a name given by the economist John Williamson (1989) in 1989 – provided for ten economic policy guidelines:

- Fiscal policy discipline;
- Redirection of public expenditure priorities towards fields offering both high economic returns and the potential to improve income distribution, such as primary health care, primary education and infrastructure;

- Reform of the tax system, aimed at enlarging the tax base and reducing the marginal rate;
- Interest-rate liberalization;
- A competitive exchange rate;
- Trade liberalization;
- Liberalization of inflows of foreign direct investment;
- Privatization of state-owned companies;
- Deregulation;
- Protection of private property rights.

Then, the name also received an informal meaning, identifying a number of policies aimed at elevating the role of the free market to the detriment of government interventions in the economy, according to the guidelines of neo-liberal orientations.

The actual working of the IMF has been criticized from several standpoints, often for opposite reasons. On the one hand stand those who (e.g. the Meltzer Commission, 2000) highlight that the IMF's readiness to act in the crises may introduce a sort of moral hazard for investors: relying on rescues by the IMF, agents may feel relieved of their responsibilities and take excessive risks, as in the case of the systemic crises of emerging countries. Therefore, according to this view, the interventions by the Fund to solve a financial crisis should be strongly limited. On the other hand stand those who call for larger interventions by the IMF and, mostly, more appropriate interventions for the actual needs of the country hit by a crisis. For example, Stiglitz (2002) chastises the IMF, as its interventions would jeopardize globalization, due to its failures in three important areas: a) the governance of the crises (e.g. the Asian crisis where, by imposing its conditions, countries in crisis would have adopted wrong policies); b) its attention, considered as too low, to the problems of poor countries/population strata; c) the policies recommended by the Fund with respect to the transition to the market economy in the former communist countries have been considered excessively quick. More generally, Stiglitz accused the IMF of having transformed from Keynes' creature aimed at fighting against global depressions – also due to market failures – to a centre for the promotion of ultra-liberalistic solutions that are typical of a 'market fundamentalism'.

Although IMF reform has been under discussion for many years, no practical solutions have been found yet. The most important impediment seems to be the fact that launching incisive measures requires the formation of a wide consensus, which can hardly be obtained. In fact, with its 17 per cent of votes of the Fund Council, the USA alone has the power of veto, as reform measures require the 85 per cent qualified majority.

Part II
Liberalization, Crises and Mega-Corporate Bankruptcies

Part II describes the main financial crises that, more and more frequently and virulently, have been occurring since the Great Depression. Two types of crisis have been identified: the macroeconomic crises (Chapter 8) and the mega-corporate bankruptcies (Chapter 9). The Great Crisis triggered by the subprime mortgage meltdown – which seems to mark the end of this political-economy cycle of finance – is discussed in Part III, Chapter 10.

6
The Great Depression of the 1930s

The Great Depression of the 1930s is the deepest crisis faced by contemporary economies. Sometimes, it is also referred to as the 'Great Crash'. Economic historians use the term 'Great Depression' for the prolonged deflationary phase from the 1870s to the 1890s but we will use the term to indicate the crisis of the 1930s, following the stock market crash at Wall Street of 1929. Though the Great Depression hit many countries, its epicentre was in the United States. To have an idea of the depth of the phenomenon, suffice it to observe that from the pre-crisis peak to the minimum touched in the course of the crisis US industrial production collapsed by 60 per cent. Such a dip was larger than the fall recorded in the other affected countries (Austria, Belgium, Canada, Czechoslovakia, Denmark, Finland, Germany, Greece, Hungary, Italy, Japan, the Netherlands, New Zealand, Poland, Romania, the United Kingdom and several others). In addition, the USA was also the last country to emerge from the depression with industrial production resuming its pre-crisis level only by 1937 (Romer, 1993).

As happened in several other crises, the increase in the interest rates controlled by the central bank was the trigger of the crisis. The Federal Reserve was increasingly worried that major speculation was inflating the stock market boom. Furthermore, the USA was experiencing reserve outflows, partly due to the depreciation of the French franc. Thus, from January 1928 the Fed started lowering its money supply. Accordingly, the Fed's monetary restriction determined higher interest rates. In turn, highly leveraged companies faced increasing debt service difficulties and curtailed their production. According to the official dates calculated by the National Bureau of Economic Research the recession began in August 1929. However, the recession became much deeper after the special events the USA experienced from the end of October of that year.

The stock index of Wall Street, the Dow Jones, in three sessions – the famous 'Black Thursday' (24 October) and the subsequent 'Black Monday' and 'Black Tuesday' – lost approximately one-third of its previous value. After an ephemeral recovery between November 1929 and April 1930, the drop in share prices continued for almost two years and a half. When it touched the minimum, on 9 July 1932 (eight months before the end of that recession), the Dow Jones index had lost 89 per cent of the value it had reached at its 1929 peak. This stock market crash was the longest and heaviest throughout the financial history of the USA. The crack of Wall Street came about at the end of a prolonged speculative phase – that had noticeably accelerated since mid-1928 featuring widespread euphoria and the belief on the part of investors that a new 'Era' had begun in which the prices of the stocks could reach ever higher levels.

Through various channels of transmission, the crisis quickly spread to the banking system and to the real sector. The deep recession induced households and companies to postpone their expenditures because of both the significant drop in their financial wealth and the conspicuous increase in the uncertainty about future incomes. This link between the drop in stock prices and the choices as to consumption – by the household sector – and of investment – by the company sector – is a fundamental ingredient to explain the Great Depression.

After a brief economic recovery at the beginning of 1931, between April of that year and July 1932 US industrial production recorded a contraction of some 43 per cent. During 1932, the US unemployment rate approached one-quarter of the labour force. There was also a deflationary spiral at work which, between 1929 and 1932, dragged production prices down by 40 per cent. The Great Depression was also heightened by four waves of banking instability. The first, relatively moderate, materialized in the autumn of 1930. A new wave of bank insolvencies happened in the spring of 1931. The autumn of 1931 featured a third phase of banking instability. Finally, the fourth wave of bank distress and closures hit the US economy in 1933, as the new Roosevelt administration took office. Overall, banking instability levied a toll on depositors and shareholders close to 2.4 per cent of 1929 GDP.

Some additional figures help give an idea of the devastation caused by the Great Depression. Thirteen million US employees became unemployed, taking the unemployment rate from the pre-crisis value of 3 per cent to 25 per cent in 1932–33, if we calculate it on the whole labour force, and to 37 per cent, referring to non-agricultural employees only. US household average income dropped by 40 per cent between

1929 and 1932, when 34 million – out of the total US population then of 128 million – Americans belonged to families in which no family member had a stable wage income, to the point that over 60 per cent of US citizens lived below the poverty line by 1933 and some 2 million in the country had no stable dwelling. Besides the harsh drop in industrial production, between 1929 and 1932 corporate profits plummeted from $10 billion to $1 billion. Over the same three years, house constructions plunged by 80 per cent and house prices lost over one-quarter of their pre-crisis value. By the end of 1933 the number of failed banking institutions reached approximately 11,000 out of the almost 25,000 banks operating in 1929. In addition, in the early 1930s, from a country welcoming large immigration flows, the USA became a country of net emigration.

The crisis quickly spread from the USA to the rest of the world. In Europe, the country that was hit the most was Germany where, between 1929 and 1932, industrial production slumped by 41 per cent; by 1933, the year in which the crisis was deepest in the country, France had an industrial production level 26 per cent below its 1929 level. Great Britain, mainly thanks to its wise decision to devalue the pound sterling relatively soon in the crisis, was the least affected among the main European countries, suffering – with respect to 1929 – a drop in industrial production of 14 per cent by 1931, the worst year for the country, to start its own recovery thereafter. Similar to France, Italy reached its trough in 1933, with a drop of 23 per cent in industrial production vis-à-vis 1929. However, Italy had already been through its own crisis since 1927, when the return of the national currency to gold convertibility at an overvalued parity had caused a home-grown recession. Between 1927 and 1934 its per capita GDP plummeted by 36 per cent; there were also drops of 28 per cent in consumer prices and of 40 per cent in wholesale prices.

Returning to the US case, officially the Great Depression ended in March 1933. However, in spite of the high rates of growth experienced thereafter, the country's industrial production recovered up to its pre-crisis levels only by 1937. The USA overcame the depression owing to the 'New Deal', a set of economic policies engaged by the Roosevelt administration. The stimulus plan was four-pronged, featuring expansive fiscal policy and monetary policy packages, the abandonment of the **gold standard** for the external value of the US dollar and a pervasive stabilization of the banking system. This last leg of the New Deal was achieved through the passing of the Emergency Banking Act, enforcing a four-day bank holiday, during which the banking system was deeply reorganized allowing only the sound banks to reopen for business.

On its part, the depreciation of the dollar allowed by the abandonment of the gold standard increased the nominal value of the gold reserves that the Treasury could then use to back its bond issues. In turn, the Treasury deposited the funds it raised via those issues at the Fed. Also thanks to this mechanism, the US monetary base grew by 12 per cent between April 1933 and April 1934 and by an additional 40 per cent between April 1934 and April 1937. The remarkable increase in the supply of money was a key driver behind the strong surge in investment – thanks to the reduction in real interest rates – that eventually kicked the US economy into running at full steam again.

There was, however, a new dip in 1937. In the four years after Franklin Delano Roosevelt took office in 1933 annual real GDP growth averaged over 9 per cent and unemployment fell from 25 per cent to 14 per cent. But the USA experienced a new – though shorter – serious recession in 1937–38, with unemployment returning to 19 per cent. According to the scholars who have studied this phase (Romer, 2009), this was caused by fiscal and monetary policies prematurely taking a contractionary stance.

6.1 The debate on the causes of the Great Depression

Arguing on the causes of the Great Depression has fed one of the most long and vocal debates in the history of economic thought. We will now try synthesizing the most credited views (Danske Bank, 2009):

1 *Credit boom.* Through the 1920s the US economy experienced high rates of growth of loans to households (related to both consumption and real estate financing) as well as to the corporate sector. As happens over and over again, credit booms also end up financing very risky agents. When the macroeconomic environment sours, these agents become insolvent and the related losses for the banks may stretch to the point of endangering the stability of the economy.

2 *Distress and closure of the banks.* Between 1930 and 1933, as already mentioned, close to half of the banks in business before the crisis went bankrupt. The deep uncertainty on the health of many of the banks set in motion a dangerous vicious cycle: fearing to lose their savings should their bank go bankrupt, depositors massively withdrew their deposits from the banking system, forcing also the sound banks to sell part of their assets at fire-sale prices, thus endangering the stability even of healthy banks. What's more, as evidenced

by Bernanke (1983), bank closures phase out the unique external financing modality for small businesses, which are normally unable to issue stocks or bonds on financial markets. When a bank is closed, the long-term relationships it held with borrowing businesses and the soft information it accumulated over time on the borrowers are lost. Accordingly, all of a sudden, it is as if those enterprises had become more informationally opaque or, in other words, their information asymmetries – as described in the first part of the book – had soared. Indeed, when those borrowers that have lost their banking counterpart apply for a loan at another bank they will face a higher probability of being denied credit because of the increased asymmetries of information they have with the new bank. Also, the specific structure then prevailing for the US banking system should be mentioned as an aggravating factor. At the time, most US banks consisted of small banks devoted to lending to agriculture. This made banks highly sensitive to local shocks and to bank runs. According to many economists, the Fed should have intervened to avoid the numerous bank closures and prevent a contraction in the supply of money and of credit. On the contrary, the Fed refrained from large-scale interventions to support the banking system. In fact, the Fed followed the 'liquidationist' view put forward by the then Secretary of the Treasury Andrew Mellon, who held that the closure of frail banks was a necessary condition to restore the soundness of the banking system.

3 *Tight monetary policy*. Partly related to the previous point, a further ingredient of the Great Depression was the restrictive monetary policy stance enacted by the Fed. Milton Friedman and Anna Schwartz (1963), in their famous essay *A Monetary History of the United States, 1867–1960*, vividly describe the mistakes of the Fed. During the Great Depression the supply of money underwent a 25 per cent contraction due to various factors. The bankruptcies of the banks gave rise to substantive losses for depositors, who were covered by no deposit insurance at the time, something that is today available in most advanced economies. The uncertainty on the true state of health of many banks induced an increasing number of depositors to withdraw their deposits from the banks and to hoard cash. Also, healthier banks – not suffering deposit runs – became more cautious about lending to households and enterprises while preferring to keep liquid to counter possible deposit drains. And the Fed failed to offset – via the creation of new money – the reduction in the amount of

money in circulation in the economy. The monetary contraction delivered higher real interest rates and further depressed investment. The great merits of Friedman and Schwartz's analysis were even openly acknowledged by Governor Bernanke (2002), when he explicitly recognized the responsibilities of the Fed in the Great Depression: 'Let me end my talk by abusing slightly my status as an official representative of the Federal Reserve. I would like to say to Milton and Anna: Regarding the Great Depression. You're right, we did it. We're very sorry. But thanks to you, we won't do it again.'

4 *Tight fiscal policy*. To lower the public debt accumulated during the first years of the crisis – because of the drop in fiscal revenues – the Revenue Act was passed in 1932 causing the largest increase in taxation in US history. Taxes on the highest income brackets jumped from 25 to 63 per cent and corporate taxes rose by 15 per cent. There was an obvious contractionary effect on aggregate demand, prolonging the depression.

5 *Deflationary spiral*. As mentioned, during the Great Depression production prices plummeted by 40 per cent. The deflationary spiral contributed to intensifying the severity of the crisis. In this respect, the most enlightening contribution was that by Irving Fisher (1933), who identified two transmission channels from the reduction of prices to the real sector of the economy. First, when prices decline, consumption and investment plans are postponed waiting for the prices to touch bottom. In addition, the price reduction increases real interest rates. Second, when prices decrease, the real burden of debt for the borrowing households and enterprises grows because wages and profits are also decreasing. The reduction in income, when households and firms are heavily indebted, leads many borrowers to distress to the point of giving rise to a wave of bankruptcies with negative consequences for the banking system too.

6 *Protectionism*. To counter the negative impact of the crisis, the USA chose to enact protectionist trade policies. These policies – labelled 'Beggar thy neighbour' – were believed to favour national producers. However, since also other countries were adopting such policies, the final effect was to curtail international trade and exacerbate the real effects of the crisis.

7
From Bretton Woods to Financial Globalization

As already stated, the Great Depression of the 1930s led to stricter rules and a larger involvement of the public sector in the economy. In particular, with reference to the new financial rules, each nation adopted country-specific banking rules. In the USA, for instance, the authority chose a specialization model, and the regulatory approach of the New Deal limited competition in the banking and financial system to guarantee more stability. In 1927, the McFadden Act had already stiffened the rules on the establishment of a national banking system and ruled that the opening of new branches in a state other than that of the origin of the financial institution was only possible subject to the approval of the affected state. In 1933, Regulation Q set a ceiling on bank deposit rates and prevented the banks from competing in the field of retail funding. The same year, the Glass-Steagall Act classified banking institutions as commercial banks and investment banks, thus putting an end in the USA to the existence of universal bank. After World War II, the creation of the national monetary and financial frameworks was reconciled with the international monetary guidelines provided by the Bretton Woods agreements. As a consequence, the control of the international monetary order shifted from the United Kingdom – which had kept it for a long time (de Cecco, 1974) – to the United States. The two main elements of these agreements, signed in 1944 and named after the US town situated in the State of New Hampshire, were: a) the implementation of a 'gold exchange standard' monetary system in which the dollar was the reserve currency, that is the one that could be converted into gold (exchange ratio: $35/ounce), while the other currencies had a fixed exchange rate to the dollar, which could only be modified in exceptional cases; b) the establishment of the International Monetary Fund and the World Bank, which were expected to grant, respectively,

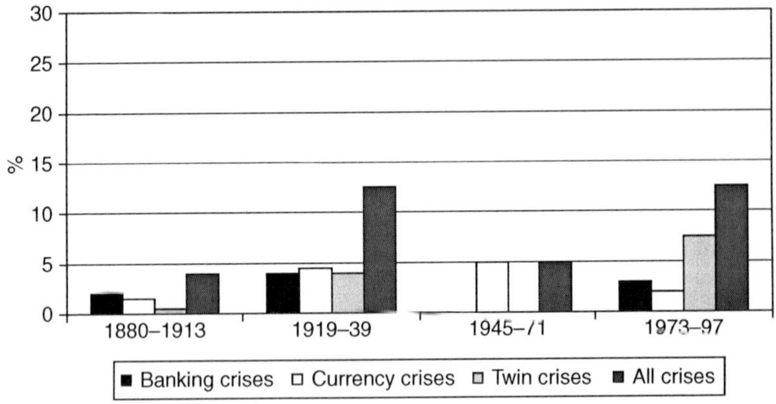

Figure 7.1 Crisis frequency in industrial countries (percentage probability per year)
Source: Bordo et al. (2001)

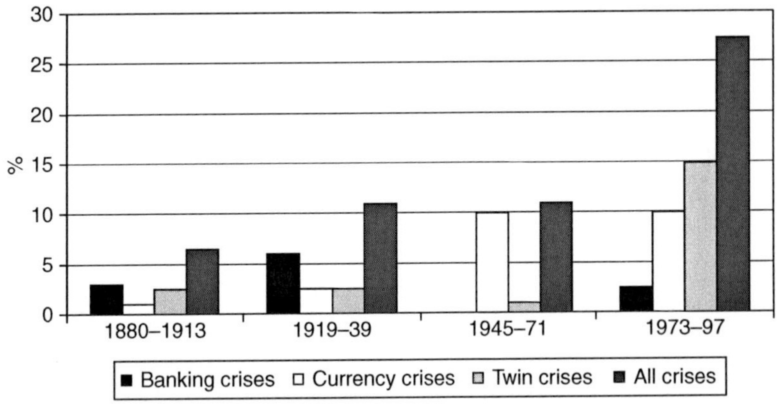

Figure 7.2 Crisis frequency in emerging countries (percentage probability per year)
Source: Bordo et al. (2001)

short- and long-term credit to their member states. More specifically, the IMF was expected to give liquidity to the countries experiencing temporary balance of payments deficits, thus preventing the competitive devaluations that had exacerbated the Great Depression. The new regulations guaranteed financial stability and, between 1945 and 1971, systemic crises were very rare in the emerging economies, as well as in the industrialized countries (see Figures 7.1 and 7.2) (see Bordo et al., 2001).

Nowadays, the main culprit behind the occurrence of more and more frequent and virulent crises is to be found in the inconsistent system that has resulted as the international monetary and financial order – established after the crisis of the 1930s and the war and coherent with the objective of preserving financial stability – progressively lost its internal consistency with the abandonment of the gold exchange standard (in August 1971) and the widespread deregulation and financial innovation phenomena which started in the 1980s.

8
Recent Financial Crises

The macroeconomic crises can be divided into three different types: a) excess demand crises (section 8.1); b) regulatory inconsistency crises (section 8.2); c) systemic crises (sections 8.3 to 8.7). The excess demand crises are discussed with reference to Latin America in the early 1980s, when the currency crises were the unavoidable consequence of incompatibility between growth-oriented economic policies and fixed exchange-rate regimes (first-generation models). The regulatory inconsistency crisis is discussed with reference to the US S&L (Savings and Loan) debacle, in which the lack of experience of the banks and authorities, in a framework of pervasive deregulation, allowed the S&Ls to undertake excessive risks, eventually leading to a very expensive financial crisis for US citizens. As far as the systemic crises are concerned, a new phenomenon arose in the 1990s; with hindsight, it marked the beginning of the most acute and probably final phase of this political-economy cycle of finance. These crises of unprecedented severity, compared to the ones of previous decades, affected emerging countries: Mexico (in 1994), East Asia (in 1997–98), Russia (in 1998), Argentina and Turkey (in 2001). The systemic crises may be further divided into crises in the emerging economies and crises affecting the industrialized countries. With reference to the former, the first systemic crisis occurred in Mexico in 1994 (section 8.4), followed by East Asia in 1997 (section 8.5), Russia in 1998 (section 8.6), Turkey and Argentina in 2001 (section 8.7). With reference to the industrialized countries, some of them – for example the Nordic countries – suffered severe systemic financial crises during the 1990s (section 8.3), but Japan was the only nation that experienced a very deep and prolonged systemic crisis (section 8.8), starting in 1990.

8.1 The Latin American crisis of the 1980s

The origin of the Latin American crisis of the 1980s can be found in the end of the gold exchange standard and the following growth of the **eurodollar market** (i.e. the market of the monetary and financial transactions in US dollars mainly taking place in Europe). In fact, this market played a crucial role in recycling the current account surplus accumulated in the 1970s. Large surpluses were recorded in the oil-exporting countries as a result of the two oil shocks that had significantly increased the oil price. Eventually, the recycling of petrodollars on the eurodollar market led to the excessive borrowing by Latin American countries that caused their crisis.

The Middle East oil exporters deposited their dollar profits in US and European banks, which, in turn, granted enormous amounts of credit to the governments and state institutions in the developing countries (DCs), especially in Latin America, eager to receive cheap loans. However, the whole process was stopped by the global recession in the early 1980s. The significant drop in the exports of the borrowing countries, combined with the appreciation of the US dollar vis-à-vis their national currencies and the increasing interest rates at international level, drained the foreign currency reserves that these countries needed for their international financial transactions. Hence, the borrowing countries started to feel the pressure of the foreign debt repayment, especially because the rising global interest rates had been applied to them. These problems were also exacerbated by the funds transferred abroad by private entities and other institutions in the DCs.

In August 1982 Mexico stopped its repayment of foreign debt, and other heavily indebted Latin American countries followed suit: Argentina, Brazil, Chile and Venezuela. The potential insolvency worried the creditor countries and the USA in particular. For the first time after the war, the authorities in the industrialized countries realized that the banks did not have enough capital to make up for the potential insolvency of the over-indebted developing countries. Moreover, they also became aware of the lack of international bankruptcy procedures and authorities that could coordinate the solution of the crisis.

The international financial system was rescued from this first severe crisis thanks to some targeted debt-rescheduling agreements. The main actors involved in the crisis, that is, the governments, the banks, the IMF and the World Bank, joined forces to restructure the debt of the insolvent countries. Restructuring committees, composed of hundreds of creditor banks worldwide, were established, while the credit-restructuring activities to the benefit of the over-indebted developing countries were entrusted to the Paris Club.

The creditor banks accepted the granting of new credit to the countries in trouble and the postponing of the repayment of debt, in exchange for the commitment of the borrowing countries to meet the stabilization and structural-adjustment plans signed with the IMF and the World Bank and aimed at solving the internal imbalances that had led to the crisis. Typical measures in the IMF-led stabilization plans included drastic cuts in public spending to reduce the fiscal deficit, restrictive monetary policies to tame inflation and significant exchange rates devaluation to encourage exports; on the other hand, the structural-adjustment programmes led by the World Bank focused on long-term structural adjustments.

Initially the restructuring seemed to work, but then the debtor countries in Latin America faced new difficulties in the mid-1980s. The banks feared a new insolvency of the over-indebted countries and withdrew the new credits. As a new and more effective strategy was urgently needed, the Brady Plan – named after the then US Secretary of the Treasury – was launched in October 1985. The plan aimed at relaunching growth in 15 over-indebted developing countries, thanks to the new loans (amounting to $29 billion) granted by the banks and the international institutions in exchange for the structural reforms to be undertaken in the DCs, such as the privatization and economic deregulations.

However, the strategy failed because the promised new loans were not fully disbursed and, in any case, foreign debt was a heavy burden for the indebted countries. Hence, in March 1989 a new Brady Plan was issued, which marked a significant change in the US approach to the debt crisis. Since the heavy foreign debt was still present, the new plan shifted from the disbursement of new loans to the creditor banks' voluntary reduction of the debt and/or interest payment, also in this case in exchange for reforms in the developing countries benefiting from this initiative. The plan was successful. The indebted countries in Latin America implemented substantial economic reforms and in 1991, for the first time after the beginning of the crisis in 1982, foreign capital inflows to these countries exceeded the related outflows. So the crisis ended, but the 1980s are often referred to in Latin America as the 'lost decade' because of this long crisis (as we will see, the same expression was also used in Japan during the 1990s).

8.2 The Savings & Loan crisis

The US S&L crisis (S&L refers to the Savings & Loan and the Savings Banks, sometimes called Thrift Institutions) is a typical example of how inappropriate regulatory framework and poor supervision go hand in hand with unfavourable macroeconomic and financial market evolutions. In addition, the financial innovation that emerged after the S&L crisis is an important aspect that links this event with the subprime crisis. In fact, the S&L crisis encouraged the creation of a strong mortgage loan securitization market.

8.2.1 From the origins to the 1970s

The S&Ls were established in the nineteenth century to grant loans to the building sector, raising funds through fixed-term deposits based on an intermediation model similar to that of the building societies in Great Britain.

In the 1930s, the Great Depression severely hit the S&Ls, even though their number decreased less than the number of other banks (White, 1997). For instance, between 1929 and 1933, the number of banks dropped from 24,504 to 14,440, while the S&Ls went down from 12,342 to 10,596 only.

Subsequently, several reforms were implemented, based on the assumption that the bankruptcy of the S&Ls had exacerbated the crisis of the real estate market (Barth and Regalia, 1989). To restore financial stability, in 1932 the S&Ls went under the control of the Federal Home Loan Bank Board (FHLBB) and in 1934 most of them were insured with the Federal Savings and Loan Insurance Corporation (FSLIC). On the contrary, commercial banks underwent the controls of the newly created Federal Deposit Insurance Corporation (FDIC).

After the war, the S&Ls grew rapidly as a result of economic growth, the low inflation rate, the ban on banks opening new branches in states other than the state of origin and the increased coverage of deposit insurance schemes. It follows that the market share based on total assets of the S&Ls went up from 6 per cent in 1950 to 13 per cent in 1970.

However, the credit crunch in the mid-sixties (1966) caused the first difficulties. The restrictive monetary policy raised the interest rates well above what the S&Ls could offer on their deposits according to the limitations posed by the FHLBB. To curb the deposit reduction, the Interest Rate Control Act in 1966 extended Regulation Q (the public control regime on deposit rates), applied to the banks since 1933, to the S&Ls.

Nonetheless, as the assets of the S&Ls mainly included 30-year fixed-rate mortgages, their main weakness was in the impossibility of raising lending rates in spite of increased returns. Hence, the FHLBB proposed the introduction of adjustable-rate mortgages (ARMs), but Congress denied this opportunity to the federal S&Ls – which held 60 per cent of the total S&L assets – for consumer-protection reasons.

Other frictions occurred in 1969–70, when a new monetary squeeze raised interest rates well above Regulation Q limits. Once again the crisis was resolved by raising the deposit insurance limits, from $20,000 in 1969 to $40,000 in 1975. The problems had only been postponed.

8.2.2 The first crisis

The trouble for the S&Ls emerged in two crisis phases during the 1970s and 1980s. The first phase took place in the late 1970s, when the limits of the bank rate controls emerged; as a result of the second oil shock and the monetary squeeze implemented by the Governor, Paul Volcker, short-term interest rates doubled between 1978 and 1980. To make matters worse, the S&Ls were also affected by increasing competition on the part of the money-market funds. This led to the possibility of issuing six-month certificates of deposit (CDs) remunerated at market rates. Thanks to this innovation, the S&Ls were able to regain retail funds, although the costs increased because the yield of CDs was linked to the market interest rate. As their ROA – return on assets – was linked to the historical returns, the operating profits of the S&Ls became negative in the two-year period 1981–82.

Overall, the first crisis of the S&Ls was due to a maturity mismatch between assets and liabilities and to the interest-rate increase caused by Volcker's anti-inflation monetary squeeze. In such a framework, the main regulatory error was to prevent the S&Ls from transferring the higher rising fund costs onto their lending rates, through index-linked mortgages. As already mentioned, it was politics that opposed a more consistent market regulation.

8.2.3 The wrong reaction to the first crisis

Between 1980 and 1982, the S&Ls were given more opportunities to allow them to solve their economic problems (Barth and Bradley, 1989). Reagan's presidency had a twofold effect: on the one hand, his free market approach encouraged the deregulation; on the other hand, it hindered acknowledgement of the S&L crisis, fearing the worsening of the public deficit it would cause (Winston, 1993). The S&Ls were authorized to issue credit cards; to grant simple loans, business credit and mortgage loans to businesses; to link the land mortgages to variable interest rates (only for the S&Ls with a state statute); to manage **futures** and **options**; to underwrite very low-quality bonds (junk bonds) and share certificates; and to introduce a return (unprecedented in the USA) on the current accounts on which cheques can be issued (NOW accounts). In 1980 the insurance on the deposits was increased, for all the US banks, from $40,000 to $100,000 for private accounts: that is, a value that was three times higher than the 1934 amount. Finally, Regulation Q was abolished.

In addition to the enlargement of their activities, thanks to a lobbying initiative the S&Ls were also granted other measures to facilitate their business expansion: a) many of them moved away from their cooperative structure to collect new capital; b) the supervisory authorities reduced the 'net wealth' requirement, which was equivalent to a 3–5 per cent deposit capital ratio; c) the accounting criteria got weaker and shifted from historical costs to rules allowing the overestimate of assets, the loss amortization period was extended and the goodwill was included in the equity.

Between 1981 and 1982, the widespread reduction of interest rates seemed to improve the situation. In 1983–85, the S&Ls took advantage of US expansion to reach a remarkable growth: their total assets increased by 18.6 per cent in 1983 and 19.9 per cent in 1984. They aimed at reducing the effect of the fixed-rate mortgage (FRM) loans on their balance sheets, taking advantage of the new activities. Especially in the southern states the new activities were spurred by the growing price of real estate and oil (the two indexes went up from 70 to 113 between 1977 and 1985 and from 32 to 108 between 1977 and 1981, respectively).

8.2.4 The second crisis

The collapse of oil and real estate prices started the crisis of the S&Ls, especially in the southern states. The oil-price index dropped to 40 in 1984, while the business real estate indices in the south and south-west decreased from 100 in 1982 to 59 and 66, respectively, in 1989. The S&Ls' non-performing loans increased, while the real value of the guarantees went down, especially for those institutions that were highly exposed in the commercial real estate sector. Five key regulatory measures were taken to tackle the crisis: a) a limitation in assets growth; b) limitations in maturity transformation and stricter capital requirements; c) limits in owned shares; d) more reliable accounting criteria; e) more resources were made available to the supervisory authorities. As a result, between 1986 and 1987 the S&Ls' growth slowed down and 'non-traditional' activities had a smaller impact on their balance sheets.

However, the situation was already critical: in 1987 S&Ls' net profit turned into a negative figure and Congress established the Financing Corporation to recapitalize the FSLIC through a multi-annual plan of bond issues. In 1988 the crisis became evident: S&L assets decreased by 0.9 per cent and 205 S&Ls were wound up or merged, which involved some 7.5 per cent of the assets in the sector. The measures that had to be taken even included FSLIC insolvency (Krugman, 1992; Barth et al., 1990). Hence, a structural reform in the S&L regulatory system was needed.

During the second crisis of the S&Ls, the losses were mainly caused by assets deterioration. Risky investment strategies were implemented as a result of the reduction in the minimum capital required by the supervisory activities (Dewatripont and Tirole, 1994). The lack of a deposit insurance system with risk-specific premiums amplified the moral hazard issue.

8.2.5 Re-regulation

In 1989 the FSLIC and the FHLBB were abolished and the S&Ls went under the control of the Office of Thrift Supervision. The minimum capital requirements were increased and a new federal agency, the Resolution Trust Corporation (RTC), was established with the aim of managing the crises of the insolvent S&Ls; with losses highly concentrated in Texas (*c.* 50 per cent of the total losses).

The S&Ls with more diversified investments faced fewer problems (Odgen et al., 1989). The risky activities were hindered by establishing that for an S&L to be considered such, 70 per cent of its total assets had to be invested in the real estate sector. The main reason was that between 1980 and 1988 S&L assets invested in this sector had dropped from 71 to 54 per cent, the mortgage loans from 66 to 39 per cent, while the MBS (mortgage-backed securities) went up from 5 to 15 per cent. Indeed, the S&Ls that had been wound up were characterized by a higher percentage of 'non-traditional' activities (e.g. business mortgage loans, investment in shares, land) and disbursed variable-rate mortgage loans (Williams et al., 1991).

The crisis was caused by a wide range of factors: a) the deposit insurance premiums were not proportionate to the risk, thus causing moral hazard problems; b) the accounting standards were weakened and the reduction in the resources available to the supervisors after the deregulation delayed the involvement of the authorities (Thomson, 1993); c) increased competition in the US banking market where, at the end of the 1980s, the credit intermediaries granted 40 per cent less credit to non-financial businesses which, together with non-banking institutions, played a key role in funding the industrial sector (nearly 27 per cent).

The cost of the S&L crisis was very high: in 1992 the US bank non-performing loans (mainly caused by the S&Ls) were almost 3 per cent of the total bank loans.

8.2.6 US real estate funding after the S&L crisis

The crisis significantly reduced the number of the S&Ls, which dropped to 2100 in 1991, that is, half the number of 1980. Between 1984 and 1994, the market share of S&L assets, compared to the total including also the total assets of the commercial banks, decreased by nearly one-third, from 30.7 to 20.4 per cent. Keeping the final holders of the mortgage loans and the relevant liabilities (MBS) into consideration, starting from the early 1980s a significant shift from the intermediaries to the markets took place. In 1980 the S&Ls alone were at 54 per cent (plus 17 per cent for the commercial banks); this share dropped to 23 per cent in 1994 (27 per cent for the commercial banks). The intermediaries went down from approximately three-quarters to one-half of the real estate market in terms of its financing, which in the meantime had grown from $1000 billion to $4000 billion (FHLMC, 1996).

The crisis was not the only reason why S&Ls no longer had mortgage loans in their portfolios; the securitization of mortgage loans – which will be dealt with in Part III, together with an analysis of the subprime mortgage meltdown – also played a key role. Here, reference is made to the federal agencies and to the link between their development and the need to solve the S&L crisis, while establishing the new structure of real estate funding as a result of the S&L crisis.

Mortgage securitization follows a standardized formula whereby the bilateral credits of a bank are turned into financial assets that can be traded in multilateral markets. The bank (originator) gives its portfolio of loans to be securitized to an external entity, the **special-purpose vehicle (SPV)**, the only corporate object of which is the management of the securitization transactions; the SPV issues the bonds that are guaranteed by the capital value and the expected interest flow on the securitized loans and sells them to the final investors; the bonds are accompanied by additional guarantees (credit enhancement – often provided by an operator external to the originator bank) and their risk category is indicated by the rating agency according to the characteristics of the securitized loans, the credit enhancement amount (credit support as an additional or supplementary guarantee) and the rating of the entity that provides the credit enhancement. The creation of the

SPV keeps the securitized loans separate from the others in the bank portfolio. The credit enhancement is of paramount importance to give the bonds issued by the SPV an investment grade that is such that they can be included in the portfolio of the institutional investors. The institutions that can grant low-cost credit enhancement during the initial market-creation phase play a fundamental role, as such support might be more expensive.

Hence the key role of the federal agencies entrusted with the facilitation of loan disbursement for residential houses: the Federal National Mortgage Association (Fannie Mae), the government Home Loan Mortgage Association (Ginnie Mae) and the Federal Home Loan Mortgage Corporation (Freddie Mac). In 1938, under Roosevelt's presidency, Fannie Mae was established with the aim of creating a **secondary market** for residential loans (with specific reference to the government civil building programmes), the lack of which was particularly evident during the Great Crisis. In 1968 Fannie Mae was split: the insurance activities to fund the residential building programmes supported by the government were transferred to Ginnie Mae, the new *ad hoc* federal agency. Though still under federal control and subject to the government's appointment (as a general stakeholder) of some of its directors, Fannie Mae was privatized and dealt with only the private mortgage loans to support the development of a secondary market for these liabilities. With the aim of increasing the secondary market potential, in 1970 the US Congress established a new company, Freddie Mac, whose main field of action was related to the private residential loans made available to the market.

These effects were the result of the limited availability of residential loans in the second half of the 1960s. Indeed, the increase in short-term interest rates induced the first wave of disintermediation for the S&Ls, cutting the supply of mortgages. With hindsight, one might say that the reforms implemented in the 1970s on the one hand reduced the sensitivity of the real estate funding market by creating the secondary market of mortgage loans and MBSs, but on the other hand they also reduced the need for an urgent review of S&L regulations.

Here are a few figures to understand the extent of the mortgage securitization phenomenon. At the end of 1995 the MBS on the private residential loans granted by Fannie Mae and Freddie Mac amounted to nearly $900 billion. The overall MBS market (which did not even exist 20 years earlier) was worth $1800 billion, that is, half the amount of the circulating Treasury bonds in the USA.

The problems of the S&Ls in the 1980s strengthened the residential loan securitization process for two main reasons. First, the need to guarantee funding while keeping S&L trading as limited as more entities entered this market to play the originators' role and then transfer the mortgage loans to the secondary markets. Second, and even more important, the S&Ls were forced to release their assets, thus starting an enormous increase in the loans available for securitization (Bradley et al., 1995).

As a result of the increasing importance of the secondary market, many believed (FHLMC, 1996) that the intermediation cost affecting the US mortgage loans would have significantly decreased and the new residential building funding system would have become more efficient. This opinion was widespread until the beginning of the subprime mortgage crisis and should now be reviewed (this subject will also be dealt with in Part III).

8.3 The Scandinavian crisis

After the Great Depression, Sweden, Finland and Norway were the first industrialized countries to be hit by a systemic financial crisis. Because of the remarkable similarities between the three crises, we describe only the Swedish case, but a similar pattern also applied to the other two Nordic countries.[1]

The Scandinavian crisis fully reflects the interpretation (illustrated in section 1.1 above) characterized by financial liberalization, capital inflow, high growth of credit and economic boom followed by a crash.

From the 1950s to the mid-1980s, the Swedish banking system was heavily regulated (Englund, 1999). The main regulations regarded the assets, 50 per cent of which had to be used to underwrite public bonds, and the interest rates on loans, which could not exceed a specific ceiling. But, in 1985, the government and the central bank, encouraged by some high-profile economists and bureaucrats, started an intense process of financial deregulation which led to the removal of the assets and rates restrictions. As a consequence, private borrowing grew rapidly and, in just five years, its stock outstanding went up from 85 per cent to 135 per cent as a ratio to GDP. Most of the new debt was in foreign currency because the fixed exchange rate chosen by the Swedish authorities seemed to prevent any exchange risk. The increased borrowing was also encouraged by both negative real interest rates, caused by the high inflation rate, and tax relief on investments. Many new loans were poured into the real estate and equity markets, where the prices were rapidly going up (see Figures 8.1 and 8.2). The increase in the value of the collaterals further expanded the supply of credit thanks to the

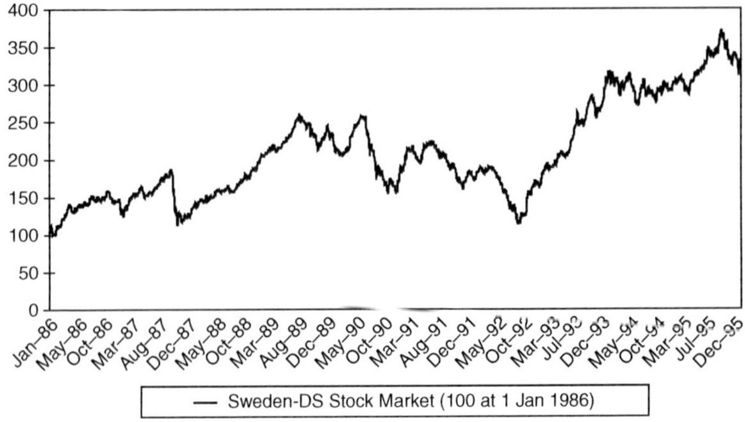

Figure 8.1 Sweden stock market index
Source: Thomson Datastream

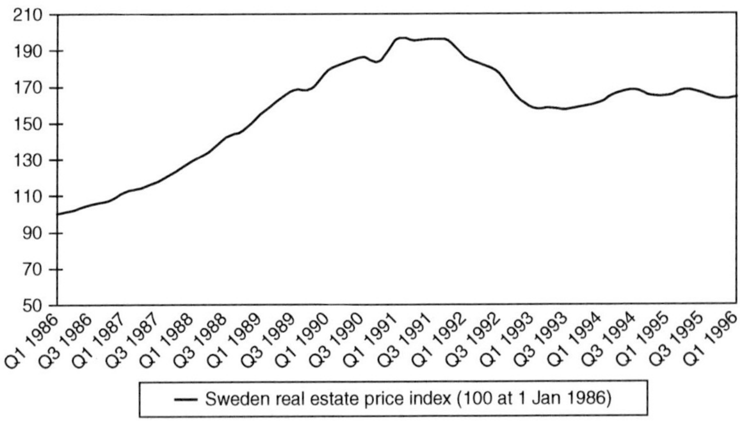

Figure 8.2 Sweden real estate index
Source: Thomson Datastream

balance-sheet channel (see section 4.2.1 above). However, the flood of money simply overwhelmed the capacity of financial institutions and regulators to handle it. After 40 years of heavy regulation, the banks and the regulatory institutions did not know how to work on deregulated and highly competitive markets. Specifically, the main deficiencies were in the assessment of the clients, the projects and the collaterals.

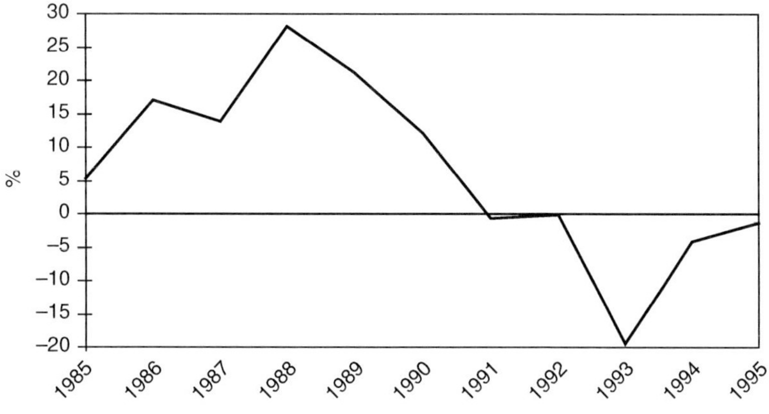

Figure 8.3 Banks' claims on private sector (1Y percentage change – Sweden)
Source: Thomson Datastream

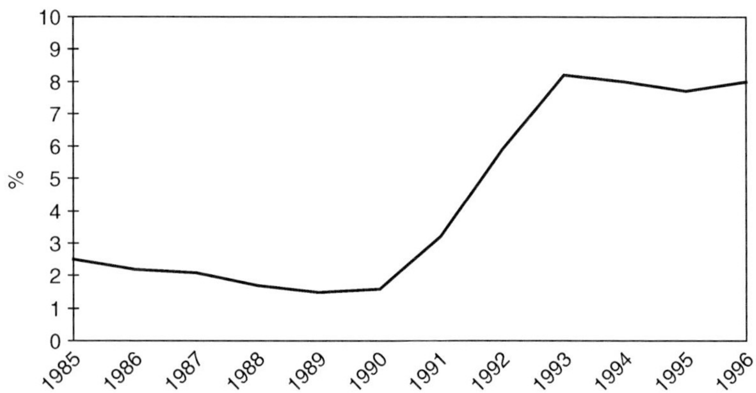

Figure 8.4 Unemployment 1985–96 (percentage – Sweden)
Source: Thomson Datastream

Therefore the results of some years of deregulation were a speculative bubble, high private borrowing and an excessive credit growth (see Figure 8.3).

Financial deregulation also affected the real economy. Consumption grew more than disposable income and the savings ratio collapsed. The rate of unemployment reached unprecedented lows (see Figure 8.4), thanks to the real estate bubble that spurred the demand for domestic goods and services. Moreover, inflation curbed exports, the buoyant

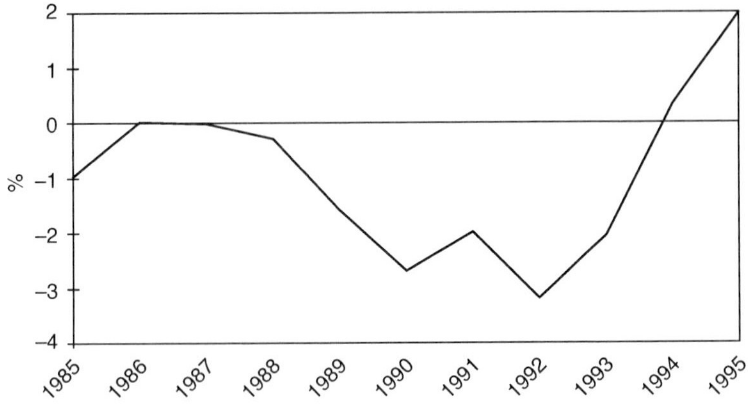

Figure 8.5 Current account balance (percentage of GDP – Sweden)
Source: Thomson Datastream

domestic demand encouraged imports and the current account reached a negative value (see Figure 8.5).

But the economic boom stopped all of a sudden in 1989. In order to curb inflation, the Riksbank (the Swedish central bank) increased its policy interest rate exactly when German reunification pushed up international interest rates (see Figure 8.6). As recounted by Jonung et al. (2008), the real interest-rate increase – from −1 to +5 per cent in just two years – triggered Fisher's debt deflation (see section 1.1 above). So assets prices collapsed, financial wealth decreased and the real weight of debt increased (because the nominal value of the debt had not changed). The attempt to reduce the indebtedness by selling the assets made the situation even worse. In fact, during the second half of 1989, the equity and the real estate markets both dropped (see Figures 8.1 and 8.2).

The losses on these two markets jeopardized financial stability. In September 1990, the financial company Nyckeln could not renew its short-term liabilities (*marknadsbevis*) due to its exposure on the real estate market. In just a few days, the *marknadsbevis* market was drained and the financial companies were forced to resort to the traditional banks they had established links with during the boom. Unfortunately, due to inappropriate credit policies, the banks also had low-quality assets.[2]

In the autumn of 1991 the liquidity problems turned into solvency problems when two major Swedish banks, the Första Sparbanken and the Nordbanken, had to resort to capital injections in order to meet their minimum requirements. The Swedish government had to underwrite new

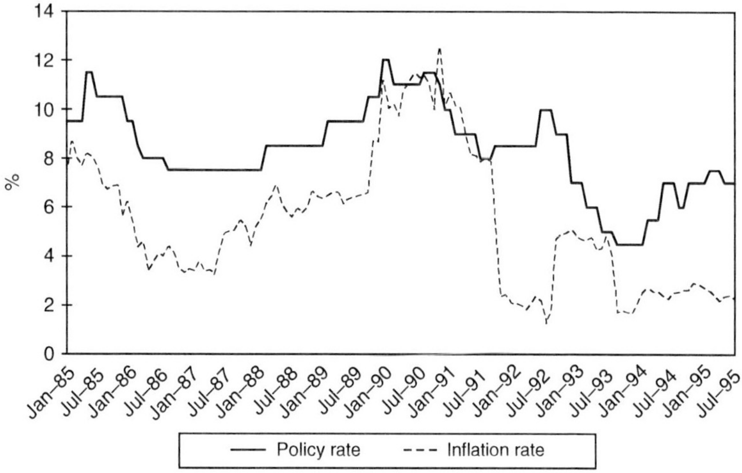

Figure 8.6 Policy rate and inflation (Sweden)
Source: Thomson Datastream

shares of the Nordbanken and guarantee the loan issued by the Första Sparbanken. However, these measures did not ease the crisis, which became even more severe in September 1992, following the bankruptcy of the Gota Bank. Hence, the turmoil turned into a systemic crisis and the government had to undertake firm, transparent and resolute actions. Due to the lack of a deposit insurance mechanism, the government guaranteed the liabilities of all Swedish banks and, between the end of 1992 and the beginning of 1993, nationalized the Nordbanken and the Gota Bank. Moreover companies specialized in credit management (bad bank) were established to deal with non-performing loans of these two banks. The Bank Support Authority was also established to support the other banks in trouble.

The financial crisis hit the real economy severely as the financial losses triggered the deflationary spiral on consumption (see section 1.1 above). The demand for goods, and durable goods in particular, dropped and in just a few years the real interest rate increased from a negative value to more than 8 per cent. The aggregate demand reduction caused a significant increase in the unemployment rate, from 2 to 8 per cent.

According to second-generation currency crisis models (see Chapter 2), severe domestic recession challenges the sustainability of the fixed exchange rate. On the one hand, the central bank should reduce the interest rate to ease the recession, but on the other hand, it should

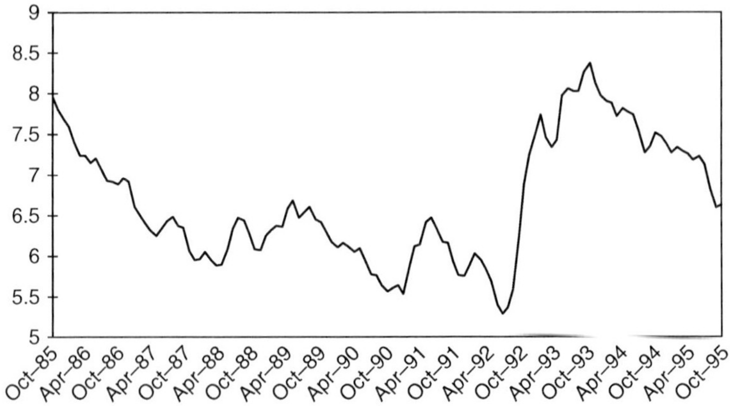

Figure 8.7 Krona to US$ (Sweden)
Source: Thomson Datastream

increase the interest rate to protect the exchange rate from speculative attacks. In the case of Sweden, the interaction between the real, bank and currency crises was strengthened by the remarkable stock of foreign liabilities accumulated by the private sector in the 1980s.

While Finland abandoned the fixed exchange rate, and Italy and Great Britain left the European Monetary System (EMS), the Swedish central bank decided to maintain the exchange rate. However, in September 1992 the overnight rate reached 500 per cent and, following some speculative attacks, the central bank was forced to abandon the fixed exchange rate on 19 November 1992 (see Figure 8.7). This decision was taken when the crisis reached its peak; however, it also marked the beginning of the recovery. Between 1990 and 1993, the Swedish GDP went down by more than 5 per cent, but in just a few months the interest rates went back to less than 8 per cent and the remarkable depreciation of the krona (30 per cent in 1993) favoured exports and helped the Swedish economy to overcome the crisis.

8.3.1 Managing the crisis

Many consider the bank crisis management approach of Sweden as a model. Indeed, its success was based on four main elements (IMF, 2009a):

1 The establishment of the Bank Support Authority (BSA). The new body did not depend on any other financial authority (Ministry of

Finance, central bank and supervisory authority) and was ı by a team of experts who aimed solely at the solution of tı crisis, without any political interference;

2 The use of stress tests based on a three–five-year period to verify the individual banks' solvency;
3 The classification of the banks into three groups, according to the results of the stress tests:
   A Sound banks, with regulatory capital exceeding 8 per cent of their assets;
   B Banks in trouble, with regulatory capital temporarily below 8 per cent;
   C Banks that had practically gone bankrupt.
4 The nationalization of the group C banks, the assets of which were divided between good and bad assets. The loan assessment was entrusted to the BSA, which performed a very conservative estimate on a voluntary basis. A specialized firm (bad bank) was established for each bank and was transferred the bad assets.

The government decided to rescue the banks, but not their shareholders, who had their rights wiped out unless they could provide the funds needed to recapitalize the banks in trouble.

The government allocated 88 billion kronas (nearly 5 per cent of the GDP of Sweden at the time) and estimated 10–15 years for the restructuring. The efforts mainly focused on two banks and the corresponding bad banks: Nordbanken and Securum AB, on the one hand, and Gota Bank and Retriva, on the other. Only the Gota Bank was freshly nationalized, because the Nordbanken already had government participation before the crisis.

A key element of the plan was the high recovery rate on non-performing loans. The loan types were quite homogeneous – mainly mortgage and business loans – thus facilitating the assessment process. Moreover, the sale of the collaterals was staggered over time, with the aim of preventing a further price reduction and an increase in the losses.

At the end of the restructuring process, the total cost (65 billion, *c.* 4 per cent of GDP) and the required time (only three years – from 1993 to 1996) were less than initially expected.

The success of the restructuring plan was also the result of the limited losses on loans (13 per cent of the total loans at the peak of the crisis), of the total cost of the crisis (less than 4 per cent) and the relatively simple assessment of bad debts. These conditions simplified the restructuring process, differently from crisis cases which proved more expensive and featured a more difficult evaluation of the non-performing loans of the banks (such as with the Great Crisis triggered by the subprime mortgage meltdown). Moreover, the krona depreciation speeded up economic recovery and helped to ease the banking crisis.

8.4 The Mexican crisis of 1994–95

The Mexican crisis of 1994–95 marked the beginning of the most acute and probably final phase of this political-economy cycle of finance. Also, this crisis fully reflects the interpretation (illustrated in section 1.1 above) characterized by financial liberalization, capital inflows, high growth of credit and economic boom followed by a crash.

Since 1945, the five attempts made by the Mexican authorities to implement a fixed exchange rate have many similarities: periods of economic expansion, accompanied by the appreciation of the real exchange rate and the deficit of the current account, which after a few years ended up in a heavy depreciation, the outflow of capital and economic contractions. However, an in-depth analysis of the financial crisis of 1994 shows some new elements. Thanks to previous structural reforms, starting at the beginning of the 1990s, Mexican inflation reached US levels (see Figure 8.8) and public debt went down from 50 per cent to 20 per cent of the country's GDP (see Figure 8.9). Many companies were privatized, several sectors were deregulated and the NAFTA (North American Free Trade Agreement) agreement with the USA and Canada allowed Mexico

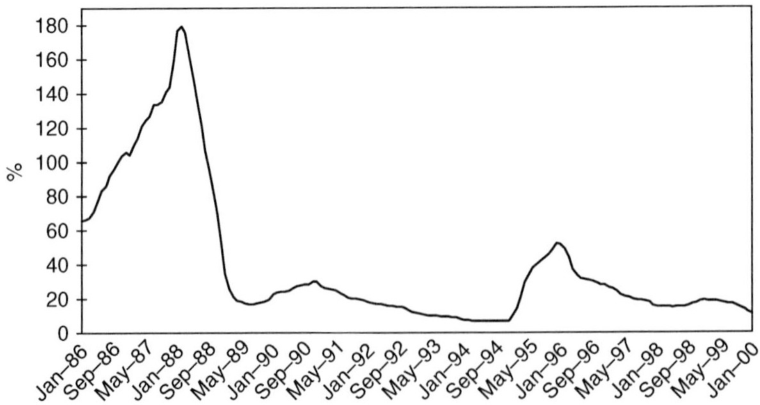

Figure 8.8 Consumer Price Index annual inflation rate (Mexico)
Source: Thomson Datastream

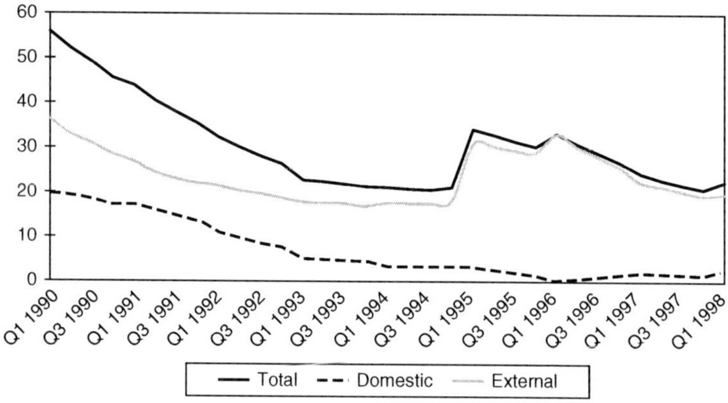

Figure 8.9 Net public debt (percentage of GDP – Mexico)
Source: Thomson Datastream

to enter into a large trading area, with excellent growth prospects based on free trade policies.

The only uncertainty was due to the appreciation of the real exchange rate resulting from the inflow of foreign capital, attracted by good economic fundamentals, which increased both the aggregate demand and domestic prices. The subsequent increase (decrease) of imports (exports) resulted in a deficit of the current account. The main concerns did not come from the amount of the deficit, which could have been absorbed by the gradual devaluation of the nominal exchange rate, but by its funding. Between 1990 and 1994, only 25 per cent of foreign capital was used for long-term domestic investment, while the remaining 75 per cent was targeted to short-term financial investments, split as follows: 25 per cent shares purchased by foreign investors, 50 per cent government and national bank bonds. At the end of 1993 the latter were four times higher than the value of the currency reserves in the vaults of the central bank. As a consequence, the Mexican financial vulnerability was very high because the capital inflows might have stopped, thus causing a severe liquidity crisis. Moreover, because of the fixed exchange-rate regime, the flight of the investors would have challenged the currency reserves of the central bank.

The crisis followed the pattern described by the second-generation models: even though the exchange rate was compatible with the economic fundamentals of the country, the Mexican depreciation was the result of a sudden loss of confidence in the ability of the country to meet its financial obligations. As a result, the investors did not renew their short-term loans and the government became insolvent. The Banco de Mexico reacted to the capital outflow by reducing its reserves, thus encouraging the speculative attack.

8.4.1 Understanding the crisis

The microeconomic instruments illustrated in Chapter 3 allow a full understanding of the role of the banking system in the Mexican crisis.

Starting from the mid-1980s, Mexico undertook an intense financial liberalization process to get rid of the (lending and deposit) interest-rate ceilings and the limitations imposed on the banking business. This approach led to a growth in bank loans, mainly as a result of foreign capital inflows, which was in turn encouraged by the decision of the Mexican government to implement a fixed exchange rate to eliminate the currency risk for the investors. As a consequence, from the end of the 1980s until the beginning of the financial crisis, lending to the private sector grew to 45 per cent (see Figure 8.10).

The expansion was so rapid that many low–quality projects were also funded, due to a twofold inefficiency (Mishkin, 1996). The Mexican banks could not properly manage the risks they were facing also because, as already mentioned, many of them were nationalized in 1982 and most loans were granted to the government. When these institutions were privatized in 1990, their ability to screen good clients was very low. Moreover, the rapid growth of the banking assets came as a surprise to the bank supervisory bodies in such an institutionally weak context, to the point that they could not prevent excessive exposure to risk by the banking system. On their part, the depositors and investors felt reassured by

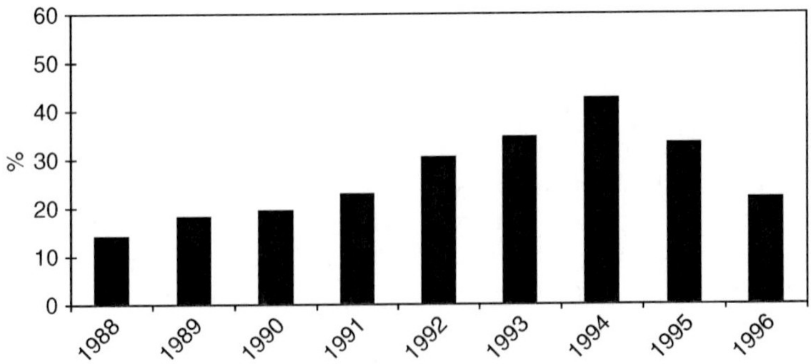

Figure 8.10 Bank credit to private enterprises (percentage of GDP – Mexico)
Source: Thomson Datastream

the public guarantees (i.e. the explicit deposit guarantee or the implicit expectation that the government would never let a bank go bankrupt) and did not appropriately monitor the Mexican banks. As a result, the soundness of the banking system got much worse between 1990 and 1995 and the non-performing loans grew from 5 to more than 15 per cent of total outstanding loans.

The financial crisis was triggered by two shocks that hit the Mexican economy in 1994. In February, as the Fed decided to increase its interest rates to stifle domestic inflationary pressure, some of the capital originally targeted for Mexico was repatriated to the USA. In March the presidential candidate Luis Colosio was killed and the uncertainty about Mexican political stability skyrocketed. To roll-over public debt, the government was forced to convert the Treasury bond denominated in local currency (CETES) into short-term dollar bonds (Tesobonos). In 1994, in a context in which the total net public debt amounted to 21 per cent of GDP, approximately 85 per cent was denominated in foreign currencies (see Figure 8.9). The combination of these two factors significantly reduced foreign capital inflows.

The first- and second-generation models of exchange-rate crises show that the fixed exchange rate can be maintained if the capital outflow is tackled by increasing interest rates and not by reducing foreign currency reserves. However, the Mexican monetary authorities, worried by the weakness of the banking system, decided to avoid a restrictive monetary policy because an increase in the interest rates would have also increased the bad debt and it was foreseen that many banks would have gone bankrupt. Hence, the central bank decided to use its foreign currency reserves to counterbalance the capital outflows, thus increasing the risk of a speculative attack. The interventions in the currency market were burdensome: in 1994 the reserves dropped from $30 billion to less than $5 billion (see Figure 8.11) and the Mexican government became illiquid on its short-term foreign currency liabilities.

The unavoidable speculative attack forced the government to devalue the peso by 15 per cent on 20 December 1994. However, the results were not as expected because the devaluation was not sufficient to make up for the existing imbalances, and the expectations of further devaluation triggered a severe financial crisis. The investors started to convert pesos into foreign currency, which reduced the currency reserves of the central bank even more, to the point that the government was forced to move away from the fixed rate and let the peso fluctuate on the currency markets. The enormous capital outflows pushed the dollar from 3.3 to more than 7 pesos in just a few months (see Figure 8.12).

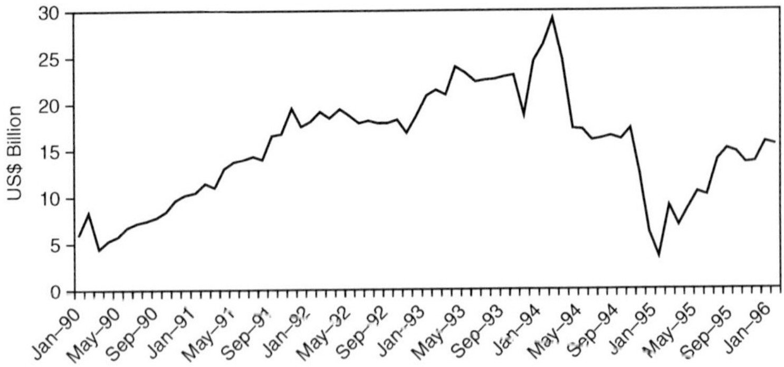

Figure 8.11 International reserves (US$ billion – Mexico)
Source: Thomson Datastream

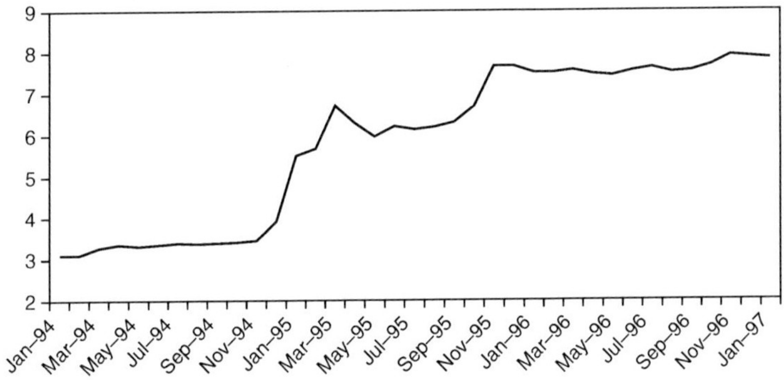

Figure 8.12 Mexican pesos to US$
Source: Thomson Datastream

The heavy depreciation of the exchange rate pushed import prices up, which increased the inflation rate (see Figure 8.8). To curb the depreciation and to stifle inflation, the central bank significantly increased interest rates, up to 100 per cent. At this juncture, as we will see again in the 1997 Asian crisis, the microeconomic mechanisms described in Chapter 3 were triggered. Because of the short-term debt contracts and their foreign currency denomination and as the information asymmetries grew, the currency crisis became a severe financial one. The peso depreciation reduced the net assets of the banks and enterprises because, on the one hand, the foreign currency liabilities increased but, on the

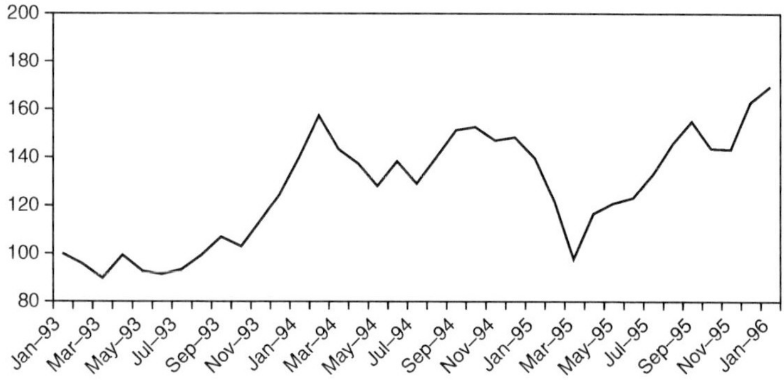

Figure 8.13 Stock market (100 at 1 January 1993 – Mexico)
Source: Thomson Datastream

other, the value of the assets in the local currency did not change. The soundness of the household and company sectors was also weakened by the increasing interest rates and the collapse this caused on the stock market (almost 40 per cent at the beginning of 1995) (see Figure 8.13).

Screening low-risk from high-risk debtors became more and more difficult (because of heightened adverse selection). Moreover, the reduced borrowers' net worth decreased the value of the collaterals that, in turn, encouraged their investments on risky projects because, in case of failure, the debtors' loss would have been smaller (increased moral hazard). The information asymmetry issue weakened the foundations of the banking system, which was trying to cope with the sudden increase of non-performing loans (15 per cent in 1995). Less funds became available to the economy and the resulting short, though severe, recession further weakened the banking system. Hence, the government had to guarantee the deposited funds and prevent widespread bank runs. To avoid a worsening of the crisis, the USA and Canada granted a $52 billion loan that allowed the Mexican government to remain solvent. Nonetheless, the Mexican GDP dropped by 7 per cent in 1995. Subsequently, the Mexican recovery started the following year.

8.5 The East Asian crisis of 1997–98

The East Asian crisis of 1997–98 also fully reflects the interpretation (illustrated in section 1.1) characterized by financial liberalization, capital inflows, high growth of credit and economic boom followed by a crash.

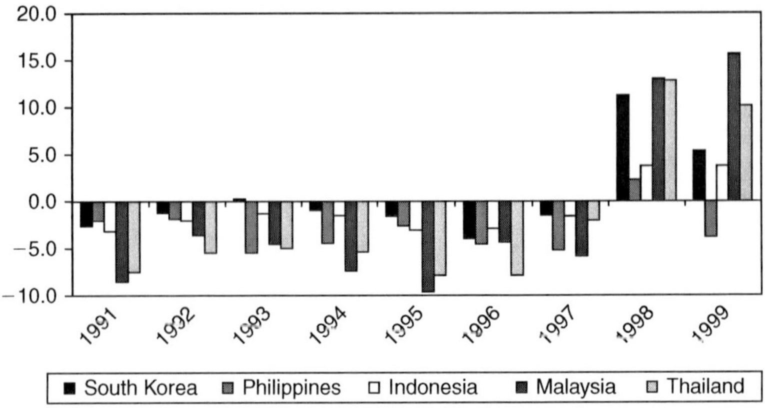

Figure 8.14 Current account (percentage of GDP – Asia)
Source: International Monetary Fund IFS

However, even if it followed the line of the Mexican crisis, the crisis in East Asia was a clear intensification in the pathology of systemic crises. This is for two reasons: a) its extension (the crisis did not affect a single country, but an entire region); and b) the high reputation of the region before the crisis, confirmed by definitions such as 'Asian tigers'.

The first signal of instability appeared in 1993, when the real exchange-rate appreciation contributed to worsening the current account balances in all five countries affected by the following crisis: in 1996, in percentage to the GDP, the current account deficit was almost 8 per cent in Thailand, 5 per cent in the Philippines, 4 per cent in Malaysia and South Korea, and 2 per cent in Indonesia (see Figure 8.14). The leverage (in term of ratio between debts and capital), which was even 3.5 for the South Korean enterprises, was also quite high for the other countries: 2.3 in Thailand, 1.8 in Indonesia, 1.3 in the Philippines and 1.2 in Malaysia (see Figure 8.15). Companies were excessively indebted in the short term: in 1996, in comparison with 26 and 45 per cent, respectively for the USA and Germany, the ratio between the short-term debt and total debt was 48 per cent in the Philippines, 53 per cent in Indonesia, 57 per cent in South Korea, 63 per cent in Thailand and 64 per cent in Malaysia (see Figure 8.16). Also, a high share of total debt of private firms, ranging between a minimum of 40 per cent in Indonesia and a maximum of 47 per cent in South Korea, was denominated in foreign currency in all five countries. Furthermore, 30 per cent of total debt of private firms in South Korea, Malaysia and Thailand – and a little less in

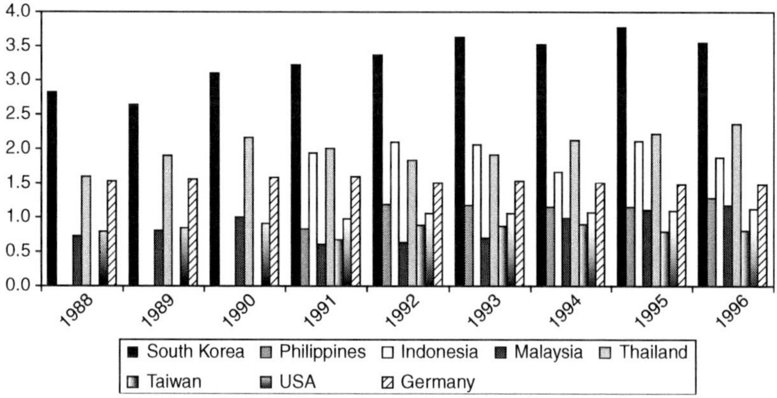

Figure 8.15 Leverage for six East Asian countries, Germany and the USA
Source: Claessens et al. (1999)

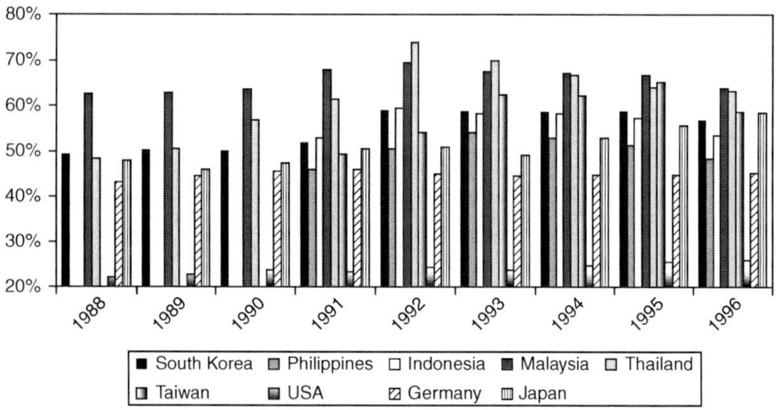

Figure 8.16 Short-term debt share for six East Asian countries, Germany and the USA
Source: Claessens et al. (1999)

the other two countries – was short-term debt in foreign currency (see Figure 8.17). The significant exposure of these firms to exchange risk – due to their high debt in foreign currency, mainly with no coverage of exchange risk – was combined with an equally concerning exposure to interest-rate risk – due to its broad short-term debt component.

So, just a few months after the World Bank had praised their development model – defining it as the 'economic miracle of East Asia' (World

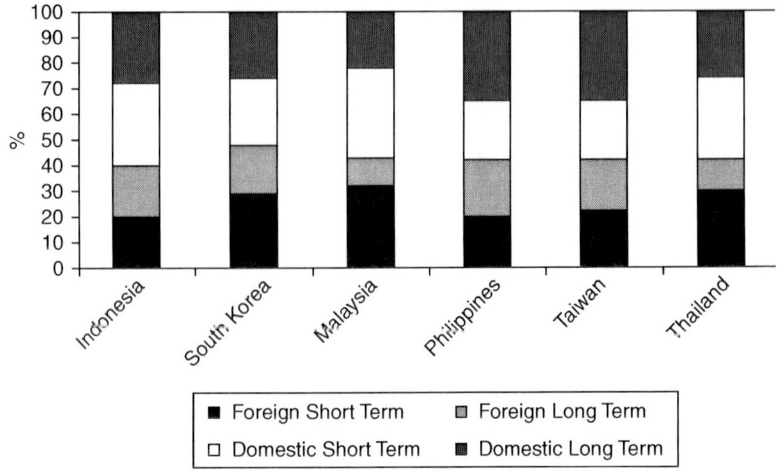

Figure 8.17 Distribution of debt in six East Asian countries (foreign vs domestic and short vs long term)
Source: Claessens et al. (1999)

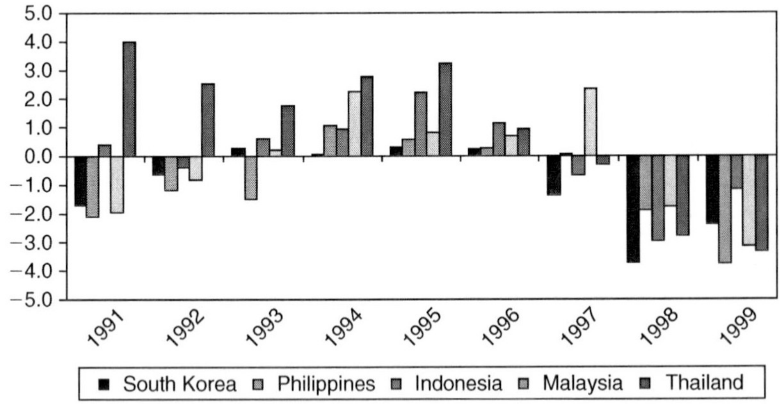

Figure 8.18 Government deficit (percentage of GDP – Asia)
Source: International Monetary Fund IFS

Bank, 1996), due to high growth with high private savings rates, public finance surpluses (or small deficits; see Figure 8.18) and low inflation rates (see Figure 8.19), in contrast with the fragility that led to the crisis in Latin America during the early 1980s – East Asia was affected by the crisis, which burst as a currency crisis initiating in Thailand.

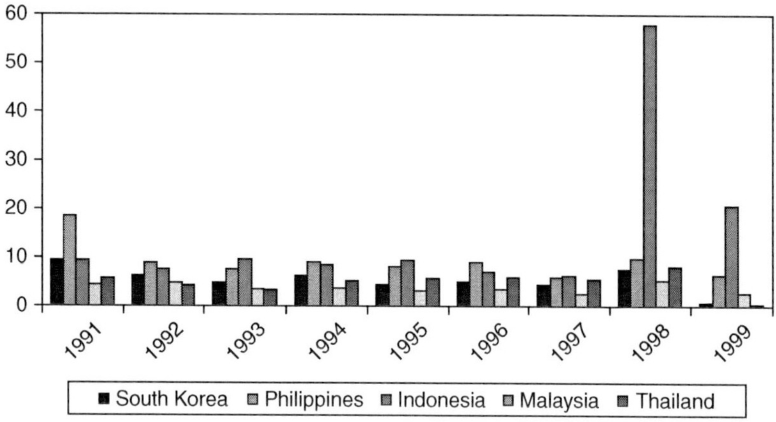

Figure 8.19 Inflation rate (Asia)
Source: International Monetary Fund IFS

The concerns about Thailand had already started in 1995–96 upon the appearance of signals of loss of external competitiveness – deficit of current accounts – in combination with a public deficit at 3 per cent of the country's GDP in 1995. As was the case in Mexico, large short-term capital inflows also supported a boost of credit with annual growth rates of more than 20 per cent during the period 1993–96. The credit boost was partly directed to low-quality investments and determined a quick growth of stock and real estate prices. In turn, luring investors with ample capital gains, the sharp growth of these prices attracted even more capital from abroad. Moreover, credit was flowing into a production sector that was already highly indebted – at the end of 1996 the leverage of Thai firms was 2.3, as against 1 in the USA and 1.5 in Germany – through intermediaries subjected to a low and inadequate extent of supervision. Additionally, most of the capital generated credit that residents took in foreign currency with no coverage of exchange risk, having the expectation that the parity of their national currency with the US dollar would be maintained. Therefore, inflows of short-term capital financed loans for long-term investments – with a dangerous change of maturity – and this credit, whose quality was partly doubtful, brought exchange risk with it.

In July 1997, a speculative attack forced Thai authorities to capitulate, as they had drained foreign currency reserves and the only choice they had was to abandon fixed parity and devalue the Thai bath by more than 20 per cent.

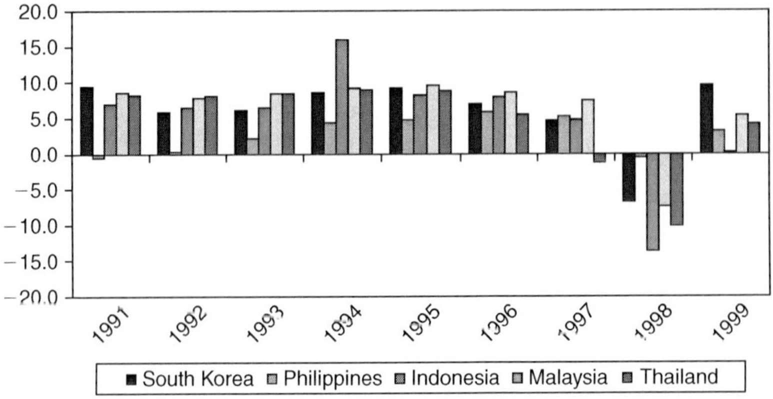

Figure 8.20 GDP growth (Asia)
Source: International Monetary Fund IFS

Despite the intervention of international financial institutions, the crisis did not end in Thailand, but spread by contagion to several other countries in the region, which were forced, one by one, to abandon their fixed exchange rate with the US dollar: first to suffer contagion were Indonesia – where the political/institutional instability linked with the fall of Suharto compounded the financial crisis – and South Korea and, although more mildly, the Philippines and Malaysia were affected too. Compared with pre-crisis values (1996), at the peak of the crisis (January 1998) the exchange rates with the US dollar were depreciated by 320 per cent for the Indonesian rupee, 120 per cent for the Thai bath, 90 per cent for the South Korean won, 80 per cent for the Malaysian ringit and 60 per cent for the Philippine peso.

The exchange-rate depreciation was combined with generalized crashes of the stock market indices, and the real growth rate of GDP collapsed from 1996 values of 5.5 per cent in the Philippines and Thailand, 7 per cent in South Korea, 8 per cent in Indonesia and 9 per cent in Malaysia to 1998 values of −13 per cent for Indonesia, −10 per cent in Thailand, −7 per cent for Malaysia and South Korea, and −1 per cent in the Philippines (see Figure 8.20). The repercussions of the crisis were also felt in Hong Kong, Singapore, Taiwan and Japan, while the persistence of capital controls spared China.

As in a long-lasting marriage, what united the Asian tigers in the long period of bursting growth during the 1980s and early 1990s also united them in bad luck. So, for foreign investors, East Asia quickly changed from riches to rags as a block, with international capital leaving the region just at the time when it was needed the most.

8.5.1 Understanding the crisis

The East Asian crisis is a striking example of a twin crisis: third-generation crises of exchange rate and bank system linked together in an explosive mix, independently from the part the initial spark comes from (Kaminsky and Reinhart, 1999). In this type of crisis, as mentioned above, exchange-rate depreciation and interest-rate increase have dramatic consequences. When the crisis starts as an exchange-rate crisis, the depreciation of the national currency increases the liabilities of the credit system – due to its exposure to the exchange risk, either directly (if the banks borrowed in foreign currencies and lent in the domestic currency without hedging) or indirectly (if the companies, having borrowed in foreign currencies without hedging, become distressed and inflate the banks' non-performing loans) – and if authorities try to defend the exchange rate with restrictive monetary policies, they just worsen the situation of heavily indebted borrowers, generating trouble on the part of bank assets.

Alternatively, the crisis can start from the financial system, if investors recognize that it has become too fragile, realizing that financial liberalization allowed the undertaking of excessive risks by the financial institutions, and also as a result of inadequate regulation/supervision. In the specific East Asian case, this was added to dangerously close relationships between governments and financial institutions (especially in Indonesia and South Korea), which generated a typical moral hazard problem, due to implicit guarantees for the borrowers.

As an additional alternative, the crisis of the banking system can be triggered by the expected bursting of the bubble – of stock and/or real estate prices – or by a deposit run. Once it starts, the bank crisis generates inflation expectations – due to liquidity increase from rescue interventions by the authorities – which trigger a speculative attack on the fixed exchange-rate regime. Bank difficulties amplify the problems of information asymmetries (adverse selection and moral hazard) in the credit market, up to blocking the financial markets. The reduction in the supply of credit limits the investment capacities of businesses, trailing the economy into a severe recession.

Finally, the microeconomic instruments illustrated in Chapter 3 also allow full understanding of the role of the banking system in the East Asian crisis. The deterioration of the banking system triggers the financial crisis through various mechanisms. Because of losses on loans, banks sharply reduce the supply of credit, depressing economic activities. Also, with a very fragile banking system, the central bank finds it extremely unpalatable to protect the exchange rate against a speculative attack by increasing interest rates, as this would provoke the bankruptcy of many banks.[3] When investors realize the fragility of the banking system, their incentives to launch a speculative attack considerably increase.

Due to the exchange-rate depreciation, the issues of information asymmetries become very serious. Considering that in emerging economies debt is mainly at short term, the depreciation increases the risks of adverse selection through increasing the burden of debt and/or reducing the value of business assets. This effect was particularly accentuated in Asia, where even many very solid businesses have bankrupted after the depreciation. Also, the depreciation fires inflation, which shoots interest rates up, increasing the tensions on financial markets, with very negative effects on the real economy.

Finally, the depreciation further weakens the banking system if, as it happens, its liabilities are mainly in foreign currency, whereas its assets are in domestic currency. This provokes an additional reduction of credit.

Due to the joint effect of East Asian currencies' depreciation and considerable interest-rate increase through the region, in September 1998 about 30 per cent of the listed firms of the five countries were technically insolvent, with peaks of 65 per cent in Indonesia and 40 per cent in South Korea (Claessens et al., 1999).

The effect of the diffused difficulties of indebted firms and the materialization of both currency and maturity mismatching risks, the banking systems of the five countries stopped working properly. The financial crisis hit two-thirds of financial intermediaries in Thailand, half in Indonesia and South Korea, one-quarter in Malaysia and 10 per cent in the Philippines (Bongini et al., 2001). This required, when bankruptcy was not declared, significant government intervention to save the banks. The financial cracks of banks as well as monetary and regulatory squeeze on intermediaries, worsening the situation of the borrowers via the balance-sheet channel (see section 4.2.1 above), led to a widespread credit crunch – that is, a unilateral reduction in the supply of credit – which, in turn, contributed to spreading and worsening the crisis. The credit crunch damaged the economy, limiting the availability of external funding for 'good' businesses – causing their bankruptcy or limiting their activity below their potential – and affecting the small and medium-sized enterprises (SMEs), in particular. Domaç et al. (1999) listed nine indicators which allow identification of the credit crunch and they found factual indications of its occurrence in East Asia between 1997 and 1998 (see Table 8.1).

Table 8.1 Summary of bank behaviour in the countries affected by the crisis

	Indonesia	South Korea	Malaysia	Philippines	Thailand
1 *Degree of increase in real interest rates following the crisis*	Negative real rates until summer 1998; high real rates thereafter	High until summer 1998; moderately high there-after	Moderately high in the earlier part of 1998; then declines	Moderately high in the latter part of 1997; downward trend in 1998	Moderately high in 1997; downward trend in 1998
2 *Increase in the spread between lending rate and interest rate on risk-free assets*	Yes (but moderate from summer 1998)	Yes	Yes	Yes	Yes (at least temporary third quarter 1997)
3 *Extent of decline in the growth of real loans*	No significant change in 1997 but sharpest drop in 1998	Sharp decline in first half of 1998	Sharp decline in 1998	Downward trend in 1997; drop in 1998	Slight upward trend in 1997 and sharp decline in 1998
4 *Evidence of flight to quality by depositors*					
4.1 Among domestic banks	From private banks to state banks	From local banks to nationwide banks	From merchant banks and finance companies to commercial banks	From private banks and saving banks to commercial banks	From small banks to large banks
4.2 Domestic to foreign banks	Yes	Yes	Yes	NA	Yes
5 *Evidence of flight to quality by banks (e.g. via larger holding of Treasury securities)*	Yes	Yes	Yes	Yes	NA

(*continued*)

Table 8.1 Continued

	Indonesia	**South Korea**	**Malaysia**	**Philippines**	**Thailand**
6 *Evidence of disproportionate contraction in loans to SMEs*	Yes	Yes	No obvious decline but drop in share of small-size loans	Yes (loans drop more in regions where SMEs are concentrated)	NA
7 *Increase in the rejection rate of loan applications*	NA	NA	Yes	NA	NA
8 *Shortening in the maturity of financial intermediation*	Yes, strongly so	Yes	Yes	No, contrary evidence	NA
9 *Evidence on contraction in pre-committed loans*	NA	Yes	Yes	NA	NA

Source: Domaç et al. (1999)

Two more contributions worth being mentioned show that the restriction in the supply of credit: a) led to bankruptcy not only of 'bad' firms, but also part of the 'good' ones (inefficient bankruptcies) with high debt because they were in sustained growth (Bongini et al., 2000); and b) has distributive (inefficient) effects, affecting the SMEs in particular (Domaç and Ferri, 1999).

With regard to the policies to counter the crisis, a harsh debate took place, where the various positions taken depended on the interpretation of the origin of the crisis. On the one hand, there were those who questioned the icon of the economic miracle, claiming that the origin of the crisis lay in the weak fabric of East Asian capitalism, which was full of conflicts of interest and over-indebted firms (e.g. Krugman, 1998). On the other hand, there were those (e.g. Radelet and Sachs, 1998; Furman and Stiglitz, 1998) who claimed that the crisis was mainly the result of irrational market behaviour, pushed by a rushed financial liberalization, which left those countries at the mercy of short-term speculative flows. While the former judged that the crisis was entirely justified and that rigorous macroeconomic policies were appropriate, the latter observed that, as the crisis affected economies with high private debt – due to the fact that their growth was sustained – fiscal/monetary restriction policies were harmful and worsened the debt-deflation spiral. Thus, Stiglitz (2002) even accused the IMF of having worsened the onset of the crisis, instead of solving it, with restrictive interventions in situations of debt-deflation, thus contributing to facilitate the contagion. With reference to the hypothesis of contagion, it should also be mentioned that the countries in crisis would have been penalized with excessive rating **downgrades** implemented during the crisis by the main rating agencies (Ferri et al., 1999). There is also an intermediate position, where both bad fundamentals and contagion played a role (e.g. Corsetti et al., 1999).

In conclusion, the Asian case confirms that often economic miracles also stumble on systemic crises. In these situations, active economic policies may be unavoidable to limit the pernicious consequences of the crisis, but they have a side effect, which is raising moral hazard for the future.

8.6 The Russian crisis and the collapse of LTCM

In the summer of 1998, the international financial markets were shocked by the Russian debt default. This crisis also reflects the interpretation of a boom and bust cycle, illustrated in section 1.1, but with some peculiar features.

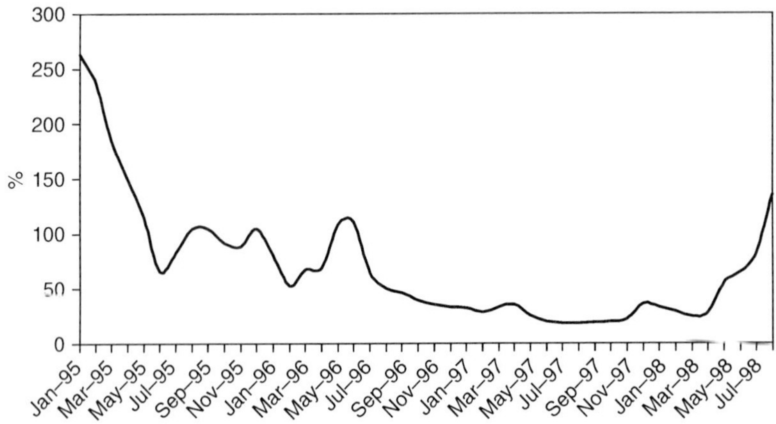

Figure 8.21 GKO yield (Russia)
Source: RECEP, Russian economic trend, various issues

After the currency crisis in 1994, Russia started a delicate process of domestic stabilization and recovery of international credibility (IMF, 1999). In the first place, with the support of the IMF, a new macroeconomic stabilization plan was set up in 1995. However, aid from the IMF was conditional on the achievement of specific objectives in terms of inflation containment; reduction of public deficit; adoption of a fixed exchange-rate regime; and implementation of structural reforms to definitively transform Russia into a market economy. In addition, the heavy public debt inherited from the Soviet Union was restructured, first with the Paris agreements in September 1997 ($60 billion) and then, one month later, with the London agreements ($33 billion). Therefore, limitations on the purchase of Russian government securities by non-residents were removed and international investors trusted in Russia again. Between November 1996 and December 1997 Russia experienced several positive developments: the government was able to place $4.5 billion Eurobonds with a relatively low **spread** which – compared with US government bonds – was between 330 and 375 base points; the interest rates on short-term government securities denominated in roubles (GKO) went from 100 to 18 per cent (see Figure 8.21) and the share of foreign subscribers of public debt reached 30 per cent (see Figure 8.22).

So, the year 1997 seemed to be the time of the so-long-awaited macroeconomic stability: a) the balance of trade showed signs of equilibrium between imports and exports; b) the inflation rate went from

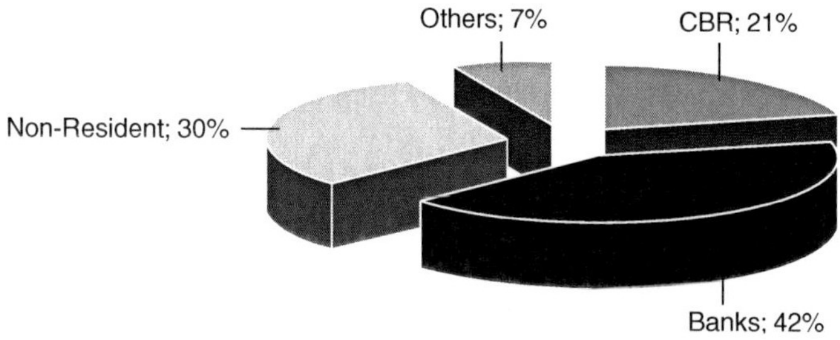

Figure 8.22 Distribution of GKO/OFZ holdings (June 1998 – Russia)
Source: Our estimates

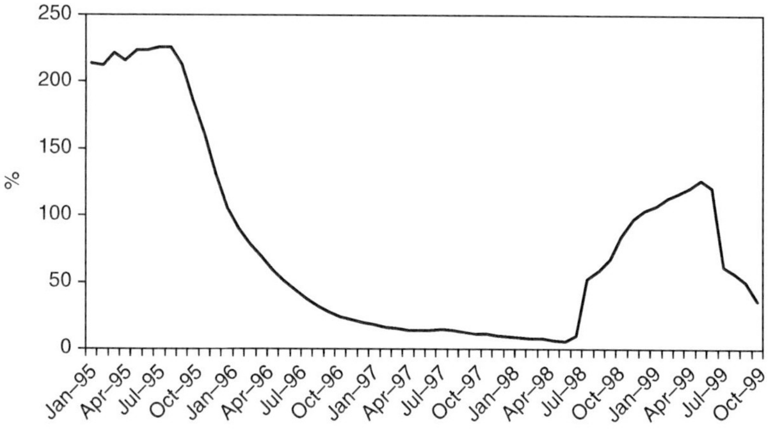

Figure 8.23 CPI annual inflation rate (Russia)
Source: Thomson Datastream

200 to 15 per cent during the period 1995–97 (see Figure 8.23); c) the exchange rate fluctuated within a limited range between 5 and 6 roubles per US dollar (see Figure 8.24); d) the high price of oil ($25 per barrel) had very positive effects on the value of Russian exports; e) GDP, for the first time since 1992, showed a positive growth (+0.9 per cent). The favourable context pushed up the stock market, which grew by more than 100 per cent during the first nine months of 1997 (see Figure 8.25).

However, many problems remained unsolved. The main concerns came from the degree of inefficiency of the fiscal system, which generated a persistent deficit (see Figure 8.26), and high public debt, mainly in foreign currency and at short term.

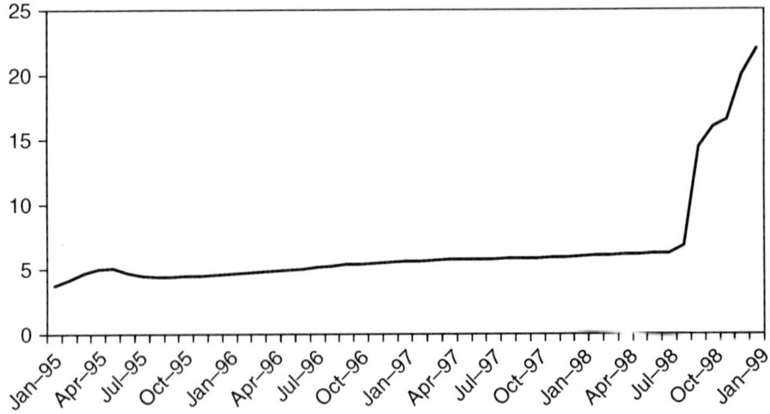

Figure 8.24 Roubles to US$
Source: Thomson Datastream

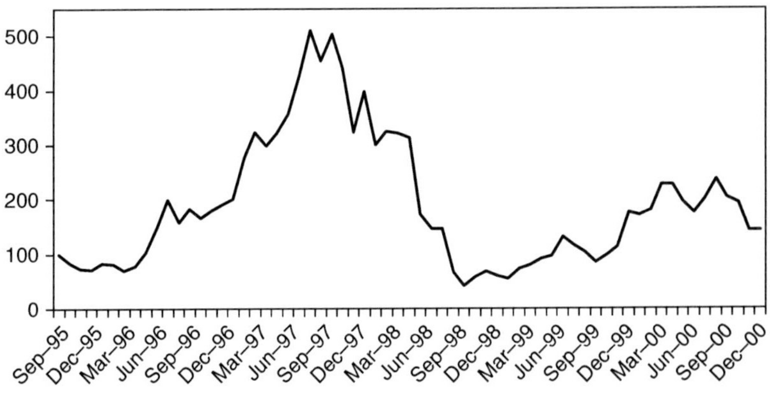

Figure 8.25 Equity index (RTS = 100 at September 1995 – Russia)
Source: Thomson Datastream

With these weaknesses, the two shocks affecting Russia in the second half of 1997 opened the way to crisis. On the one hand, the oil-price drop reduced the value of Russian exports by approximately 20 per cent and further depressed tax revenues. On the other hand, the East Asian crisis put the exchange rate of many emerging economies, including Russia, under heavy pressure. In November 1997, to roll-over the GKOs approaching their term, the central bank started a long series of interest-rate increases, while, on the currency exchange market, it lost

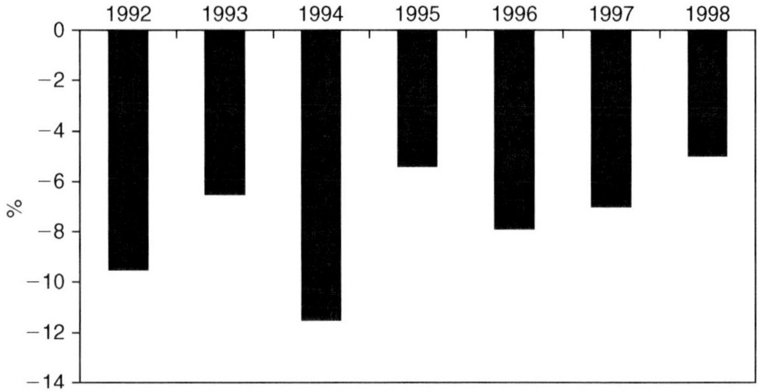

Figure 8.26 Federal budget deficit to GDP (Russia)
Source: RECEP, Russian economic trend, various issues

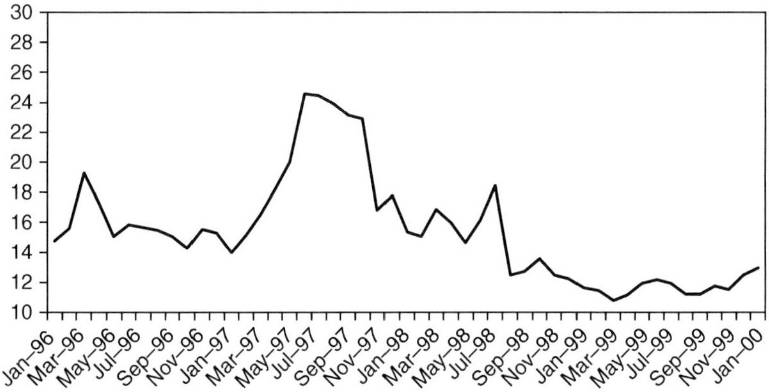

Figure 8.27 International reserves (US$ billion – Russia)
Source: Thomson Datastream

approximately $6 billion foreign currency reserves within one month to defend the rouble (see Figure 8.27).

This was added to deep political instability. In March 1998, President Boris Yeltsin dismissed all members of the government and appointed the young and inexpert Sergei Kiriyenko as Prime Minister. In May, the investors' confidence was further weakened by Kiriyenko's refusal to meet the US Secretary of the Treasury Lawrence Summers who was visiting Russia. That international incident marked the beginning of massive sales of Russian government bonds by international investors.

The macroeconomic instability was confirmed by repeated downgrades issued by the main rating agencies against Russia in March, May, June and August 1998.

The financial crisis was triggered by further interest-rate increases to roll-over public debt as, between May and June, the rate on GKOs reached 60 per cent (see Figure 8.21). To face the crisis, the government renewed its efforts on the front of structural reforms and tax revenue, while it also applied for a loan from international financial institutions to face the speculative attacks against the rouble. At mid-July, as the IMF, with the contribution also of the World Bank and Japan, granted a package of aid to Russia of approximately $17 billion, the tensions on the markets decreased for a few days. However, the crisis screwed in again, when political oppositions blocked some significant measures of the new anti-crisis plan. In mid-August 1998, only one year from its peak, the stock market had lost more than 70 per cent (see Figure 8.24), and the foreign currency reserves of the central bank were reduced by $3.5 billion more within a few days (see Figure 8.27). At this point, there were no longer many alternatives: on 17 August 1998, the government and the central bank announced a series of drastic measures: a) widening of the rouble oscillation range at $6 billion and $9.5 billion (which, in fact, turned into a devaluation); b) the unilateral restructuring of the debt denominated in roubles maturing between August and December 1999; c) 90 days of moratorium on the foreign debt contracted by commercial banks. But tensions on the rouble were not eased because the announcement, without the support of appropriate corrective macroeconomic policies, weakened even more the investors' confidence, which accelerated capital flight from Russia. On 2 September, the fixed exchange-rate regime was definitively abandoned and, in just 20 days, the rouble–dollar exchange rate reached the level of 21.

The crisis had very negative effects on the banking system. Many banks risked bankruptcy, considering that a significant share of their assets (*c.* 35 per cent) was formed by public securities (GKO) on which the government declared default. Also, due to the rouble depreciation, forward contracts in dollars signed with foreign investors before the crisis became very onerous. The counterparty risk blocked negotiations on the interbank market, paralysing also the payment system. Just a number of extraordinary measures avoided the collapse of the banking system: a) the reserve requirements were lowered; b) many short-term credits were allocated to banks which were under restructuring; c) the deposits of insolvent banks were transferred to Sberbank to avoid inflicting more losses on depositors.

The crisis also blocked the real economy with a number of social consequences. In 1998, GDP shrank by 5 per cent, the inflation rate skyrocketed to 84 per cent and on 7 October more than 100,000 people demonstrated in Moscow to express their unrest. However, Russia recovered quite rapidly from the crisis, mostly through the increase in oil price. In 1999, GDP increased by 5.4 per cent and the inflation rate went back below 40 per cent.

The Russian default considerably troubled all emerging financial markets and was among the primary causes of the (technical) bankruptcy of the LTCM (Long-Term Capital Management) hedge fund, in September 1998.

8.6.1 Understanding the crisis

The Russian crisis may be interpreted with first-generation models, considering that the main cause was the fragility of public finance. The persistent fiscal deficit and growing public debt fuelled the expectations of money-supply expansion, which would eventually cause the rouble depreciation. The central bank was able to defend the rouble against the first two speculative attacks which occurred in November 1997 and June 1998, but this was very expensive in terms of foreign currency reserves. Hence, in August 1998, when a third speculative attack was launched, the fixed exchange-rate regime collapsed.

Yet the Russian crisis also included elements of the other two generation models (Komulainen, 1999; Chiodo and Owyang, 2002). Based on second-generation models, even if the government and the central bank were ready to accept a high interest rate to defend the exchange rate, investors expected the rouble devaluation due to the economic slowdown which was materializing. In fact, before the crisis, the interest rate to allow the roll-over of government debt grew considerably.

There were also spill-over effects from the East Asian crisis that affected Russia through lower oil prices. Because of demand reduction in Asia, the oil price started decreasing considerably and the ability of Russian businesses to pay taxes was also reduced, further weakening public finances. Also, the Asian depreciation hit Russia because international investors became more risk-averse in all emerging markets.

With regard to the Russian banking system, it was more a victim than a cause of crisis. In Russia, bank assets in relation to the GDP were very low, if compared with the other emerging economies. Debt in foreign currency, although growing, was not unbearable and domestic credit did not feed consumption and investment bubbles. At the most, the negligence of the banking system may be identified in the strong exposure to GKOs and to forward contracts in foreign currency.

8.6.2 The collapse of Long-Term Capital Management

John Meriwether, who was one of the most famous Wall Street bond traders, established the Long-Term Capital Management (LTCM) hedge fund in February 1994. His partners included David Mullins, Fed Deputy-Chairman and possible successor to the Chairman, Alan Greenspan, and some of the best arbitrageurs from the academic and financial world. Robert Merton and Myron Scholes, creators of the famous Black-Scholes formula to price options, who then received the Nobel Prize for economics, completed the dream team.

In addition to the high quality of its partners, other characteristics differentiated LTCM from the other hedge funds. The minimum entry share, which could not be withdrawn for at least three years, was very high ($10 million) and commissions received by managers were higher than market average (2 per cent of assets plus 25 per cent of profits, as against an average of 1 per cent and 20 per cent; see Edwards, 1999).

Despite the selective conditions, thanks to its dream team LTCM was able to collect the record amount for a hedge fund of $1.3 billion in equities, of which $100 million came from its partners.

LTCM, as with the other hedge funds, was not heavily regulated. It had no minimum capital requirements to abide by and needed only deliver a short annual report to the SEC. LTCM also operated on all international markets mainly following a 'relative-value' trading strategy. Such strategy has very low market risk, considering that long positions on an instrument are offset by short positions on similar instruments or their derivatives. The gains of this strategy originated from small price differences which disappear when other traders also identify **arbitrage**. The most common operations implemented by LTCM concerned the purchase of Italian government fixed-rate bonds (BTPs) and the sale of German Bunds on the futures market, or the purchase of US Treasury 'off-the-run' and the sale of US Treasury 'on-the-run'.[4] The problem with such trading strategy is that the spread between the two securities is very low. For example, in August 1993, the Treasury with 30-year maturity (on-the-run) yielded 7.24 per cent, whereas the Treasury with 29 years and six-month maturity (off-the-run) yielded 7.36 per cent (Prabhu, 2001). To ensure such low spreads may generate an appropriate interest yield, it is necessary to use a very high leverage. In fact, at the beginning of 1998, the LTCM leverage value was much higher than that of the other hedge funds: with $125 billion debt and $5 billion equity, its debt–equity ratio was 25 to 1.[5] Furthermore, if the notional value of operations in derivates is considered, its leverage was even higher: at the beginning of 1998, LTCM had open positions for

$700 billion swaps and $500 billion futures in currency, for a total of $1200 billion.

Between 1994 and 1996, LTCM trading strategies generated record profits: 20 per cent, 43 per cent and 41 per cent respectively. However, these extraordinary returns were mostly due to high leverage: in 1995, return on equity was 59 per cent, but return on asset was just 2.1 per cent.

LTCM believed that, even if the ROE (return on equity) was high, the potential risk of its portfolio was very low. Based on Value-at-Risk (VaR; see Box 11.1 below)[6] calculations, LTCM informed its investors that they might lose more than 5 per cent of their portfolio one month out of five, more than 10 per cent one month out of ten, and more than 20 per cent just one year out of 50 (Lowenstein, 2000). Furthermore, according to LTCM estimations, a reduction of its equity of more than 45 per cent during one month had such low probability that it would be impossible in the history of the universe. Unfortunately, this event occurred in August 1998.

After the first three years of amazing results, in 1997 LTCM yielded only 17 per cent as against 31 per cent of the S&P 500. To go back to the returns of the first three years, LTCM took two strategies. First, it returned $2.7 billion to its shareholders, therefore increasing the leverage even more. Second, it adopted new trading strategies, in which it did not have much experience. Specifically, LTCM observed that current volatility on the equity market was higher than the historical volatility and for this reason it started selling options, betting on the reduction of stock market volatility.

During 1998 matters came to a head when Salomon Brothers' traders liquidated the bonds in their portfolios because the desk was dismissed. The situation worsened considerably on 17 August 1998, with Russia's default on approximately $13.5 billion of public debt denominated in roubles. This event caused a massive **flight to quality** on all international financial markets, which pushed spreads in the opposite direction than expected by LTCM. The fund had many open positions in which it believed that spreads between high- and low-quality securities would be reduced. However, after the default of Russia, the strong demand for high-quality securities increased their price, provoking spread widening: exactly the opposite situation on which LTCM had bet. For example, the demand for Treasury 'on-the-run' considerably increased, whereas the demand for Treasury 'off-the-run' decreased, bringing the spread from 6 to 19 basis points. Adverse market movements provoked record losses for LTCM, which amounted to $550 million on 21 August alone. Additionally, the strong tensions in the financial markets increased the volatility of the share market, while LTCM had bet on its reduction, provoking $500 million more losses. From April to September 1998, losses reduced LTCM equity from $4.5 billion to less than one. At this point, with assets value of $100 billion and more than $1200 billion in derivative instruments, a reduction of just 1 per cent of LTCM's assets value would have caused its bankruptcy.

The sale of all assets of derivative contracts in which LTCM was involved would have provoked such a reduction of market prices that it would have caused the blockage of international financial markets.[7]

To avoid this scenario, the Federal Reserve of New York organized a consortium of 14 banks which took over 90 per cent of LTCM for approximately $3.625 billion on 23 September 1998.

Even if the bailout avoided a huge fire sale of assets, it did not avoid significant losses for LTCM and for its counterparties. The largest losses were concentrated in operations of swaps and equity volatility; while the most affected counterparties were its partners and the European bank UBS, which lost, respectively, $1.5 billion and $700 million. In the year 2000, LTCM was finally closed.

8.6.3 Understanding the collapse of LTCM

In LTCM's bankruptcy there are many of the ingredients that we will find in the Great Crisis of ten years later, showing that policymakers were not able to learn the right lessons from what had happened.

Between 1997 and 1998, markets lost their bearings and international institutions unwillingly contributed to worsen the problems by applying to the Asian crisis a deflation solution in a situation of generalized debt crisis. Therefore, the initial crisis of Thailand spread through contagion to South Korea and Indonesia, and less to Malaysia and the Philippines; it even involved Hong Kong, Singapore and Taiwan, touching even Japan but sparing China, which was still protected by strict controls on capital flows. Almost all statistical regularities previously observed in the prices of securities of emerging countries failed due to the investors' stampede. This is how Merton and Scholes' **algorithms** were taken in, and only the intervention of Greenspan's Fed saved LTCM and avoided the collapse of the financial system. The debacle of these sophisticated algorithms originated from the fact that international finance was facing an extreme situation, a fat tail-distribution event that those algorithms were not able to foresee. The sudden panic of investors and financial intermediaries determined a flight to quality, which caused immediate abandonment of all risky activities to concentrate investments on Treasury securities. The flight from risk dried up liquidity of all other financial segments, in particular those of structured finance. Those who, like LTCM, bet on arbitrage strategies that supposed a spread reduction between the other securities and Treasury securities had failed: exactly the opposite was happening.

The LTCM crisis included all the lessons required to avoid what would happen ten years later. As liquidity dried up, a big intermediary from the **shadow banking system** was producing systemic damage. High leverage and very sophisticated investment strategies were the main fragilities of LTCM. Indeed, the leverage of LTCM reached 100 at the most critical moments, and its investment strategies were so sophisticated that the experts sent by the Fed needed a few weeks to understand the value of those contracts. Hence, the Fed was forced to act. However, instead of learning the obvious lesson from what had happened (make sure that no individual private institution poses systemic risks for the financial markets), the Fed adopted a model of economic policy that produced a huge problem of moral hazard. Markets were allowed to incorporate a Greenspan put in their expectations, meaning that if things went wrong, there would always be a rescue by the central bank. And, in fact, this is what happened the day after the blow-out of the dotcom bubble. Life's little irony: the investment bank Bear Stearns – which was the only one to oppose the LTCM rescue in 1998 – was the first one to pay the bill ten years later.

8.7 The crises of Turkey and Argentina

8.7.1 The crisis in Turkey

Before commenting on the tumultuous period experienced by Turkey between 2000 and 2001 – with a bank crisis in November 2000 and a currency crisis in February 2001 – it is necessary to mention the main developments of the Turkish economy in a medium–long-term perspective.

During the 1980s the reforms implemented by Prime Minister Özal signalled the transition from a state-controlled economy – with policies of import substitutions, strong controls on prices and markets – to a fully fledged market economy. Specifically, the second half of the 1980s and first half of the 1990s were characterized by the liberalization of trade, interest rates and movements of capital (completed in 1989); and by the promotion of exports and the attempt to attract direct foreign investments. All this was called the 'populist cycle', which ended with the 1994 crisis. After the crisis, GDP dropped by 6.2 per cent, but the depreciation of the Turkish lira caused a boost of both exports, mostly directed to transition economies, and investment that paved the way to recovery.

The 1989–94 expansion cycle also undermined the macroeconomic fundamentals of Turkey. The public debt skyrocketed to more than 42 per cent of GDP, creating problems of sustainability. The price dynamics also accelerated, with inflation rates above 60 per cent. These developments affected the investor's confidence in the Turkish lira, causing a strong phenomenon of currency substitution towards the dollar and the German mark.

During the 1990s, wide spreads opened between domestic and international interest rates. In the expectation of a consistent reduction of domestic rates, Turkish banks took advantage of this spread to borrow from abroad (mostly US dollars) and reinvest in Turkey. In particular, after the 1994 crisis, the significant inflow of short-term foreign capital was combined with the large phenomenon of maturity transformation: banks borrowed at short term and reinvested at long term. In this, the Turkish banks – which were largely state-owned (*c.* 50 per cent of the market) or, if private, had solid political connections – implicitly counted on the possibility that the government would cover any losses.

After the 1994 crisis, a new investment boost started, but a new recession appeared due to the fiscal and monetary policy austerity inaugurated by the Yilmaz government in summer 1997, the foreign shock of the Russian crisis (August 1998) and the Turkish earthquake in August 1999. The result was an outflow of foreign capital at short term and the intensification of currency substitution. Real interest rates increased, worsening the recession, and both phenomena tended to widen the public deficit, which, in turn, determined an increase of sovereign risk premium that further pushed interest rates upwards.

To come out of the recession, between August and December 1999 the Turkish authorities agreed a stabilization plan with the IMF. The plan was aimed at reducing the inflation rate from 65 to 10 per cent within two years through a number of major domestic reforms and restrictive fiscal policies, in combination with a planned exchange-rate devaluation. For a few months, the stabilization plan obtained the confidence of the markets and the interest-rate differential with the USA was reduced by approximately 40 percentage points (see Figure 8.28), much more than the inflation-rate reduction (see Figure 8.29).

However, because of the sustained domestic demand and resistance against cutting real wages, the inflation rate did not decrease with the same speed as the exchange-rate devaluation. Therefore, during the year 2000, there was a real appreciation of the Turkish lira, which led to

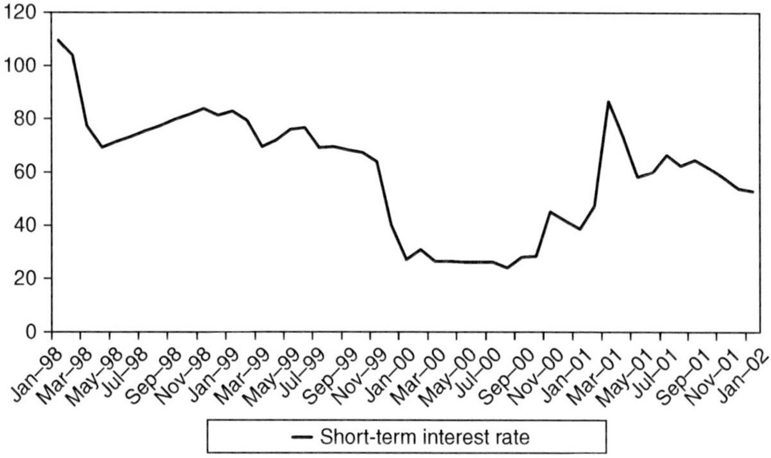

Figure 8.28 Interest-rate spread: Turkey vs USA
Source: IMF

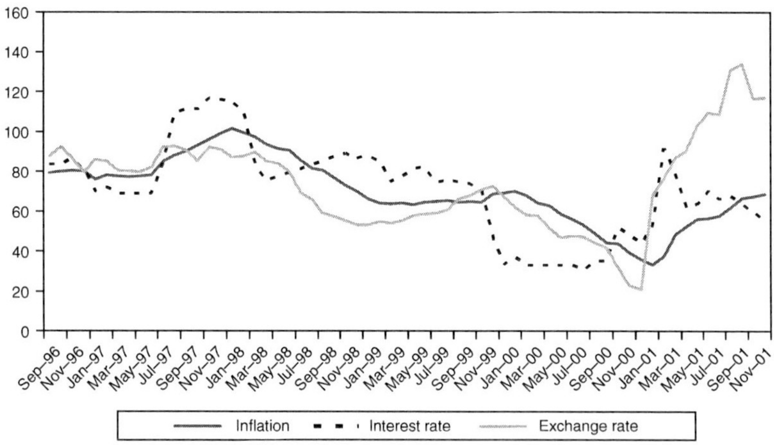

Figure 8.29 Inflation, interest rate and exchange rate: Turkey vs USA
Source: IMF

increased imports and, also due to the simultaneous oil-price increase, to a worsening of the current account deficit.

The first Turkish crisis occurred in December 2000. At the end of November, a series of investigations on corruption in the banking system led to receivership measures against a medium–large-sized bank

(Demir Bank). Mistrust regarding the financial system spread and within two weeks mistrust turned into panic with bank runs and an exchange-rate crisis. The mechanism was simple: both foreigners and Turks withdrew their deposits in fear of bank bankruptcies and converted them into foreign currency in fear of devaluation.

To prevent the situation becoming irreversible, on 6 December the IMF acted with a new opening of credit of $10 billion – with an immediate tranche and another tranche planned for 2001 – which renewed some confidence and started a rate decrease. The support of the IMF was conditional on the commitment of the government to strengthen the financial sector, strengthen the budget to face bank recapitalization and to accelerate privatizations.

However, at the beginning of 2001 there was a second wave of the crisis. The dispute between the Prime Minister and the President of the Republic about the creation of an extra-governmental body of investigation on corruption in the banking system intensified fears among the public. This time there were political concerns, but the dispute had originated from problems in the banking sector. The fear of a government crisis provoked an immediate response by the public, who also feared the blockage of the IMF loan: within just one day, Turkey lost one-fifth of its foreign currency reserves and rates went up to 3000 per cent. Three days after the political dispute, the Turkish lira was left to fluctuate, and in just one day the national currency lost 36 per cent of its value. A new plan agreed with the World Bank and the IMF and the appointment of Kemal Derviş (previously Vice-President of the World Bank) as plenipotentiary Minister of the Economy were required to bring back the depreciation of the Turkish lira, in March, from fluctuation around 30 per cent and interest rates over 10 per cent. However, the repercussions of the crisis, especially on the level of investors' confidence, did not end in the short term.

The high depreciation of the Turkish lira produced a considerable acceleration of the inflation rate, an unsustainable growth of public debt, which reached approximately 90 per cent of GDP, and a currency and banking crisis. There was a strong contraction of the real GDP in the second quarter of 2001, and in May the IMF added $8 billion more to its assistance programme, after the Turkish parliament passed important structural reforms, including the new law on banks.

8.7.2 The crisis in Argentina

Since World War II, Argentina has regressed from a rich economy to an emerging economy. Undoubtedly, the persistence of its marked dependence

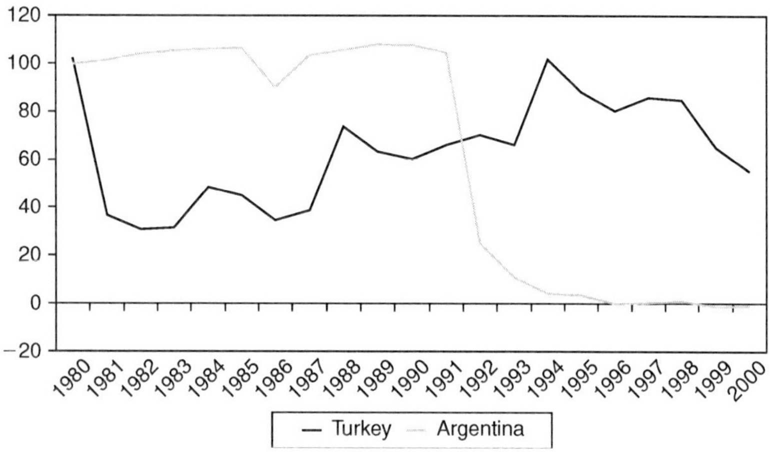

Figure 8.30 Inflation rate (Turkey and Argentina)
Source: IMF

on agriculture commodities exports, where the country had a significant production specialization, and the relative price decrease of these commodities through the decades contributed to its impoverishment. But also a contradictory political organization, as in the case of Peronism or military governments, and unstable social balances certainly played a relevant role.

As for the macroeconomic developments, Argentina experienced a period of hyperinflation during the 1970s and was involved in the financial crisis of Latin America in the early 1980s, from which it came out with the Brady stabilization plan. Hyperinflation and exchange-rate instability were still the worm of Argentina's instability during the 1980s.

At the beginning of the 1990s, with its anti-inflation plan and the adoption of the Currency Board, which decided the one-to-one parity between the peso and the US dollar, the newly appointed minister Domingo Cavallo appeared as the saviour of the country to most of the people. The plan quickly curbed hyperinflation: the inflation rate collapsed to 20 per cent in 1992, below 10 per cent in 1993 and down to almost zero in 1996 (see Figure 8.30). Through the considerable capital inflows and the reduction of real interest rates, the annual GDP growth went above 5 per cent from 1991 to 1997, with a temporary setback only for the spill-overs of the Mexican crisis in 1995 (see Figure 8.31).

However, in 1998 there was an abrupt growth deceleration and, in 1999, after the East Asian crisis, Argentina slid into recession. When

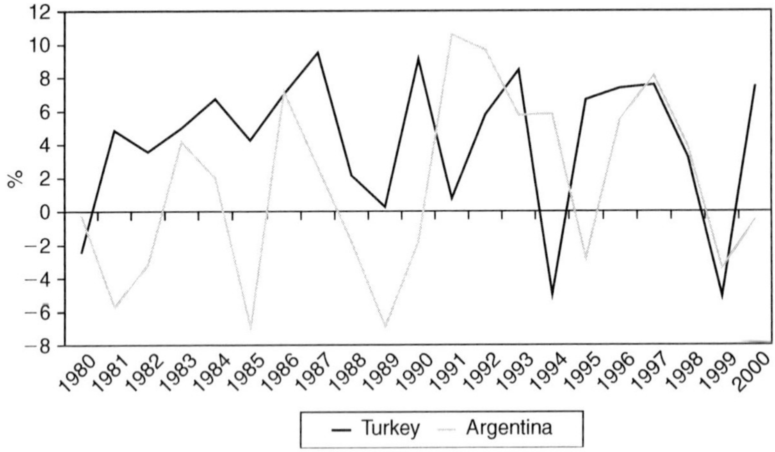

Figure 8.31 GDP growth (Turkey and Argentina)
Source: IMF

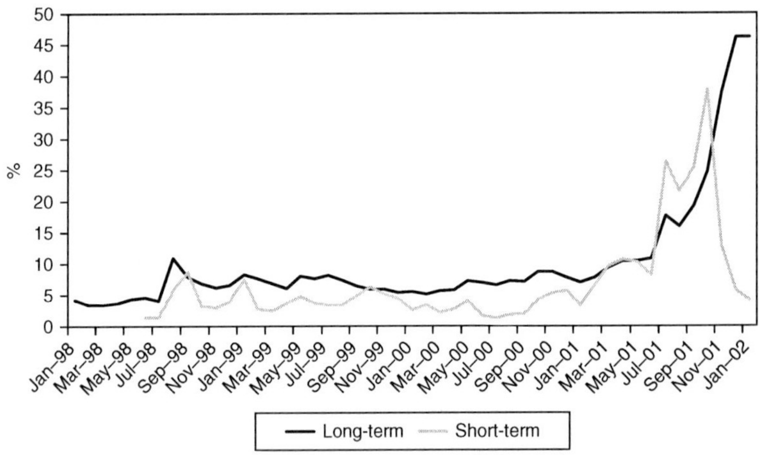

Figure 8.32 Interest-rate spread: Argentina vs USA
Source: IMF

growth stopped and a broad opposition against fiscal austerity policies appeared, doubts emerged on the actual capacity of Argentina to sustain the debt and exchange-rate parity. The short-term interest-rate spread with the USA, around 500 basis points during the first half of the year 2000, widened subsequently to almost 1000 basis points in March 2001 (see Figure 8.32). During the following three months, the spread widening stopped, but it did not go back to the initial point, due to massive outflows of deposits from the country. International reserves were reduced by 40 per cent during the first seven months of 2001 and by approximately one-quarter in July alone.

The interlocutory situation occurring between April and July 2001 reflected the government's attempt to come out of the impasse. It being impossible to raise funds on the domestic market, the Argentine authorities, with the direction of Domingo Cavallo, in order to roll-over the public debt held by international investors, could find no better solution than to convert their bonds near to maturity and their short-term debt into new long-term bonds with prohibitive interest rates. On the deficit front, Cavallo persuaded the Congress to approve a law to cancel public deficit through cutting public expenditure on the level of tax revenues. However, this involved cuts in non-interest expenditure – including public-sector wages – that were so significant that a problem of political sustainability occurred. As a result, investors' confidence slowly came back and the measure was only able – between March and July – to stop the situation being locked on a level that had become highly precarious.

In August, the IMF accelerated the disbursement of a $1.2 billion instalment planned for September and committed itself to providing further loans for $8 billion in return for the government commitment to rationalize transfers between central and decentralized public administrations and search for voluntary debt restructuring on the market. The IMF widely granted additional loans with the idea of allowing the country to avoid referring to financial markets in such a difficult period or, at least, reducing the roll-over risk of international private loans. The assumption of the IMF was that investors' confidence in Argentina could soon return, not only through its intervention but also mostly by virtue of the commitment to cancel the public deficit. In turn, it was expected that the return of confidence would reduce real interest rates and trigger a new growth phase.

Unfortunately, these assumptions were wrong. The interest-rate differential of Argentina as compared with the USA began to grow again from August and increased to 2000 basis points in October and to 2500 basis points in November, just before the crisis. After he tried, with no success, to obtain further support from the IMF, Minister Cavallo was forced to resign in December. In a situation of rioting among the population, the government was forced to declare the suspension of the convertibility of the peso with the US dollar with unit parity; and banks and markets were closed. The widespread riots, which included fatalities, led to the resignation of President de la Rúa. In a crescendo of socio-economic and political unrest, the Peronists took power back from the opposition. The Congress elected President Saá, who also resigned after a few days because of a split in the Peronist movement. Subsequently, the previous governor of the province of Buenos Aires, Eduardo Duhalde, was elected President, and although problems kept appearing, the situation gradually improved.

On the exchange rate, two groups were opposed in this period: on the one hand, those who pressurized for full 'dollarization' of the Argentine economy; on the other hand, those who wanted free fluctuation of the peso. The first group mostly consisted of finance representatives, while the second group mainly included industrial representatives.

Initially, Duhalde decided to fix a new parity at 1.4 pesos per dollar. But the markets clearly indicated that the parity was going to be exceeded and, eventually, the authorities decided for free fluctuation of the peso. In time, the ordered freezing of deposits in dollars appeared as less and less sustainable.

In the meantime, Argentina declared default on its debt. The default affected a vast audience of international investors. Moreover, like the case of Russia in 1998, suspension of payments by Argentina occurred without a resolution mechanism, which would have allowed finding a fair solution for the country in default and for the investors, without increasing the problem of moral hazard. Actually, a suspension of payments not on a unilateral base but 'authorized' by the IMF was at the core of the new approach to the governance of international crises, as suggested in the 'Krueger doctrine' (see Box 8.1).

8.7.3 Similarities between Turkey and Argentina

Among the many interesting common features between Argentina and Turkey, the most important is that both countries were considered as 'the poster boys of the Washington consensus' (Eichengreen, 2002). Before the stabilization, the two countries went through a period of low growth: in Argentina, GDP growth was negative on average and hit 1 per cent between 1980 and 1990, while a marked deceleration of growth towards the end of the 1990s occurred in Turkey. In both countries, growth accelerated after the stabilization; reducing real interest rates boosted domestic demand. Therefore, despite the simultaneous rebound of exports, in both Argentina and Turkey, the recovery worsened the deficit of the current accounts (see Figure 8.33), thus increasing the dependence on the inflow of international capital. Finally, both countries launched plans for the reduction of public deficit, privatization of public businesses and the strengthening of the national banking system.

Box 8.1 The Krueger doctrine

It was not by chance that on 26 November 2001 – with the Turkish crisis over and that of Argentina in its most acute phase – Anne Krueger, the influential then First Deputy-Director General of the IMF representing the USA, put forward an interesting and innovative proposal, discussed by the IMF's Executive Directors' Board on 6 December. Even though the proposal was shelved, it is important to review it as it represents one of the most interesting signals of the awareness of the problem of systemic financial crises in emerging economies. Had it been adopted, the history of the financial crises thereafter would have probably been different from what we actually saw.

Krueger noted that 'at the moment, too many countries with insurmountable debt problems wait too long, imposing unnecessarily heavy economic costs on themselves and on the international community that has to help pick up the pieces' ... and, also, 'We lack incentives to help countries with unsustainable debts resolve them promptly and in an orderly way' (IMF, 2001). Krueger proposed adopting a scheme, taken to the sovereign level from the company bankruptcy law, that would allow sovereign debtors to enjoy temporary protection from their creditors while they tried to restructure their debt via bona fide renegotiation with creditors. According to the proposal, the country entering a crisis would require the IMF to allow a temporary standstill (probably for a few months) of their debt payments, a period during which the country would try renegotiating its debt and rolling it over. Any postponement in the temporary payment standstill would require IMF approval. It was also conceived that the plan might require imposing temporary exchange-rate controls to impede capital flights from the country. According to Krueger, the 'primary objective in creating a formal mechanism of this type would be to create incentives for debtors and creditors to reach agreement on their own accord, so the mechanism would rarely need to be used'. The sovereign debt restructuring mechanism was to be based on four prospective principles:

1 Creditors should not be allowed to disrupt negotiations by seeking recourse in their own national courts;
2 Debtor countries would need to provide assurances that they were negotiating in good faith and treating all creditors equally;

(*continued*)

Box 8.1 Continued

3 Private creditors would need to be encouraged to lend new money by receiving some guarantee that they would be repaid ahead of existing private creditors;
4 Once agreement on a restructuring had been reached by a large enough majority of creditors, the rest would be bound to accept the terms.

Anne Krueger was aware that, before launching such a mechanism, some technical questions had to be answered, including:

- how to provide a legal basis for the mechanism;
- who should operate the mechanism;
- how the standstill would be formally activated;
- how to ensure the debtor country behaved appropriately during the negotiations;
- what financing the IMF should provide after the restructuring;
- to what type of debt the standstill should apply.

This proposal came close to what others had proposed after the East Asian crisis (e.g. Miller and Zhang, 2000) and would have potentially reconciled the function of international lending of last resort while attempting to get private creditors involved in the resolution of the crisis. The preamble was recognizing that the systemic nature of the crisis determines a situation of illiquidity for the country, which, though potentially solvable on a longer time horizon, might instead be forced to default if required to pay back immediately. In the event, the lending of last resort interventions by the IMF and the other international institutions risks being ineffective – leading in through the main door what will immediately fly away through the window – if payments are not temporarily suspended and temporary capital controls are not enforced. Getting private creditors involved – making them share the crisis losses – in the debt restructuring would have corresponded to enforcing the principle of 'bailing in', the opposite of 'bailing out', under which private creditors bear no loss. As such, the 'bailing out' aggravates the moral hazard of the private creditors, and tends to make them irresponsible – generating a vicious circle in which the countries burdened with unsustainable

(*continued*)

Box 8.1 Continued

indebtedness keep receiving credit at prohibitive terms, leading them to 'betting for resurrection', which generally amplifies the dimension of the crisis. On the contrary, the 'bailing in' would have provided incentives to responsible behaviour on the part of the private creditors, thus lowering the extent of the crisis.

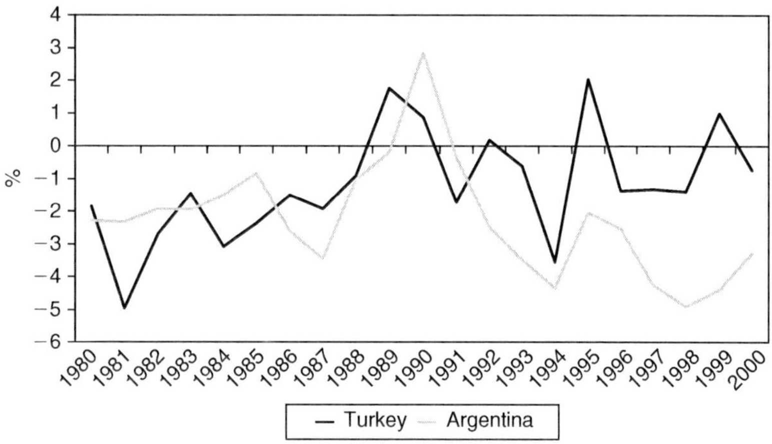

Figure 8.33 Current account balance (percentage of GDP – Turkey and Argentina)
Source: IMF

However, it is also true that the experiences of Argentina and Turkey did not entirely match. Upon stabilization, Argentina was coming out of a long period of hyperinflation, whereas the inflation rate in Turkey, although it was steadily higher than 50 per cent, had never degenerated into hyperinflation. If stabilization in Argentina took place at the beginning of the decade (in 1991), stabilization in Turkey took place only in 1999. Furthermore, while stabilization in Argentina was based on a strong connection with the US dollar, by choosing the Currency Board, stabilization in Turkey was based on the adoption of a moving parity, as compared with a basket including both the US dollar and the German mark. Also, Argentina had entirely and quickly cancelled its inflation, whereas the Turkish inflation rate remained consistently around 50 per cent, even after the stabilization started. Finally, the Turkish crisis appeared relatively abruptly, while the Argentine stabilization lasted much longer.

Despite this, it later became clear that the weaknesses of Argentina and Turkey were similar. Fiscal adjustment was incomplete, public expenditure cuts had insufficient political support and public deficit would quickly expand once the revenues from privatizations were reduced.[8] Additionally, the disinflationary anchoring of the exchange rate affected external competitiveness, and no adjustment of exchange-rate parity could be implemented without affecting the credibility of the disinflation measure as well as the stability of the national banking system, which had accumulated foreign currency liabilities in excess of corresponding assets. Finally, the funding of current account deficits was ensured by significant capital inflows, which took the form, especially in the case of Turkey, of increasingly short-term funds. Hence, when the confidence of investors was lost, the risk of default sharply increased.

The consequence was that Argentina and Turkey were particularly vulnerable to the deterioration of international conditions. With the East Asian crisis and Russian default, the risk premium required by international investors quickly went up. There were also other additional shocks: a) the external competitiveness of Argentina was put at risk by the devaluation in Brazil, at the beginning of 1999, and by the strengthening of the US dollar; b) Turkey was hit by a devastating earthquake; c) export perspectives for both countries were influenced first by oil-price increase and then by weakened world growth.

In this unfavourable context, just a few small signals doubting about the government commitment on tax adjustment were enough to accelerate the crisis. So Turkey paid for the consequences of a dispute between the Prime Minister and the President of the Republic concerning the ways to confront corruption in the public sector; while Argentina suffered from the loss of consensus to tax cuts planned by the government. The heightening of risks in the future caused an increase in interest rates, weakening growth and showing doubts on debt sustainability. The IMF immediately acted in Turkey and, after a few months, also in Argentina through granting new loans.[9]

8.7.4 Understanding the crises

The Argentine and Turkish experiences confirm the hypothesis of the 'twin crises' (see section 2.3 above) – meaning that bank crisis and exchange-rate crisis usually come together – but with an important qualification. In the case of Turkey, the fragility of the banking system seems to be an important element at the origin of the crisis, while in Argentina the bank crisis was one of the results of the exchange-rate crisis.

In Turkey, the weakness of the banks, only partly connected with the lira situation, was one of the causes of the loss of confidence by international investors, and also by Turkish people, in the stabilization plan. It is true that the loss of confidence also originated in the inconsistency of government policies and insufficient support for expenditure-reduction policies, but the fragility of Turkish banks was well known. In turn, in addition to the weakness in the regulatory and supervisory framework, the fragility of the Turkish banking system also originated from its actual protection, with a limited degree of openness to foreign banks, which still in June 2001 only accounted for 5 per cent of the Turkish banking market. On the contrary, in Argentina, the privatization of the banking system was pervasive and attracted many big international banks into the country, which penetrated even the retail market: between 1991 and 1998, the market share (on total assets) of foreign-owned banks increased from 14 to 53 per cent. Hence, the birth of 'dollar liabilities' in the economy and, mostly, in the Argentine banking system was not the result, as in Turkey, of the attempt of fragile banks to make easy profits by betting on filling the gap between domestic and foreign interest rates. It is true that the crisis also provoked widespread distress phenomena in the Argentine banking system, but this seems to be the consequence of the exchange-rate crisis, instead of being one of the factors causing the exchange-rate crisis.

However, probably the most important lesson of the Argentine crisis refers to the compatibility of the economic policies framework, including the exchange-rate policy. The main difference between the Argentine stabilization and the Turkish stabilization was in the duration of the experience: ten years the former, and just one the latter. This means that even the consequences of the final abandonment of the stabilization plan were enormously heavier for Argentina than for Turkey. Also the capacity of Argentina to make its stabilization last so long leads us to question the immediate causes that brought it to its end: the appreciation of the dollar and even more the devaluation in Brazil in 1999. This stresses the importance of trade connections in the spreading of crises (see section 2.3 above) and specifically the problem of consistency between free movements of capital, fixing of the exchange rate and trade freedom. Argentina was commercially integrated at the highest level with Brazil, within the Mercosur, while the intensity of its trade with the USA was limited. The economy of Argentina lost competitiveness with the US dollar appreciation from 1996, but this issue exploded in 1999, when Brazil devalued its currency causing a huge shock of competitiveness for Argentina. Although Argentina tried to protect itself with selective trade restrictions against Brazil, that was not enough and Argentina entered recession. Moreover, despite the high devaluation of the Brazilian real at the beginning of 1999, Brazil only had a limited return of inflation, which – by virtue of a limited pass through from exchange rate to domestic prices – also remained below 10 per cent during the following three-year period.

8.8 The Japanese depression

From the Great Depression of the 1930s to the Great Crisis of 2007–09, the Japanese economic and financial crisis was the most important affecting an industrialized country. It was surprising for its duration and intensity, for the extent of efforts made to solve it, but also for their ineffectiveness. It started in the early 1990s and continued on alternate phases up to the first years of the new century, so that the 1990s are called 'the lost decade' in Japan. The impact of this complex crisis brought Japan from being a 'model' country – the one that developed the most after World War II – to a 'big chronic sufferer' unable to come out of stagnation.

Although with very peculiar characteristics, the Japanese crisis can also be interpreted as illustrated in Part I, characterized by deregulation, financial innovation, credit expansion, speculation bubble and deep recession. The difference here is that the exchange rate did not play a relevant role.

As for the macroeconomic developments before the crisis, Japan had experienced exceptional growth after World War II until the 1980s. GDP grew by 6 per cent on average, almost double that in the USA and in the current EU zone, largely thanks to its export dynamics. The Japanese market share on world exports went from almost zero in 1946 to around 7 per cent during the 1980s. So, world markets were inundated with Japanese products. Western countries had the impression that Japan had a superior production model and tried to imitate it (Forester, 1993).

The favourable macroeconomic scenario, characterized by high economic growth and low inflation rate, stimulated a strong expansion of credit that pushed up the stock and real estate market (Kanaya and Woo, 2000). The level of the Nikkei 225 stock index went from 5000 in the early 1980s to 37,000 in 1990, and in 1991 the price of land in the six main cities was four times higher as compared with ten years before (see Figure 8.34).

Meanwhile, liberalization and financial-innovation processes were also intensified and led to reduced control on interest rates and lending, deregulation of capital markets, the gradual removal of restrictions

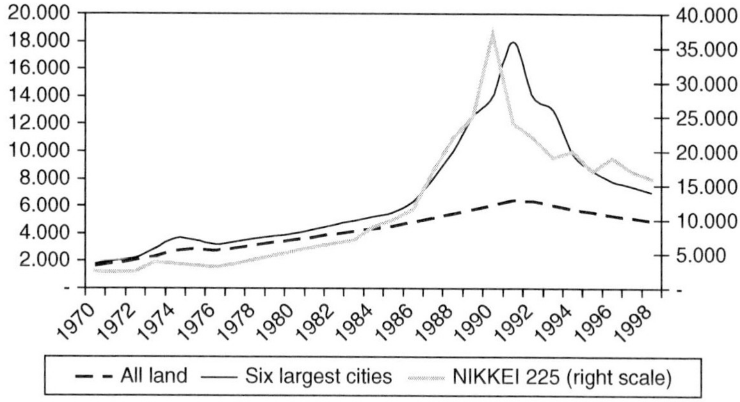

Figure 8.34 Japan double bubble
Source: our elaboration

for access to the bond market by the firms and the creation of the **commercial paper** market.

These developments had important consequences for the banking system, because the increased competition reduced the interest margin and pushed banks to look for alternative sources of income in more risky sectors, where they had no experience. In particular, loans to consumers, the real estate sector, and small and medium-sized enterprises significantly increased. The hike of stock and the real estate market price triggered the balance-sheet channel (see section 4.2.1 above), which strengthened the credit expansion.

As in other historical situations, the sequence of events included, first, the burst of the equity bubble and then the burst of the real estate bubble. Between 1990 and 1991, the Nikkei 225 index lost one-third of its value and further decreased to 15,000 in 1998, and down to 8000 at the end of 2002. After 1991, the drop of the land price in the main cities, although it was less abrupt, had a similar trend. The sudden slowdown of the Japanese economy – GDP growth dropped from 6 per cent to approximately 1 per cent – continued up until 1995.

In 1996, there seemed to be a significant recovery, pushed by a strong expansive fiscal action. However, the recovery was transitory. In 1997, there was a new slowdown, which degenerated into recession in 1998, when – as we have seen – Japan was also partly involved in the East Asian crisis. Despite the massive fiscal expansion, which was sharply intensified in 1998 – when the deficit/GDP ratio left the 4 per cent area, went up to almost 9 per cent and remained above 5 per cent during the following years – the growth was very low in 1999 and went back to above 2 per cent in the year 2000. But Japan fell again into recession in 2001–02 and a longer-lasting recovery started only from 2003.

The most worrying aspect of the crisis was that Japan, the first industrialized country since the 1930s, experienced a long period of deflation: its GDP deflator was zero or negative from 1994 and went back to slightly positive values only in 2008. In response to deflation, after 1996 the nominal short-term interest rate became virtually zero, and the Japanese economy was in a liquidity trap thereafter.

During the 1990s, against the background of a deep and long recession, the Japanese banking system experienced a slow and progressive deterioration, which then culminated in the systemic crisis of 1997.

The first signals of instability appeared in 1992, when the *jusen* companies got into trouble. These companies were established during the 1970s to facilitate residential credit but, after competition increased in this sector, during the 1980s they moved to loans for the building sector. The burst of the real estate bubble severely hit the *jusen* companies. In the summer of 1993 their creditors agreed upon a ten-year restructuring plan with the support of the Ministry of Finance. However, the severe and prolonged decrease in the real estate market forced the plan's designers to dismiss the *jusen* companies in 1995.

The year 1994 marked the crisis for cooperative and regional banks. The first two made bankrupt were Tokyo Kyowa Credit Cooperative and Anzen Credit Cooperative. One year later, Cosmo Credit Cooperative, Kizu Credit Cooperative and Hyogo Bank, which were particularly exposed in the building sector, suspended their activities. The debacle scared the investors, who rapidly transferred their deposits to banks with high rating and to postal accounts. To calm the situation down, the Japanese government allocated substantial funds to support the banking system and guaranteed all deposits of cooperative banks.

In 1997, the crisis also involved large Japanese financial institutions. The first institutions to be in trouble were Nissan Life Insurance and Sanyo Securities. The two events significantly shocked the interbank market, where trading had a marked contraction. Soon after, Hokkaido Takushoku Bank and Yamaichi Securities also suspended their activities. At that point, the difficulties were reflected in both the value of equities of the entire Japanese banking sector and the cost of procurement on international markets (Japan premium).

In 1998, the Long Term Credit Bank of Japan and, subsequently, the Nippon Credit Bank were nationalized. At that point, the use of a large amount of public funds to solve the financial problems could be no longer postponed. In February, 30 trillion yens were allocated to save banks and protect depositors.

8.8.1 Understanding the crisis

The crisis in Japan stimulated a multiform debate: a) on the causes of the speculative bubble, whose burst was the origin of the crisis; b) on the limits of economic policy in the case of a liquidity trap; c) on the bidirectional links between the economic crisis and the weakening of Japanese banks.

As for the causes of the speculative bubble, developing the concept of 'irrational exuberance', formulated by Greenspan in 1996 about the strong growth of the US equity price, Shiller (2000) identified the common characteristics of the various speculative bubbles in that particular situation, which separated and differentiated the prices of real or financial assets from their intrinsic value, meaning from that value that they would have in the case of efficient markets. If the US irrational exuberance of the late 1990s refers to the excessive expectations on the 'new economy', that of Japan ten years earlier was dependent on the perception that the miraculous Japanese growth could continue forever. Inducing the investors to increase their positions, which pushed up the rates and, in turn, the impression that rate increase could only continue, induced the investors to neglect the fundamentals. Also in Japan, the formation of the speculative bubble followed intense financial liberalization. The bubble burst after the central bank recalled the attention of investors to the large divergence between market value and fundamental value. So, in 1989, the governor Yasushi Mieno explicitly declared he wanted to burst the existing bubble and increased interest rates. At that point, the expectations of future increase of prices ceased and the bubble burst.

As for monetary policy, the Japan depression is the most recent case of liquidity trap. In such a situation, that is when the LM curve – which ensures the monetary market equilibrium in the well-known IS-LM model – becomes horizontal, expansionary monetary policies have no effect, as monetary demand is infinitely elastic to the interest rate; while a fiscal expansion is most effective, as the crowding-out is zero (see Figure 8.35). This happens when the nominal interest rate hits the zero lower bound and cannot go further down.

The economic literature also shows that the decision of the central banks about short-term interest-rate objective is well summarized by the so-called Taylor's rule, which is:

$$i_t = \alpha_0 + \alpha_1 \pi_t + \alpha_2 (y_t - y^*_t) + \rho i_{t-1}$$

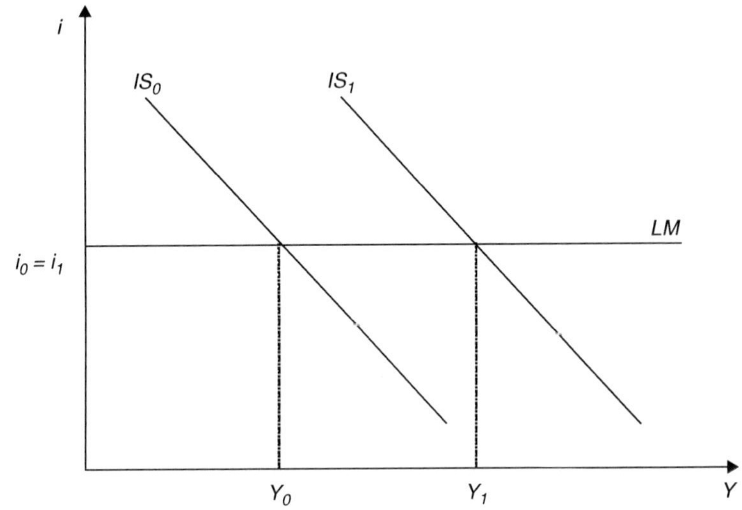

Figure 8.35 Liquidity trap

where i_t is the short-term rate selected by the central bank on the basis of parameters, which are all positive: α_1 (the weight given to the inflation objective), α_2 (the weight given to the objective of containing the output gap, which is GDP deviation from its potential level) and ρ, which expresses the wish to smoothen the interest rate (i.e. to avoid changing it too abruptly). When $\pi_t < 0$ (i.e. we are in deflation) and also the output gap is negative (i.e. we are in recession), and i_{t-1} has also been brought to zero, then Taylor's rule implies fixing $i_t < 0$, which is normally not possible.

The consequence is that the output gap becomes even more negative and the price drop intensifies, causing a deflationary spiral, which can be unstable (Benhabib et al., 1999). For some time, Krugman (2000) suggested that even in liquidity traps induced by nominal rates almost at zero and continuous deflation, it is possible to use monetary policy, assigning to it the objective of generating inflation expectations, hence lowering the real interest rate and stimulating private demand. In fact, by accelerating the creation of the monetary base, it is possible to ingenerate in the operators the expectation that in the future the monetary value will be reduced in terms of consumption (i.e. prices increase), or in relation to the other currencies (yen depreciation, herald of imported inflation). However, it seems that Krugman's recipe was never followed with determination in Japan.

Finally, on the bidirectional connections between economic crisis and the weakening of the Japanese banks, many points deserve to be highlighted as they are another distinctive element of the Japanese crisis. We should not underestimate how Japanese banks became reluctant to grant new loans, as they were prostrated by the burst of the speculative bubble. Although the crisis deflagration cannot be considered as being caused by this attitude, it certainly acted as a significant mechanism for crisis propagation and amplification.

Traditionally, the Japanese financial system is indicated as a bank-based system, where the role of banks dominates the role of the financial markets (Allen and Gale, 2000; Baba and Hisada, 2002). However, there are two requirements to ensure proper operation of a system based on banks: a) appropriate profitability of intermediaries, which ensures autonomous management choices in the case of debtor difficulties; b) appropriate resolution mechanisms from the authorities, in case the banking system loses its capacity to absorb the shocks on debtors within their own funds. All these elements were missing in the Japanese crisis.

Japanese banks have usually operated traditional intermediation, based on the offer of loans, facilitated by their operation in substantially captive markets (i.e. without competition), for historical relations with the main businesses, strengthened by the joint presence of both banks and big companies in their respective shareholding through group organizations. The intermediation model is that of the 'main bank' ruled by cross-shareholdings within the keiretsu system – industrial and financial conglomerates – that contributed to keeping almost exclusive banks' function to provide credit to big companies.

The close connections between banks and big business formed an important factor of fragility in relation to the appearance of a generalized crisis of debtors. Cross-shareholdings forms, in fact, are a mutual support mechanism between a bank and an industrial group. It also becomes hard for a bank to deny funds to an industrial group in situations where the quality of an industrial group is degraded, thereby generating an intricate conflict of interest. In turn, this worsened bank instability and increased the complexity of solving the crisis, due also to the appearance of systemic risks.

When the crisis worsened, the Japanese banks tried to diversify their activities into real estate loans – assuming a continuous growth of real estate prices – and in the stock market. However, these strategies were fruitless.

The prolongation of the Japanese crisis had, as its corollary, the continuous and growing worsening of the quality of the bank-loan portfolio.

In turn, problematic high-loan stocks reduced both capitalization and the capacity of the banking system to grant new loans, increasing the problems of information asymmetries and depressing economic activities.

The non-performing loans issue was aggravated by two environmental changes: a) the real estate boost widened bank availability to financially support this sector, with imaginable consequences after the burst of the real estate bubble; b) partial deregulation allowed bigger companies to directly tap the financial markets, inducing the banks to focus on more risky sectors, such as the SMEs and the consumer loan sector.

The burst of the real estate bubble had an immediate impact on bank availability to grant new loans: the growth rate of loans was dramatically reduced to ingenerate a real credit crunch.

According to official statistics, the amount of non-performing loans was 5 per cent of total assets in 1998 (this figure kept growing during the following years up to almost 9 per cent in 2002). If we compare this figure with the data regarding the economies of the East Asian countries involved in the crisis in 1997 (see Table 8.2), which shows 'non-performing loans/assets' or 'non-performing loans/GDP' ratios often higher than 50 per cent during the worst year of the crisis, the official amount of Japanese non-performing is not an amazing figure and it can probably be managed within its existent safety net. Furthermore, if we move the comparison towards industrialized countries, such as the USA and Sweden – which experienced systemic bank crises in the early 1990s – the difference seems to be decreasing and aggravating, therefore, the alarm signal coming from the extent of bank bad debts in relation to lending and GDP.

The Japanese supervisory authorities are often criticized as they practised excessive regulatory forbearance. Through this forbearance, the authorities did not sanction banks immediately upon the appearance of undercapitalization problems and excessive exposure to risk. The rationale for the authorities was the hope that the problems would be solved by themselves either through the banks' own action or through cyclical recovery of the economy.

In this reference, it is useful to compare the case of the Japanese crisis with the Swedish banking-experience crisis (Hoshi and Kashyap, 1999; Kanaya and Woo, 2000; Suzuki, 2002; Nakamura, 2002), for both the similarities identified in the background causes of the crises and because Sweden is a successful case of the resolution of a systemic crisis.

The common characteristics between the two crises may be summarized as: a) wide supply of credit at low cost; b) weak corporate governance of both banks and authorities responsible for their control; c) pervasive

Table 8.2 The magnitude of non-performing loans

Country	Peak of the crisis	Lending/ GDP	(Non-performing loans)/assets	(Non-performing loans)/GDP
Indonesia	1998	75	70	53
South Korea	1998	100	35	35
Malaysia	1998	140	30	42
Thailand	1998	140	50	70
Sweden	1992	60	11	7
United States	1992	60	3	2
Japan	1998	106	5	6

Source: Cooke and Foley (1999), table 3, p. 6. For Japan: FSA Economic and Social Research Institute

main-bank system, which is based on very solid connections between a business and its main funding bank; d) presence of an exogenous shock: the crisis of the EMS (European Monetary System) and the crisis of East Asia respectively.

Despite these common elements, the differences must not be underestimated. As compared with Sweden, Japan is a large economy, net creditor on the rest of the world. Therefore, it has no endogenous pressure to face the problems and weaknesses of its financial system promptly and incisively. Furthermore, the absence of bank runs or any other extraordinary event that forced the authorities and government to proceed with rapid and radical measures, for many years meant that the magnitude of the problems and the need to face them at an early stage were underestimated. In any case, playing for time characterizes the actions of most supervision authorities, including the Swedish authorities, which directly faced the crisis – when it had reached systemic dimensions – just after the declaration of serious management difficulties by the main bank of the country.

9
The Mega-Bankruptcies of the Early 2000s

As we move closer to what might be the terminal crisis – the Great Crisis of 2007–09 – of this political-economy cycle of finance, the pernicious series of systemic crises in emerging economies seems to be exhausted. This apparent tranquillity does not depend on the fact that the international financial order has found a new coherent direction. Rather, the emerging countries have experienced the danger of high dependence on foreign capital and are now trying to limit that dependence. This is the motivation behind the counterintuitive new situation in which, owing to their intense accumulation of currency reserves and of foreign assets more broadly, from 2003 emerging countries switched from being net borrowers to being net lenders (Bongini et al., 2009).

This is the phase in which a different type of crisis surfaces: the corporate mega-bankruptcies. These consist of a series of episodes that are formally distinct but are connected by a common denominator. In all of these cases, a corporation presumed to be a 'champion' – on the basis of the great prospects in its own business segment it manages to represent – convinces investors to entrust it with enormous credit to turn overnight into a 'lemon', and leaving the investors alone to face the company's bankruptcy. Only ex post do financial markets realize there was something rotten with that 'champion'. Its profits and losses accounts had been systematically forged – with the complacency, if not the connivance, of the designated audit firm – and behind those munificent dividends the company disbursed there was only a **Ponzi scheme**. In other words, the new funds the company was raising did not go to finance true investment – which the 'champion' didn't really make – but only to pay attractive returns to previous investors. However, it is well known that – as the ruin of the hedge funds run by Bernard Madoff vividly reminded us at the end of 2008 – a Ponzi scheme is sustainable only in the presence of expectations of constant increase of the capital gains, a situation that cannot last forever. Some negative shock hitting the 'champion' suffices to change those expectations and then the investors start asking questions they were shy to make earlier. Thus, invariably, the bluff is discovered but it is too late for the investors to avoid massive losses.

It was between 2001 and 2003 that a considerable number of corporate mega-bankruptcies materialized. This phenomenon was more intense in the USA, where it involved a series of well-known names: AllFirst, Enron, Global Crossing, ImClone, Qwest Communication International, Republic Securities, Rite Aid, Tyco and WorldCom. Nevertheless, Europe also experienced some significant episodes of this kind: Cirio and Parmalat in Italy; Vivendi in France. Hereafter we will focus on the two perhaps most clamorous cases: Enron, the largest energy company in the world, and Parmalat, one of the chief agro-food holdings on a global scale.

9.1 Enron

Enron was established in 1985 with the merger of the Texan Houston Natural Gas Inc. and the Inter North Inc. – a company operating in the natural gas business and having its home base in Omaha, Nebraska (Sridharan et al., 2002). In 1989 Enron started trading in natural gas and in just a few years it became the market leader in North America and the UK. Enron was following the strategic consulting of McKinsey, and Jeffrey Skilling was the chief actor behind that strategy. Initially a staff member at the consulting firm McKinsey, Skilling then became for a long time the unchallenged Chief Executive Officer of Enron. Under his guidance, Enron transformed from an energy business into a risk-management company trading in all types of financial instruments from raw materials to financial derivatives. The measure of this transformation is given by the fact that, by the year 2000, revenues relating to trading in financial instruments accounted for 80 per cent of total revenues.

To accelerate its growth, Enron chose to minimize the use of its own capital, availing itself on a large scale of *ad hoc* external vehicle entities (special-purpose entities, SPEs). Though controlled by it, these SPEs were not consolidated in the holding company's profits and losses statements. So Enron had a clear advantage in carrying out its more risky trading via these controlled but unconsolidated SPEs. For example, Enron did not need to explain to investors the motivation behind such risky undertakings. Ex post, this strategy of own-capital usage minimization, the extensive use of SPEs and off-balance-sheet financing seems indeed the main determinants of Enron's bankruptcy.

The US Generally Accepted Accounting Principles (GAAP) require, normally, the controlling company to consolidate the controlled SPEs in the holding company's profits and losses accounts. But there is one important exception. Avoiding consolidation is, in fact, allowed when the following two conditions are both satisfied: a) the SPE features an independent shareholder with at least 3 per cent of the capital at risk during the transaction, and b) the independent shareholder controls the SPE. In this respect, it was crucial for Enron to receive the approval of its inflated use of SPEs by Arthur Andersen, its mandated external auditing company. Indeed, it seems that some of Enron's affiliated SPEs would not strictly respect the GAAP requirements for non-consolidation. In addition, the inflated use of SPEs and the way these were accounted for made Enron's statements extremely complex and difficult to understand, besides building a leeway to grant covered compensation to the company's top management. One must also underline that Arthur Andersen played three different roles with Enron: a) it was its external auditor; b) it was in charge of Enron's internal audit; c) it provided Enron with consultation on fiscal matters and on other issues related to its auditing. Such a multiple relationship made Arthur Andersen prone to various potential conflicts of interest.

Furthermore, part of Enron's success depended also on the company's links with politicians. The company's president, Kenneth Lay, and its auditors paid generous contributions to the electoral campaign of several political figures. This was done with a bipartisan approach so that, quite likely, the US energy policy was shaped in ways favourable to Enron's desires.

The initial signals of the fragility of Enron's financial structure emerged openly on 16 October 2001, when the company disclosed $638 million losses for the third quarter and unveiled a $1.2 billion drop in the value of its shares. These occurrences were largely related to the SPEs managed by Andrew Fastow, Enron's Chief Financial Officer. The event acted as a catalyst attracting attention to the way Enron was financing its business operations. Very soon, other wrongdoings by the company were revealed, feeding the persistent drop in the price of its shares. Also, the US Securities and Exchange Commission (SEC) started an investigation into the possible conflicts of interest between Enron and its SPEs. On 8 November Enron gave the SEC its revised profits and losses accounts for the previous five years. This amounted to disclosing $586 million additional losses. At this time, fearing its rating would be downgraded to junk status, the management tried desperately to sell Enron to Dynegy, one of its main competitors, that initially agreed to buy it for a value of above $8 billion. However, when the transaction seemed to be drawing to a close, some independent rating agencies – but not the main three agencies Moody's, S&P's and Fitch, at the time the only ones enjoying the status of Nationally Recognized Statistical Rating Organizations (NRSRO) – downgraded Enron below investment grade. The downgrade descended from the fact that Enron's financial position was rapidly deteriorating. So, Dynegy backed out from the deal on 28 November. This news quickened the drop in the price of Enron's shares that fell below $1, down from the peak of some $90 reached in the past. By then, there was no other way out and on 2 December Enron filed for bankruptcy.

9.2 Parmalat

Headquartered in Collecchio (Parma, Italy), Parmalat was founded by Calisto Tanzi in 1962. Starting as a small firm making cold cuts and jam, Parmalat grew to become, by the end of the 1990s, one of the largest companies in the world in the segment of dairy-food and related products (Dobson, 2004; Ficarella, 2004). During the 1960s, some key innovations lay at the heart of the company's expansion: Parmalat was the first company in Italy to sell name-branded milk; in 1966 it imported into Italy the new Tetra Pak technology, by which it packaged milk with the innovative ultra-high-temperature (UHT) processing procedure. The company's expansion accelerated in the 1970s when Italy did away with the monopoly of the 'Centrali del latte' (dairy companies held by the municipalities). In addition, in those years Parmalat diversified its production into cheese, butter and dessert products, to extend into fruit juice and bakery products. It also started its internationalization, beginning with Brazil, Germany and France. In the 1990s Parmalat pursued additional diversification in the tourism business (Parmatour). By 1991 the Parmalat conglomerate had 4800 employees and had extended its sales to 30 countries.

The scaling up of foreign acquisitions in 1993 – with 17 M&As – led Parmalat to issue €8 billion bonds, one of the 30 issues organized by Fausto Tonna during his ten-year role as Chief Financial Officer. Other important expansionary steps for Parmalat were its acquisitions of Eurolat (from the Cirio Group, in 1999), of the South American activities of Kraft (in 2001) and of Unilever's South African dairy activities (in 2003).

Also, thanks to its listing on the Milan Stock Exchange, Parmalat expanded to 36,000 employees and 135 factories all over the world. In 2002 its total sales were in the order of €7.6 billion. Parmalat's accelerated growth was based on four strategic keystones: a) making large reliance on debt to finance its acquisitions; b) investing in countries having a growth potential higher than that of Western Europe; c) emphasizing diversified dairy products as well as relatively high value-added products; d) diversifying in productive segments even far away from the core activity (e.g. tourism). One of the non-trivial factors behind Parmalat's expansion was represented by its connections with politicians. The company's political linkages were with the Christian Democratic Party until the early 1990s, and – with the setback of that party – thereafter the affiliation became bipartisan.

Only a few observers suspected the fall of Parmalat was near when, in January 2003, Parmalat shares become part of the Mib30 – the Milan Stock Exchange index of the 30 companies with largest capitalization. Most investment banks placed a BUY on Parmalat's shares, though a few started airing suspicions about the complexity of the company's debt structure. Worries began to surface in February. In March, Morgan Stanley withdrew its investment rating on Parmalat and shortly after that Tonna, the Chief Financial Officer, stepped down. In September, the performance of the first half-year of 2003 showed a drop in profit of 37 per cent due to an obscure extraordinary item ('restructuring costs and other losses'). The rating agency S&P's worsened its rating outlook from 'positive' to 'stable'. In October, the CONSOB – Commissione Nazionale per le Società e la Borsa, Italy's Securities and Exchange Commission – raised questions about the items 'liquid investments' and 'other infra-group losses' as reported in the company's statements. Parmalat replied, providing details on its investments (€520 million) in the Epicurum fund domiciled in the Cayman Islands based on the buyback of (not redeemed) own bonds for an amount of €2.9 billion. The auditing firm Deloitte was unable to confirm the solidity of that investment, which received instead the support of the opinion issued by Grand Thornton, Parmalat's other auditing firm.

At that time, Parmalat gave investors conflicting messages. In the beginning, it announced it had asked Epicurum to liquidate the investment. However, Parmalat then disclosed that Epicurum would be unable to liquidate the investment and, on this occasion, it postponed repaying a €150 million bond after expiration and through the whole grace period (15 days). The stock exchange placed the trading of Parmalat's shares under a temporary halt. The hectic finale lists: a) the arrival – forced by creditors – in Parmalat's cockpit of Enrico Bondi, a manager well experienced in salvaging distressed manufacturing companies; b) the stepping down of Calisto Tanzi as President; c) the disclosure by the Bank of America that the €3.95 billion deposit posted in the balance sheet of Bonlat – a company, controlled by Parmalat, incorporated in the Cayman Islands – did not exist; d) the permanent suspension of the trading of Parmalat's shares on the stock exchange; e) the issue of a government decree (later embodied in the 'Marzano Law') featuring new interventions in favour of large companies in distress.

On 24 December 2003, Parmalat was declared insolvent – even though, under the guidance of Enrico Bondi (then appointed receiver), the company managed to continue its main industrial activities – and on the 27th, Calisto Tanzi was taken into custody. In a few days, Bondi disclosed some real data on the company: 2002 sales were artificially inflated by €1.5 billion; its gross profits were overstated by €0.6 billion; the holding's net debt was understated by €12.5 billion.

9.3 Similarities and differences between Enron and Parmalat

Even though the two companies belonged to different business segments, there are various similarities between the two crises, beyond what may be pure coincidence: both collapsed in the month of December, respectively in 2001 and in 2003. First, the two companies shared an exceedingly large reliance on unconsolidated affiliates and on doing business in offshore centres. This introduces a 'halo effect', that is, it makes the two holdings opaque as they seek to minimize their tax payments, to hide enormous liabilities and to stymie possible controls on the part of the Antitrust authorities. To that end, Enron created some 2000, de facto controlled, entities to which it entrusted approximately 45 per cent of its group total sales. Analogously, Parmalat set up a complex network of controlled entities domiciled at the Cayman Islands, in Delaware (in some respects, the most permissive US state), in the Antilles, in the British Virgin Islands, in Malta and in Luxembourg. The second key element is the extensive use of 'creative' finance, by which Enron transformed from an energy conglomerate into a de facto intermediary in financial products, while Parmalat ventured into ever more complex financial dealings.

A further crucial component is the decisive role of the mandated audit companies. Due to the distortions imparted to their behaviour by the pervasive conflicts of interest stemming from their being auditors and consultants at the same time, the audit firms allowed (if not cooperated with) the systematic forging of the two companies' statements. For Parmalat, Deloitte was the main auditor, while the most involved in the final financial scandal was Grant Thornton, the secondary auditor. In the case of Enron, the auditor, Arthur Andersen, went bankrupt together with its client.

The analysts' optimistic view of the two companies was also an important ingredient: both for Enron and for Parmalat until a few weeks before their bankruptcy, analysts (or at least a great part of them) kept suggesting that investors buy into the two companies that were approaching the end.

An additional common factor was the superficial behaviour of the credit rating agencies: the main three agencies failed to downgrade both Enron and Parmalat to below investment grade – that is, below BBB – up to a few days before their downfall. Also, in some respects, partly co-responsible with the two mega-bankruptcies were various primary banks since they kept financing Enron and Parmalat in a clearly unsustainable situation.

In the case of Parmalat, as an aggravating factor, some banks were accused of undergoing perilous conflicts of interest, placing with poorly informed investors the various bonds issued by the company that was already sailing in stormy waters. Allegedly, the two chief conflicts of interest consisted in: a) the bank having the incentive to place the bonds since the funds it raised with the issue allowed Parmalat to lower its debt against that very bank and, thus, the bank passed (part of) the 'lemon' to the investors; b) some of the bank managers might have been lured by the generous fees the company close to financial distress was willing to pay so as to place its new bond issues: for example, a top-ranking manager of the Bank of America in Milan admitted having cashed €27 million in the form of the commissions paid to them by various brokers involved in the private placement of Parmalat bonds. Last but not least, their political connections permitted Enron and Parmalat to take many more liberties in contrast to unconnected companies.

9.4 Untrustworthy auditing

The finding that the selected auditing firms – in charge of certifying that the company's statements were indeed true – cooperated with corporate strategies aimed to deceive the investors sounds like an oxymoron. This seems to reveal deep dysfunction. Unrestrained greed on the part of the managers was fed by the **stock options** mechanism as well as by other company incentives that inflated questionable behaviour.

All of this nourished a set-up where multiple conflicts of interest gave rise to an unhealthy business climate. What is more, the cases of mega-bankruptcy were so numerous that they raised a heated debate at both political and academic levels. In the USA, to rebuild trust in the financial markets, even the then President George W. Bush stepped into the arena calling for greater respect for ethics in the conduct of business and in corporate management. In March 2002, he put forth a ten-point proposal aimed at impeding the occurrence of new mega-corporate scandals.

Thanks to its being put on fast-track legislation, the heart of that proposal became effective on 30 July. The law is called Sarbanes-Oxley Act (SarBox), from the names of its proponents in the Congress and Senate. SarBox introduced the following reforms: a) creating an independent committee in charge of monitoring auditing firms; b) separating these firms' consulting activities from their auditing business; c) certification on the part of senior corporate management of the truthfulness of the company's annual statement and of the financial reports for the listed companies; d) full accounting transparency of the off-balance-sheet transactions and of the other obligations that could affect or represent deceitfully the financial condition of the company; e) scaling up the financial resources available to the SEC. Analogous legislative responses, at least in terms of new laws, did not materialize in Italy.

This legislation does not take the view that a generalized strengthening of the rules is needed to guarantee financial stability. As such, this is at odds with what would instead be recommended by those who hold the opinion that the numerous corporate mega-bankruptcies offer evidence of the dysfunction of an economic system lacking adequate control. An example of the latter view is provided by Durán (2005). He holds that those scandals are part of a generalized change in the behaviour of the top corporate managers. To pursue the maximization of shareholder value, these managers would now be willing to undertake devious behaviour, which in turn would undermine the very trust in the appropriate functioning of the market mechanism. In that sense, Duràn maintains, the neo-liberal excesses could lead the free market to its own euthanasia since they undercut market participants' trust in their counterparts. To the contrary, the prevalent view is that the phenomenon depends on just a few rotten apples, and some patches to the system will suffice to avoid that other apples become rotten as well.

Part III
The Great Crisis of 2007–09

The financial crisis triggered by US subprime mortgage defaults, which started in summer 2007, was the worst since the Great Depression, due to its effects on the international financial system and real economy worldwide, on the parties involved, the figures at stake and for the sense of doom thrown onto mainstream economic beliefs. For these reasons, we decided to devote the third part of the book to it.

10
The Great Crisis of 2007–09

10.1 The chronology of the crisis

The roots of the Great Crisis are to be found in the US financial-deregulation waves, whose harmful effects had been exacerbated by the improvident monetary policies undertaken by the Fed after the collapse of the 'new economy'. In fact, between January 2001 and June 2003, the decrease in the policy rate, which dropped from 6 to 1 per cent, encouraged American households – who expected the real estate appreciation to continue – to increase their borrowings to buy real estate properties. As a result, real estate prices skyrocketed triggering two feedback processes which amplified the effects of the monetary policy and fed the speculative bubble. The first process involved the real estate market: as a result of the growing property prices, more credit was granted to households (thanks to the increased value of collateral assets), which reinforced real estate appreciation. The second process, which was closely related to the spreading out of securitization, took place on the financial market: the growing real estate prices increased the value of the securities backed by mortgage loans, making the balance sheet of intermediaries (apparently) stronger; thus the banks could raise more funds to buy those securities, which reinforced their appreciation and guaranteed abundant liquidity to the primary mortgage market.

The growing real estate value and the increased ratio between issuance of mortgage-backed securities and origination of mortgage loans led to a significant lowering of credit standards, while the financial authorities did not recognize in time the negative effects of excessive borrowing. Hence, a growing share of new loans was granted to subjects with very low repayment capacity, the so-called subprime clients. The solvency of this new category of borrowers depended almost exclusively

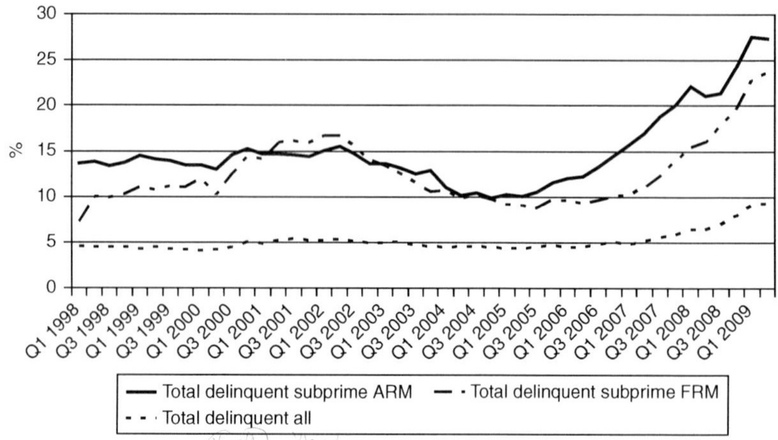

Figure 10.1 Delinquency rates
Source: Thomson Datastream

on the continuous increase in the value of the collateral (the house) getting more credit to roll-over the debt at maturity.

However, between June 2004 and June 2006, the US policy rate increased from 1 to 5.25 per cent, affecting the sustainability of mortgage debts. Thus, insolvencies started to increase, especially for subprime mortgages. Consequently, the demand for houses slowed down, curbing house-price appreciation. Moreover, in 2006, the **reset option** started to align the low initial mortgage rates to the market rate, so increasing even further the servicing cost of mortgages. At the same time, the decreasing value of the houses made it very difficult to get a refinancing loan to remain solvent. In spring 2007, the insolvency rate on the subprime mortgages exceeded 16 per cent (see Figure 10.1), thus speeding up the property price drop.

The default of the subprime segment soon affected the financial markets because many insolvent loans, or loans at risk of insolvency, were the cash flow of many structured bonds (Asset-Backed Securities and Collateralized Debt Obligations) in the hands of a multitude of international investors (such as banks, insurance companies and investment funds). In addition, between June and July, as a result of many downgrades announced by the major rating agencies, the market lost its confidence in the ability of rating to estimate the structured bond default probability. As it became suddenly clear that no sufficient information was available to evaluate those securities in a changed financial environment, the financial markets worldwide panicked.

The international financial crisis that erupted in August 2007 (see Box 10.1 for the timeline of the key events) went through five stages (BIS, 2009): a) from the beginning to Bear Stearns' rescue (August 2007–mid-March 2008); b) from Bear Stearns' rescue to the bankruptcy of Lehman Brothers (mid-March 2008–mid-September 2008); c) from the bankruptcy of Lehman Brothers to the collapse of the international financial markets (mid-September 2008–end October 2008); d) from the collapse of the financial markets to the world recession (end October 2008–mid-March 2009); e) from the world recession to the first signs of the recovery (mid-March 2009–onwards). These five phases are clearly evident in Figure 10.2, which also shows the international stock market index and the Ted spread (the latter, calculated as the difference between the three months' **Libor** rate and three months' government bonds, is used to gauge the credit risk on the interbank market).

10.1.1 Phase 1 (August 2007–mid-March 2008)

On 9 August 2007 the subprime crisis became global: three European investment funds were frozen because it was impossible to determine the value of the securities linked with the US subprime mortgages in their portfolios. Therefore, panic became widespread on the international financial markets. The high degree of opacity of the structured financial instrument (traded mainly on unregulated markets or over-the-counter markets) made it impossible to single out just those related to the subprime mortgages. Hence, a wide range of securities were no longer traded, liquidity disappeared from several markets, prices collapsed, bid-ask spreads increased and stock markets recorded mounting losses (see Figure 10.2).

The market of **asset-backed commercial paper** (ABCP) was the first one to be hit by the crisis. The increasing insolvency rates on the subprime mortgages reduced the quality of the collaterals, thus increasing the interest-rate spread on those securities (see Figure 10.3), and also caused a significant reduction in market transactions (see Figure 10.4). Hence, the 'shadow banking system' operators no longer succeeded in the rollover of the short-term borrowing on the commercial paper markets and were forced to draw on their credit lines with several US and European banks. Then, the crisis also affected the commercial banks, whose difficulties became clear in the interbank market as their counterparts were no longer willing to grant liquidity because of the fear they might have needed it, too. The interbank interest rates (**Euribor** and Libor) increased to the point that the central banks had to be involved (see Figures 10.5 and 10.6). On 9 August 2007 the European Central Bank (ECB) undertook

Box 10.1 Timeline of key events

2007	
9 August	Problems in mortgage and credit markets spill over into interbank money markets when issuers of asset-backed commercial paper encounter problems rolling over outstanding volumes, and large investment funds freeze redemptions, citing an inability to value their holdings.
12 December	Central banks from five major currency areas announce coordinated measures designed to address pressures in short-term funding markets, including the establishment of US dollar swap lines.
2008	
16 March	JPMorgan Chase agrees to purchase Bear Stearns in a transaction facilitated by the US authorities.
4 June	Moody's and Standard & Poor's take negative rating actions on **monoline** insurers MBIA and Ambac, reigniting fears about valuation losses on securities insured by these companies.
13 July	The US authorities announce plans for backstop measures supporting two US mortgage finance agencies (Fannie Mae and Freddie Mac), including purchases of agency stock.
15 July	The US Securities and Exchange Commission (SEC) issues an order restricting 'naked short selling'.
7 September	Fannie Mae and Freddie Mac are taken into government conservatorship.
15 September	Lehman Brothers Holdings Inc. files for Chapter 11 bankruptcy protection.
16 September	Reserve Primary, a large US money-market fund, 'breaks the buck', triggering large volumes of fund redemptions; the US government steps in to support insurance company AIG (and is forced to repeatedly increase and restructure that rescue package over the following months).
18 September	Coordinated central-bank measures address the squeeze in US dollar funding with \$160 billion in

(*continued*)

Box 10.1 Continued

	new or expanded swap lines; the UK authorities prohibit short selling of financial shares.
19 September	The US Treasury announces a temporary guarantee of money-market funds; the SEC announces a ban on short sales in financial shares; early details emerge of a $700 billion US Treasury proposal to remove troubled assets from bank balance sheets (the Troubled Asset Relief Program, TARP).
25 September	The authorities take control of Washington Mutual, the largest US thrift institution, with some $300 billion in assets.
29 September	UK mortgage lender Bradford & Bingley is nationalized; banking and insurance company Fortis receives a capital injection from three European governments; German commercial property lender Hypo Real Estate secures a government-facilitated credit line; troubled US bank Wachovia is taken over; the proposed TARP is rejected by the US House of Representatives.
30 September	Financial group Dexia receives a government capital injection; the Irish government announces a guarantee safeguarding all deposits, covered bonds and senior and subordinated debt of six Irish banks; other governments take similar initiatives over the following weeks.
3 October	The US Congress approves the revised TARP plan.
8 October	Major central banks undertake a coordinated round of policy rate cuts; the UK authorities announce a comprehensive support package, including capital injections for UK-incorporated banks.
13 October	Major central banks jointly announce the provision of unlimited amounts of US dollar funds to ease tensions in money markets; euro-area governments pledge system-wide bank recapitalizations; reports say that the US Treasury plans to invest $125 billion to buy stakes in nine major banks.
28 October	Hungary secures a $25 billion support package from the IMF and other multilateral institutions aimed

(*continued*)

Box 10.1 Continued

	at stemming growing capital outflows and easing related currency pressures.
29 October	To counter the protracted global squeeze in US dollar funding, the US Federal Reserve agrees swap lines with the monetary authorities in Brazil, South Korea, Mexico and Singapore.
15 November	The G20 countries pledge joint efforts to enhance cooperation, restore global growth and reform the world's financial systems.
25 November	The US Federal Reserve creates a $200 billion facility to extend loans against securitizations backed by consumer and small-business loans; in addition, it allots up to $500 billion for purchases of bonds and mortgage-backed securities issued by US housing agencies.
2009	
16 January	The Irish authorities seize control of Anglo Irish Bank; replicating an approach taken in the case of Citigroup in November, the US authorities agree to support the Bank of America through a preferred equity stake and guarantees for a pool of troubled assets.
19 January	As part of a broad-based financial-rescue package, the UK authorities increase their existing stake in the Royal Bank of Scotland. Similar measures by other national authorities follow over the next few days.
10 February	The US authorities present plans for new comprehensive measures in support of the financial sector, including a Public-Private Investment Program (PPIP) of up to $1 trillion to purchase troubled assets.
10 February	G7 Finance Ministers and central bank Governors reaffirm their commitment to use the full range of policy tools to support growth and employment and strengthen the financial sector.
5 March	The Bank of England launches a programme, worth about $100 billion, aimed at outright purchases of

(*continued*)

Box 10.1 Continued

	private-sector assets and government bonds over a three-month period.
18 March	The US Federal Reserve announces plans for purchases of up to $300 billion of longer-term Treasury securities over a period of six months and increases the maximum amounts for planned purchases of US agency-related securities.
23 March	The US Treasury provides details on the PPIP proposed in February.
2 April	The communiqué issued at the G20 summit pledges joint efforts by governments to restore confidence and growth, including measures to strengthen the financial system.
6 April	The US Federal Open Market Committee authorizes new temporary reciprocal foreign currency liquidity swap lines with the Bank of England, ECB, Bank of Japan and Swiss National Bank.
24 April	The US Federal Reserve releases details on the stress tests conducted to assess the financial soundness of the 19 largest US financial institutions, declaring that most banks currently have capital levels well in excess of the amount required for them to remain well capitalized.
7 May	The ECB's Governing Council decides in principle that the Eurosystem will purchase euro-denominated covered bonds; the US authorities publish the results of their stress tests and identify ten banks with an overall capital shortfall of $75 billion, to be covered chiefly through additions to common equity.

Source: BIS (2009)

a short-term liquidity initiative worth €45 billion, followed by five more initiatives, for a total value of €250 billion. The Fed also took similar measures. Nonetheless, the interest rates on the interbank markets and commercial paper remained very high for the rest of the month.

On 19 September the crisis hit Northern Rock. The British bank was relying heavily on wholesale short-term funding, and the lack of liquidity on the international financial markets was challenging its solvency.

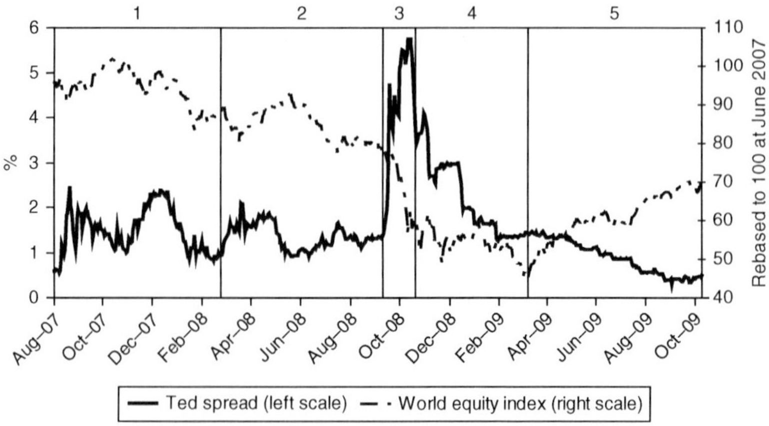

Figure 10.2 The five stages of the crisis
Source: Thomson Datastream

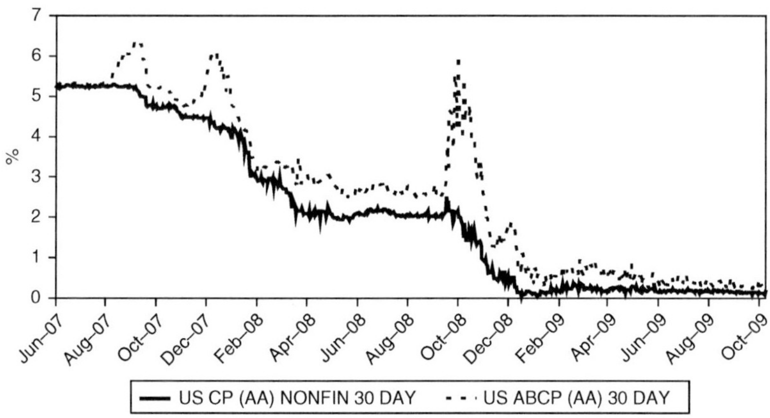

Figure 10.3 US commercial paper discount rates
Source: Thomson Datastream

Panicked depositors made long queues outside the bank's branches, evoking movies of the 1930s. The gravity of the crisis was confirmed by the large losses announced by the international banks in October. However, the market turmoil was temporarily eased by the **sovereign wealth funds'** recapitalization of the banks worst hit by the crisis.

In November the situation got painful again as it became clear that the total losses caused by the subprime mortgage crisis (*c.* $200 billion)

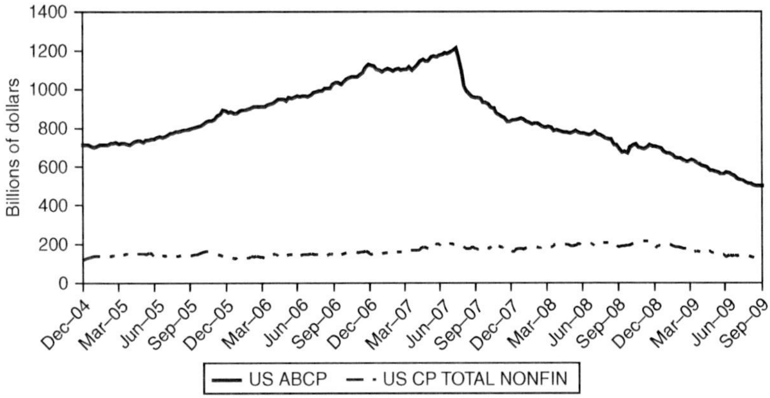

Figure 10.4 US commercial paper outstandings
Source: Thomson Datastream

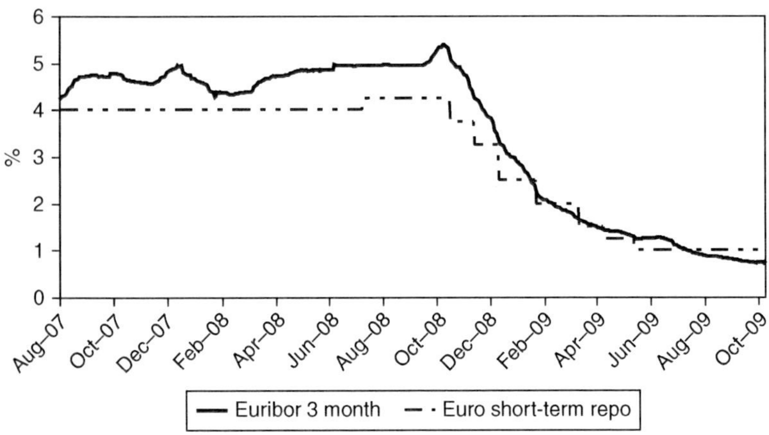

Figure 10.5 Euribor vs ECB policy rate
Source: Thomson Datastream

were largely underestimated. Many banks were forced into a new wave of write-downs that caused more strain on the markets.

At this juncture, extraordinary measures were needed to avoid a dangerous deflationary process. Two options were available: a) giving the brokers the liquidity they needed, so that they were not forced to sell some of their assets; b) buying the securities that the brokers were willing to sell, thus preventing a drop in prices. The Fed initially followed the

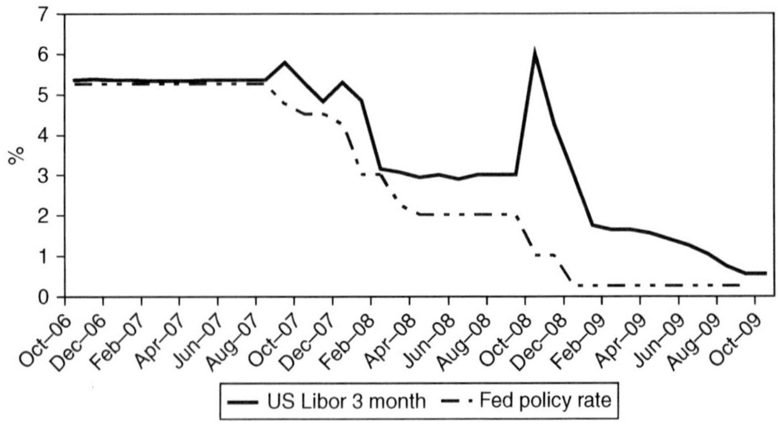

Figure 10.6 US Libor vs Fed policy rate
Source: Thomson Datastream

first option, but without any visible improvements; shortly afterwards it followed the second option too. Moreover, the US central bank implemented many new monetary policy instruments to support the financial markets (see Table 10.1). For instance, on 12 December it launched a Term Auction Facility (TAF) programme, targeted at the commercial banks, with significant advantages compared to the discount operations. As this instrument is used by the ECB on a regular basis, it merely made available more short-term liquidity to European banks, without changing the policy rate.

Following these initiatives, short-term interest rates recorded a significant reduction, but the situation got worse again at the end of January 2008. The financial markets were shocked by the potential downgrade of some major **bond insurers**. This prospect scared the markets which, between 21 and 22 January, reported unprecedented losses and forced the Fed to further reduce the policy rate by 75 basis points in the first emergency meeting ever called since 1982. At the same time, on the other side of the Atlantic, the ECB kept the rate steady.

After a period of apparent calm, new fears emerged in March. The liquidity crisis affected an increasing number of banks and on 11 March the Fed announced a new credit line (Term Securities Lending Facility, TSLF), whereby government bonds worth $200 billion would have been exchanged for other less liquid debt securities. Moreover, a few days later, the Fed, with the Primary Dealer Credit Facility (PDCF), committed itself to also granting short-term loans to the investment banks. As the rate on

Table 10.1 Forms of Federal Reserve lending

	Regular OMOs	Discount Window[1]	Term Discount Window Program (announced August 17, 2007)	Term Auction Facility (announced December 12, 2007)	Primary Dealer Credit Facility (announced March 16, 2008)[2]	Transitional Credit Extensions (announced September 21, 2008)	Reciprocal Currency Arrangements (first announced December 12, 2007)[3]
Who can participate?	Primary dealers	Depository institutions	Primary credit-eligible depository institutions	Primary credit-eligible depository institutions	Primary dealers	U.S. and London broker-dealer subsidiaries of Goldman Sachs, Morgan Stanley, Merrill Lynch	Select central banks to lend on to banks in their jurisdiction[3]
What are they borrowing?	Funds	Funds	Funds	Funds	Funds	Funds	U.S. Dollars
What collateral can be pledged?	U.S. Treasuries, agencies, agency MBS[9]	Full range of Discount Window collateral	Full range of Discount Window collateral	Full range of Discount Window collateral	Full range of tri-party repo system collateral[10,11]	Full range of Discount Window collateral and tri-party repo system collateral[11]	Central banks pledge foreign currency and lend against eligible collateral in their jurisdiction
Is there a reserve impact?	Yes	Yes	Yes	Yes	Yes	Yes	Yes
What is the term of loan?	Typically, term is overnight–14 days[14]	Typically overnight, but up to several weeks[16]	Up to 90 days[17]	28 days or 84 days[15]	Overnight	Overnight	Overnight to 3 months
Is prepayment allowed if term is greater than overnight?	No	Yes	Yes	No	N/A	N/A	Yes
Which Reserve Banks conduct	FRBNY	All	All	All	FRBNY	FRBNY	FRBNY
How frequently is the program accessed?	Typically once or more daily	As requested (standing facility)	As requested (standing facility)	Every other week, or as necessary	As requested (standing facility)	As requested (standing facility)	Typically on schedule with FRBNY TAF auctions or as requested by central banks
Where are statistics reported publicly?	Temporary OMO activity[18]	H.4,1 – Factors Affecting Reserve Balances[19]	H.4,1 – Factors Affecting Reserve Balances[19]	TAF activity[18]	H.4,1 – Factors Affecting Reserve Balances[19]	H.4,1 – Factors Affecting Reserve Balances[19]	H.4,1 – Factors Affecting Reserve Balances[19]

1 Discount Window includes primary, secondary and seasonal credit programs.
2 The AMLF, CPFF, PDCF and TSLF will remain in operation through February 1, 2010 as announced on June 25, 2009.
3 ECB and SNB announced December 12, 2007; BOC, BOE, and BOJ announced September 18, 2008; RBA, Sverige Riksbank, DNB, and Norges Bank announced September 24, 2008; Reserve Bank of New Zealand announced October 28, 2008; Banco Central do Brazil, Banco de Mexico, Bank of Korea, and Monetary Authority of Singapore announced October 29, 2008.
4 The MMIFF will remain in operation through October 30, 2009 as announced on June 25, 2009.
5 The Federal Reserve Board is prepared to increase the size of the TALF to as much as $1 trillion and broaden the eligible collateral to encompass other types of newly issued AAA-rated asset-backed securities as announced on February 10, 2009.
6 Through the CPFF the FRBNY provides financing to an SPV that purchases eligible three-month unsecured and asset-backed commercial paper from eligible issuers.
7 Eligible institutions expanded on January 7, 2009 to include U.S.-based securities-lending cash-collateral reinvestment funds, portfolios, and accounts (securities lenders); and U.S.-based investment funds that operate in a manner similar to money market mutual funds, such as certain local government investment pools, common trust funds, and collective investment funds.
8 Through the MMIFF the FRBNY will provide senior secured funding to a series of private sector SPVs to finance the purchase of certain money market instruments from eligible investors.

(continued)

Table 10.1 Continued

	Securities Lending	Term Securities Lending Facility (announced March 11, 2008)[2]	ABCP Money Market Fund Liquidity Facility (announced September 19, 2008)[2]	Commercial Paper Funding Facility (announced October 7, 2008)[2]	Money Market Investing Funding Facility (announced October 21, 2008)[4]	Term Asset-Backed Securities Loan Facility[5] (announced November 25, 2008)
Who can participate?	Primary dealers	Primary dealers	Despository institutions, bank holding companies, U.S. branches and agencies of foreign banks	Eligible CP issuers[6]	Eligible Money Market Mutual Funds and other money market investors[7,8]	All U.S. persons that own eligible collateral
What are they borrowing?	U.S. Treasuries	U.S. Treasuries	Funds	Funds	Funds and subordinated note	Funds
What collateral can be pledged?	U.S. Treasuries	U.S. Treasuries, agencies, agency MBS, and all invesment grade debt securities[10]	First-tier ABCP	Newly issued 3-month unsecured and asset-backed CP from eligible U.S. issuers	U.S. dollar-denominated certificates of deposit, bank notes and commercial paper issued by highly rated financial institutions	Recently originated U.S. dollar-denominated AAA ABS, CMBS and legacy CMBS[12,13]
Is there a reserve impact?	No (loans are bond-for-bond)	No (loans are bond-for-bond)	Yes	Yes	Yes	Yes
What is the term of loan?	Overnight	28 days[15]	ABCP maturity date (270-day maximum)	3 months	N/A	3 or 5 years
Is prepayment allowed if term is greater than overnight?	N/A	No	No	N/A	N/A	Yes
Which Reserve Banks conduct	FRBNY	FRBNY	FRB Boston	FRBNY	FRBNY	FRBNY
How frequently is the program accessed?	Daily	Every four weeks	As requested (standing facility)	As requested (standing facility)	As requested (standing facility)	Twice a month, alternating between non-mortgage backed ABS and CMBS collateral types
Where are statistics reported publicly?	Securities lending activity	Term securities lending facility activity[18]	H.4,1 – Factors Affecting Reserve Balances[19]	H.4,1 – Factors Affecting Reserve Balances[19]	H.4,1 – Factors Affecting Reserve Balances[19]	TALF activity[18]

9 Reverse repos are collateralized with U.S. Treasuries.
10 PDCF and TSLF collateral expanded on September 14, 2008.
11 Includes non-U.S. dollar denominated securities.
12 Includes auto loans, student loans, credit card loans, small business loans guaranteed by the U.S. SBA, mortgage servicing advances, business equipment relate loans or leases, vehicle fleet leases, floorplan loans and commercial mortgages. Collateral was expanded on March 19, 2009, May 1, 2009 and May 19, 2009.
13 Legacy CMBS includes to U.S. dollar-denominated CMBS issued before January 1, 2009.
14 Open market operations are authorized for terms of up to 65 business days.
15 28-day and 84-day terms may vary slightly to account for maturity dates that fall on Bank holidays.
16 Primary credit loans are generally overnight. Loans may be granted for term beyond a few weeks to small banks, subject to additional administration.
17 Maximum maturity of term increased from overnight to 30 days on August 17, 2007, and to 90 days on March 16, 2008.
18 Data only available for days when operations are conducted.
19 Data published on Thursday, as of close of business on Wednesday.
Source: Federal Reserve Bank of New York (July 2009)

this type of operation was the same as applied to the commercial banks at the discount window, this initiative also marked the opening of Fed facilities to the investment banks. This decision came under heavy scrutiny because the investment banks were not subject to Fed regulations and, in theory, would not be entitled to use public funds. During these days the markets experienced significant strains because of the difficulties of Bear Stearns. One of the five most important investment banks was in trouble because it could not roll-over its short-term loans due to the deterioration of its assets. Bear Stearns was a counterpart in many derivatives transactions and its bankruptcy might have started a dangerous domino effect. Thus, on 24 March, JPMorgan Chase received $29 billion from the Fed to buy Bear Stearns and partially reassure the markets.

10.1.2 Phase 2 (mid-March 2008–mid-September 2008)

During this phase the US financial system was significantly challenged. The liquidity problems turned into solvency problems, because the subprime mortgages were just the tip of the iceberg and the prolonged downturn in house prices forced many investors to write-down a wide range of securities. As a result, total losses rapidly increased to more than $500 billion.

Fannie Mae and Freddie Mac, the giant of the mortgage market, were badly hit by the crisis and in just a few months their market value went down by more than 70 per cent. So, on 13 July, the US Treasury was forced to purchase the shares of the two companies and to increase the traditional funding line. Nonetheless, the fear of bankruptcy did not disappear. The share price kept decreasing and on 7 September the American Treasury had to nationalize the two financial companies, which hold more that 50 per cent of the mortgage loans originated in the USA. The collapse of Fannie Mae and Freddie Mac generated even more concern about the stability of the US financial system, and the operators shifted their attention to the large investment banks. Lehman Brothers suffered the most because of its exposure on the real estate market through complex derivatives transactions. The markets were looking forward to some initiatives by the US authorities, similar to the ones they had already undertaken for Bear Stearns, but no such measure was taken. On 15 September, Lehman Brothers, after being in business for 150 years, announced the largest bankruptcy in US history with liabilities of $613 billion.

10.1.3 Phase 3 (mid-September 2008–end October 2008)

Lehman's bankruptcy marked the beginning of the worst period of the crisis. On 16 September the Fed was forced to lend $85 billion, which would be renegotiated on several occasions, to AIG (American International Group). The largest insurance company in the world was on the edge of bankruptcy due to its hazardous dealing in CDS (**credit default swap**) derivatives offering the counterparties insurance against default on many structured securities linked to the US real estate market.

Lehman's bankruptcy also seriously challenged money-market funds. As the Reserve Primary, one of the major US funds, devaluated short-term debt securities worth $780 billion, many people withdrew their money and the managers were forced to sell some of their assets, at a time of scarce liquidity. This drain was stopped thanks to the involvement of the US Treasury, which announced a guarantee on funds liabilities.

Later on, the Fed authorized Morgan Stanley and Goldman Sachs, the last two 'pure' investment banks after Merrill Lynch had been bought by the Bank of America, to turn into commercial banks. This put an end to a form of capitalism that had dominated Wall Street for more than 30 years. The crisis also hit Washington Mutual, a chief US savings & loan institution, which was then rescued by the government and later sold to JPMorgan Chase.

It became clear that resorting to *ad hoc* actions could not solve the crisis. In fact, a comprehensive strategy was needed to tackle the problem. During the last week of September, the Treasury Secretary Henry Paulson submitted a plan whereby the government would buy the financial market securities that were causing the bankruptcy of many banks up to $700 billion. The US Congress did not initially approve the plan, with subsequent losses on all international stock exchange markets. The state of agitation continued even after the second week of October, when the plan was eventually approved.

At the end of September the crisis hit the European financial system, too. The lack of liquidity forced Iceland to nationalize the Glitnir bank, Germany to support Hypo Real Estate, the Benelux to rescue the financial giant Fortis and support the Dexia Group, the UK to nationalize Bradford & Bingley, and Ireland to guarantee the deposits of the six main national banks. On 8 October, with an unprecedented initiative in the history of international monetary policy, eight central banks (including the ECB, the Bank of England and the Bank of Canada), inspired by the Fed, cut policy rates by 50 basis points. On the same day, the British government announced a plan for the nationalization of a significant portion of its banking system, worth more than €460 billion. A few days later, **Ecofin**, chaired by Nicolas Sarkozy, met in Paris on an urgent basis in order to agree upon additional guarantees on bank deposits and liabilities.

These initiatives partially reassured the markets but the problems rapidly spread to Eastern Europe. The trade deficit of Estonia, Lithuania and Latvia was approximately 12–15 per cent of GDP as against 4–6 per cent in Slovakia, Slovenia, Hungary and Poland. Over the past few years, the deficit had been funded through foreign capital, especially from Sweden, Austria and Italy. However, because of the disruption to the international credit markets, these countries experienced a significant outflow of capital, which put the exchange rates under pressure. Hungary, Ukraine and Iceland were granted an emergency loan by the International Monetary Fund, amounting to nearly 10 per cent of GDP.

Between October and November, the subprime crisis completed its world tour contaminating also Asia and Latin America. The brisk global economic slowdown, through a sudden drop in the demand for raw materials, negatively impinged on export-oriented economies such as Chile, Peru, Argentina, Brazil and Venezuela; but even Australia, Japan and Singapore did not escape unscathed. Also China, after decades of impetuous and continuous growth, saw its growth prospects plunge to the lowest level in five years.

10.1.4 Phase 4 (end October 2008–mid March 2009)

In spite of the timely and heavy government interventions, this phase was characterized by a significant degree of uncertainty about the stability of the international financial system.

The public financial stability plans encouraged the recovery of the stock markets, but the continuity of the latter was still hindered by the lack of specific details on the actions, the effects of the crisis on the real economy and the high degree of uncertainty about financial intermediaries' balance sheets. In January 2009, the IMF estimated $2200 billion of total write-downs related to the financial crisis.

The central banks, after the experience of the Great Depression, reacted jointly and consistently to the crisis. Within the context of a significant reduction of the aggregate demand and a drop in the inflation rate, policy rates were slashed to almost zero. In December 2008, the Fed established a 0–0.25 per cent range for the policy rate and announced its willingness to keep it steady, pending clear recovery signs. From October to March, the ECB cut the reference interest rates by 2.75, down to 1.5 per cent.

The tension on the interbank market eased and the public rescue of some of the main international banks pushed the spreads down to pre-crisis levels (see Figure 10.2).

10.1.5 Phase 5 (mid-March 2009–autumn 2009)

This phase was characterized by a slow return to normality in many key market segments: volatility went down, the equity markets improved (see Figure 10.2) and the premium on corporate bonds decreased.

This reversal trend was triggered by fiscal and monetary efforts that were made to stop the crisis. More specifically, markets welcomed the implementation of non-conventional monetary policies. On this front, the central banks resorted to three main instruments: a) additional liquidity; b) establishment of extra reserves in the commercial banks (quantitative easing); c) outright purchase of public or private bonds (credit easing). The first measure had already been undertaken during the first three phases of the crisis to ease the liquidity crisis, while the last two were undertaken during phases 4 and 5 to reduce the medium and long-term interest rates. In particular, after participating in the commercial paper market as a direct counterpart, between phases 4 and 5 the Fed started to buy MBSs (mortgage-backed securities) and long-term government bonds. And the ECB, on 4 June, announced the technical details of the programme to buy €60 billion of covered bonds.

In the first weeks of March these initiatives were followed by some good financial data announced by the main US banks. The favourable period was further strengthened by the London summit of the G20 group, whereby the main leaders of the world announced their readiness to support the real economy, and by the renewed capacity of the banks to access long-term funding without a government guarantee.

At this point, the worst period of the financial crisis seemed to be overcome, but during the last phases new concerns emerged on the real economy because the default of the industrial companies might give dangerous feedback to the banks' balance sheets. In fact, the industrialized countries were in the middle of the crisis and only some emerging economies maintained positive growth figures, though smaller than in the previous years. During the two quarters that marked the end of 2008 and the beginning of 2009, the US GDP dropped by 5.5 and 6.7 per cent, respectively. During the same period, there was an even bigger drop in Europe: −7 per cent and −10 per cent, respectively. The figures were even worse in Japan: −15 per cent and −13 per cent. The emerging economies were also hit by the crisis, thus challenging the well-known 'decoupling' thesis. In Russia GDP was stable at the end of 2008, but collapsed at the beginning of 2009 (−9.8 per cent). During the first quarter of 2009, GDP decreased by 1.6 in Brazil, while a slowdown was recorded in China and India, though these emerging giants still kept growing at +6.1 per cent and +4.1 per cent respectively.

In summer 2009 some encouraging signals (green shoots) emerged, indicating that, probably, the recession–deflation spiral had stopped. The oil price was going up again, industrial production had started to grow again in many areas in Asia and also business confidence had bounced back. One of the most favourable signals was the OECD (Organisation for Economic Co-operation) leading indicator, whose downtrend had stopped. The indicator became positive again for the Eurozone and, though still negative, it showed some signs of improvement in the USA and Japan. As far as the BRIC countries (Brazil, Russia, India and China – the most dynamic emerging economies) were concerned, China and India were back to increasingly positive figures, while Brazil and Russia were recovering somewhat, even though their GDP growth figures were still negative.

The unprecedented efforts made by governments and central banks were by then showing favourable effects, but at the time of writing, the international economy was still weak (see Box 10.2).

10.2 From liquidity crisis to financial crisis: amplification mechanisms

The losses on the US real estate market have had disrupting effects. In October 2007 the estimated losses on the subprime mortgages amounted to just $250 billion, but the loss on the world GDP estimated by the IMF was $4700 billion and the losses on the international equity markets totalled approximately $26,400 billion, that is, 100 times more than the losses on the subprime mortgages (Blanchard, 2008)! How is it that losses amounting to a few hundred billion dollars in just one segment of the US real estate market caused enormous losses in the international financial markets? In this section we discuss the origin of the liquidity crisis and the mechanisms that amplified its negative effects.

Overall, the origin of a liquidity crisis is often triggered by exogenous events that highlight pitfalls in the models used to evaluate financial assets (in the subprime crisis, one example is the loss of trust in the ratings' ability to estimate the default of the financial assets originated via the securitization of mortgages). As a consequence, the investors move their capital away from riskier securities, the prices of which drop below the fundamental value, to the safest ones, the prices of which go up. This process is known as 'flight to quality' and could be associated with a shortfall of liquidity in the financial markets. In such a framework, one of the main amplifying mechanisms is based on the information asymmetries between skilled and unskilled investors, the severity of

Box 10.2 The output losses and fiscal costs of the financial crisis

Gianluigi Ferrucci
Senior Economist, European Central Bank[a]

As we have seen thoroughly in Part II of this book, the consequences of financial crises are very severe, typically involving significant bank losses and costly financial bailouts. Financial crises are also associated with sharp economic downturns and sizeable fiscal burdens, which only in part derive from the need to support the banking sector (Haugh et al., 2009).

The severity of the downturns depends on the initial strain to the financial system and, to some extent, on the policy response. Analysing a number of banking crises in industrial countries in the post-war period, Reinhart and Rogoff (2008) find that the drop in annual output growth from peak to trough may be significant, even in excess of 5 per cent, and growth may remain below pre-crisis trends for several years. Losses of this magnitude are associated with major events, such as the banking crises of Finland and Sweden in 1991 and of Japan in 1992 (described in Part II). In the majority of cases, output growth tends eventually to return to its pre-crisis level, suggesting that crises may not affect permanently the growth potential of the economy (Abiad et al., 2009). But, for example, following the banking crisis of 1992 in Japan, output growth never recovered to its pre-crisis levels.

This Box analyses the output losses and fiscal costs of the financial crisis triggered by the subprime meltdown. Specifically, it examines how a dramatic escalation of the financial crisis in September 2008 has determined a global downturn of unprecedented proportions in the post-war period. It then discusses the fiscal costs of the crisis, which have been especially large in advanced economies. It concludes by looking beyond the more immediate costs and asking whether the crisis will leave deeper scars on the supply potential of the affected economies. Predicting the shape of the recovery is clearly difficult, but past episodes may provide some guidance on which policies can be more helpful in preventing larger output losses in the medium term.

(*continued*)

Box 10.2 Continued

The sharpest downturn of the post-war period

Following the outbreak of the US subprime crisis in August 2007, world economic activity weakened. But the real turning point was the default of Lehman Brothers in September 2008, and the emergence of wider fears about the solvency of other systemically relevant financial institutions, primarily in the United States and in the EU. These events were eventually the catalyst for a sudden aggravation of the strain in financial markets, which quickly spilled over to the real sector, both in the United States and in the rest of the world.

Several transmission channels were at play.[b] The mix of corrections in the housing market, difficulties in short-term financing and adjustment in households' balance sheets contributed to the collapse of the demand for durable goods (particularly cars and appliances), which accounts for a large share of manufacturing output. The adjustment in global inventories further aggravated the dynamics of the downturn, leading to a sharp contraction in industrial activity. External trade also reacted strongly, falling by more in this crisis than during a comparable phase of the Great Depression (Eichengreen and Irwin, 2009). There is broad agreement that financial innovation has played a key role, as it allowed US mortgages to be converted through securitization into securities, which were partly sold to international investors. As the ratings of these products did not fully reflect their inherent risks, US-specific risks were allowed to be spread globally, leading to a particularly strong transmission of credit problems in the US mortgage market to the rest of the world. Finally, confidence linkages across economies have been powerful transmission channels, leading to higher business-cycle synchronization across economies and a greater sensitivity to common shocks.

These forces precipitated the world economy into the sharpest downturn of the post-war period (see Figure 10.7). Few economies were left unscathed, although the intensity of the downturn varied significantly across countries, depending on the exposure and vulnerability to the initial shock. Advanced economies were hardest hit, reflecting the strength of their reciprocal financial and trade ties, which were powerful channels of international contagion during the crisis. Emerging economies also suffered, but the size of the output losses was comparatively smaller, reflecting in most cases the fact

(*continued*)

Box 10.2 Continued

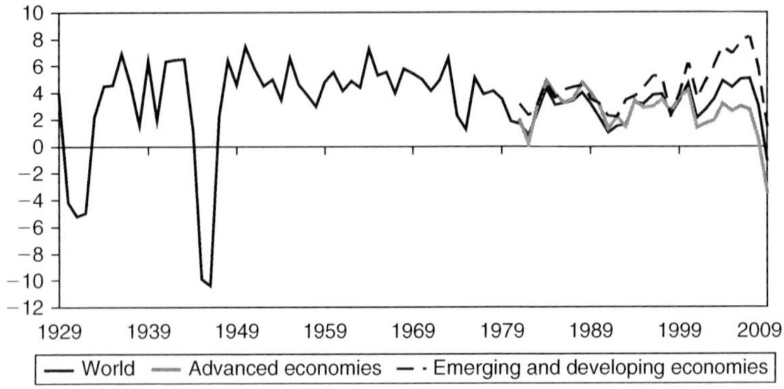

Figure 10.7 Real GDP growth (annual percentage change)
Source: International Monetary Fund, World Economic Output, April 2009
Note: Data for 2009 are estimates

that they were more sheltered from the initial shock and also the initiatives of the international financial system to provide liquidity support. As the crisis hit the very heart of the global financial system, its consequences turned out to be particularly pervasive. In addition to this, and somewhat paradoxically, technology advances and globalization in the past few decades may have facilitated the transmission of the shock and amplified its consequences, by favouring a closer integration of the global economy.

Recent data provide some tentative indications that the major economies may have bottomed out in the second half of 2009, and that growth may have resumed in some cases. However, the recovery is still modest and it is largely the result of temporary expansionary policies that will have to be unwound at some point.

Fiscal costs

The fiscal costs of the crisis are likely to cast a long shadow on the future performance of the global economy. The pace of deterioration of government balances in many advanced economies has been extremely fast, albeit the extent of this deterioration has varied across countries. Generally speaking, countries that have been hardest hit by the crisis (the United States, the United Kingdom, Ireland, Spain) have also seen the sharpest deterioration in their fiscal positions.

(continued)

Box 10.2 Continued

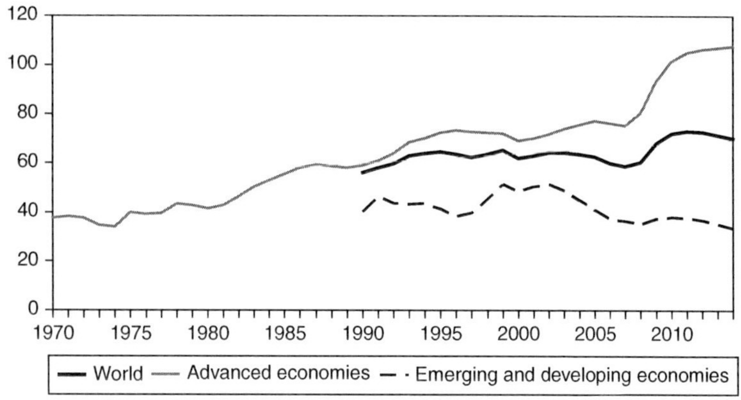

Figure 10.8 General government public debt (percentage of GDP)
Source: International Monetary Fund, World Economic Outlook Database, April 2009

Public deficits have widened on the back of two main forces. First, as the recession gained pace, tax revenues have fallen in tandem with the contraction in the tax base (income and profits). Second, public spending has increased as governments have turned to fiscal policy to support demand in the downturn. In addition to spending related to automatic stabilizers such as unemployment benefits, large discretionary stimulus packages have been introduced in several economies, notably in the United States, the United Kingdom and Japan. In some cases, governments also implemented capital injections in distressed banks and granted debt-financed guarantees.

The end result has been a large increase in government debt. In advanced economies, public debt rose from 75 per cent of GDP in 2007 to 80 per cent in 2008, and, at current trends, it is projected to overtake 100 per cent of GDP by 2010, according to estimates provided by the IMF (2009b; see Figure 10.8). In emerging economies, by contrast, public debt is expected to remain broadly unchanged over the period.

By historical standards the projected increase in public debt – about 25 percentage points of GDP between 2007 and 2010 – is not unusual following financial-crisis episodes. However, a key concern presently is that debt levels in advanced economies were already relatively high at the onset of the crisis. Furthermore, even without the

(*continued*)

Box 10.2 Continued

crisis and the related fiscal costs, public finances in these economies were already projected to come under strain in the coming years on the back of the expected increases in public spending for health care and pensions due to population aging. The crisis, therefore, will put an additional burden on public finances.

Lasting legacies

The financial crisis has had a pervasive impact on the global economy. The most immediate effects have been a sharp economic downturn, rising unemployment and a deep contraction in global trade, investment and consumption. Whether it will also leave long-term scars is more difficult to predict. One lasting legacy of the crisis is, however, already clear and relates to the need for fiscal consolidation when the recovery takes hold more firmly. The need to bring public finances back to a sustainable path may require some significant fiscal tightening in several countries.

There is an ongoing policy debate whether the crisis will have permanent effects on the growth potential of the economies most affected by the downturn. In most cases, output growth has returned to trend following a crisis – albeit it might take several years. There have also been notable exceptions, such as Japan, where GDP growth never returned to the levels prevailing before the 1992 banking crisis. Although post-crises output dynamics are hard to predict, examples of successful recoveries from past banking crises may provide some guidance on which policies should be more beneficial. More rapid rebounds have typically been associated with a favourable external environment, efforts to undertake structural reforms and actions aimed at restoring banking health, notably through appropriate programmes of bank recapitalization (Abiad et al., 2009). As the external environment is not expected to provide strong support in the forthcoming years, it appears critical to undertake policies aimed at restoring a healthy financial sector and high productivity growth.

Notes

[a] The views expressed are those of the author and do not necessarily reflect those of the European Central Bank.

[b] See the article entitled 'The Latest Euro Area Recession in a Historical Context' in the November 2009 issue of the European Central Bank's Monthly Bulletin, in particular box 2.

these asymmetries increasing with the complexity of the financial instruments. These frictions slow down the drift of the market value towards the fundamental value of the most complex financial securities for two reasons. On the one hand, the unskilled investors are forced to leave the market to get the know-how needed to evaluate the securities; on the other hand, the skilled operators, who would profit by arbitrage and could speed up the price adjustment, do not get the necessary funds.

The in-depth understanding of these mechanisms requires a clear differentiation between funding liquidity and market liquidity (Brunnermeier, 2008). The funding liquidity indicates how easily funds can be obtained on the financial market. For instance, if the market has abundant funding liquidity, the intermediaries can buy assets and fund them by issuing asset-backed securities. Differently, the market-liquidity concept indicates how easily a security can sell at its fundamental value or, in other words, when the sale of that security does not affect its going price. Small isolated sales do not usually impact on the price, but if many operators try to sell simultaneously the same type of securities, the price will be significantly affected.

In the subprime crisis, the sudden and clear reduction in financial-market liquidity, which began in August 2007, reflected the interaction between funding liquidity and market liquidity, which generated the first amplifying mechanism of the liquidity crisis: the increasing default rates on the subprime market reduced the prices of the mortgage-backed securities that, in turn, lowered funding liquidity. This forced many brokers to sell some of their assets in a phase of very low market liquidity. So, the price went down even more and the intermediaries' balance sheet kept eroding, putting at work the balance-sheet channel (see section 4.2.1 above). The widespread price drop and the increase in market volatility dried up funding liquidity in even more markets, thus triggering fire sales on a large scale.

The second amplifying mechanism is based on the bank-lending channel (see section 4.2.2 above): the high degree of uncertainty led the intermediaries to reduce the supply of liquidity, speeding up the rise in interest rates. For instance, on the interbank market, after the start of the subprime crisis, many banks needed liquidity to meet the requests coming from the sponsored **structured investment vehicles** (**SIVs**) or **conduits**. However, on the supply side, many banks preferred to hoard cash rather than increase lending for two main reasons. First, even in the case in which initially they were not involved in the crisis, the high degree of volatility led them to keep the extra liquidity so that, in case of need, they would not need to tap the interbank market for funding, where interest rates were increasing quickly. Second, credit risk on the interbank market went up all of a sudden because the difficulties of SIVs and conduits might also affect the sponsor banks. Hence, the sudden rise in interbank interest rates led to a more severe liquidity crisis.

The third amplifying mechanism is runs on financial institutions, which became evident following the bankruptcy of Lehman Brothers, which caused additional write-downs and weakened even more the balance sheet of many intermediaries. Finally, the fourth mechanism deals with the network effect and it is triggered when a financial institution is a creditor and a borrower at the same time. Thus, the fear of generalized bankruptcies forced the intermediaries to keep even more liquidity to pay off their debts, should their debtors go bankrupt. Accordingly, the joint effect of these four mechanisms literally dried up liquidity in the international financial markets and amplified the limited losses in the subprime market, to the point of causing the worst financial crisis since the Great Depression.

10.3 Transmission of the US subprime crisis to emerging markets

The financial markets of the emerging economies were initially relatively isolated from the crisis, but the risk of a deep and long global recession, which emerged after the Lehman Brothers' bankruptcy, started a downward trend for these economies as well. Dooley and Hutchison (2009) analyse the contagion mechanism using an event-study technique based on the trend of three financial markets (from 2007 until the beginning of 2009): the credit default swaps[1] market (CDS), the stock market and the currency market. The news on the financial crisis and the economic recession in the USA had a powerful impact on the emerging economies' sovereign CDS prices. More specifically, on the one hand, the news on the write-downs and downgrades about the US financial institution and Lehman's bankruptcy pushed the price of the emerging countries' CDS up, thereby indicating a higher risk of default for these countries; but, on the other hand, the news on the foreign currency funds made available by the Fed pushed it down. As for the stock market, the correlation between the USA and the emerging economies had been increasing since August 2008. The most evident cases were: South Africa and Colombia (+75 per cent),[2] Turkey (+51 per cent), China and Russia (+42 per cent). The currency market also showed a similar trend, characterized by the appreciation of the exchange rate of the emerging economies until August 2008, followed by a strong depreciation.

On the basis of this evidence, Dooley and Hutchison (2009) claim that although the efforts made by the emerging economies to decouple from industrialized countries allowed them to overcome the initial phase of the crisis, these efforts were not sufficient to spare them the effects of the worst phase. In fact, during the last quarter of 2008, the growth of the BRIC countries slowed down quite dramatically, and in the first quarter of 2009 Russia and Brazil recorded a GDP reduction, while China and India still had positive figures, though much lower than in 2007. This scenario has encouraged a lively debate in academic circles. Some people believe that the emerging economies might be less affected by the crisis and stay out of the world economic recession, since the economic situation in these countries, over the past few years, has been decoupled from that of the industrialized countries, especially the USA. This argument was supported by the following elements: a) the reduced importance of the USA as the main market for products manufactured in the emerging economies; b) the growing importance of domestic demand in these countries; c) the high growth rates of the BRIC countries; d) the improved fiscal situation in the emerging countries. On the contrary, others believe that this hypothesis is not plausible because: a) trade and financial integration between the developed and emerging countries has significantly increased over the past few years; b) the growth model of the emerging economies is still heavily dependent on exports, foreign capital inflows and the prices of raw material.

The debate has encouraged several studies to investigate the empirical evidence. Kose et al. (2008) analysed the growth rates of 106 countries in the period between 1960 and 2005 and confirm the decoupling hypothesis by showing that the economic cycles are converging within individual economic areas (developed economies vs emerging economies), but are diverging between the areas. In other words, the economic cycles of China, India, Russia and Brazil are getting closer to each other, but away from the economic cycles of industrialized countries and the USA in particular. This is quite strong evidence, but considering only the real growth rates could be misleading. For example, if the long-run growth rate is 9 per cent in China and 2 per cent in the USA, an actual growth of 5 per cent in China and –2 per cent in the USA is not indicative of diverging economic cycles between these two countries. This is because both have recorded –4 per cent with respect to the long-run trend. To take this into account, Wälti (2009) analysed the growth-rate deviation of GDP from its potential level and challenge the decoupling hypothesis by showing that the degree of synchronization of the economic cycles between the emerging and industrialized countries has not decreased over the past few years.

At the time of writing, the real economic data seem to provide some support for the decoupling thesis.

10.4 Origin of the crisis: macro elements

In the rest of this chapter we address the most debated question of the past two years: why did the crisis occur? We argue that the instruments described in Part I are also effective in explaining the Great Crisis because it is the most striking case of the boom–bust cycle characterized by financial liberalization, capital inflow, high growth of credit and economic boom followed by a big crash.

Thus, for the sake of exposition, we classified the causes of the crisis as macroeconomic and microeconomic. The macroeconomic causes deal with global imbalances and low interest rates, while the microeconomic causes deal with the impact of securitization processes, financial regulation and the rating agencies.

10.4.1 The role of global imbalances

Global imbalances are the first macroeconomic cause of the crisis. This problem was generated by the high and long-lasting current account deficit[3] in the main industrialized countries, particularly the USA, which was funded by the massive capital inflow from the emerging economies.

The causes of the global imbalances remain the subject of lively debate. Some claim that the current account deficit might be due to the low savings ratio in industrialized countries, especially the USA, which requires the inflow of foreign capital to fund investments. Another option might be that global imbalances – and the US deficit in particular – have been caused by the expectation of significant income growth in the USA, which has led the private sector to incur debts in order to smooth the income over time. The third opinion is that insufficient domestic demand in the rest of the world, and in Asia in particular, has caused an enormous capital inflow into industrialized countries. According to the fourth and most accredited explanation, the large current account deficits in the developed countries are mainly due to: a) increased surplus in the raw-material-exporting countries as a result of increased prices; b) increased economic growth in Asia which has high saving propensity; c) increased currency reserves of the Asian central banks to avoid another crisis like the 1997 one. So, between 1997 and 2007, these trends have given a significant contribution to the growth in international savings, to the point of exceeding the real investment potential in these countries and causing a 'saving glut', which has then moved to the industrialized countries (Bernanke, 2005).

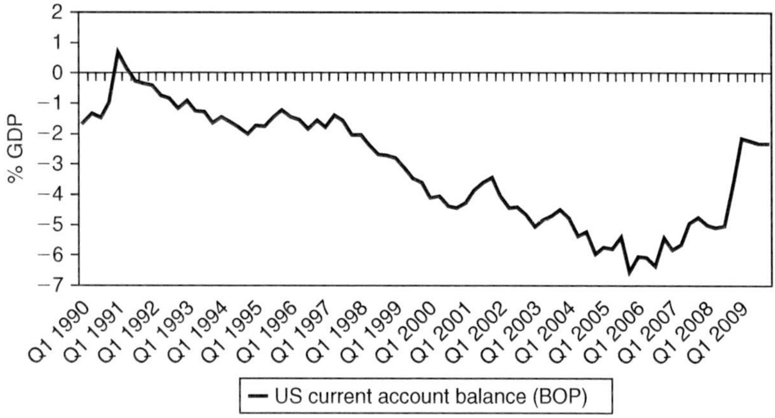

Figure 10.9 US current account (percentage of GDP)
Source: Thomson Datastream

Although the discussion on the causes of the global imbalances is still open, financial globalization – that is, international financial markets being increasingly integrated – has allowed the surplus savings to flow in many industrialized countries, such as the USA, the UK, Spain and Ireland. Since these countries had very low interest rates, investors searched for a higher yield in different markets and the real estate market in particular. For example, Aizenman and Jinjarak (2008) analysed the situation in 43 countries (25 of which were OECD countries) between 1990 and 2005 and found a very strong positive correlation between the current account deficit and real estate price increase: on average, a 4 per cent deficit increase has been associated, over the years, with a nearly 10 per cent increase in real estate prices. Specifically, in the USA house prices have increased even more: while the current account deficit went up from 1.5 per cent to more than 6 per cent of GDP between 1995 and 2005 (see Figure 10.9), household-sector borrowing grew from 71 to 100 per cent of GDP, and the prices of houses more than doubled between 2000 and 2006 (see Figures 10.10 and 10.11).

Besides fuelling a strong increase in real estate prices, the inflow of foreign capital also weakened the relation between short-term interest rates, affected mainly by the domestic policy rate set by the central bank, and long-term rates influenced much more by international factors. The first signs of this weakness and its perils emerged a few years before the beginning of the crisis. Between 2001 and 2004, the possibility of cashing in the difference between the market value of property

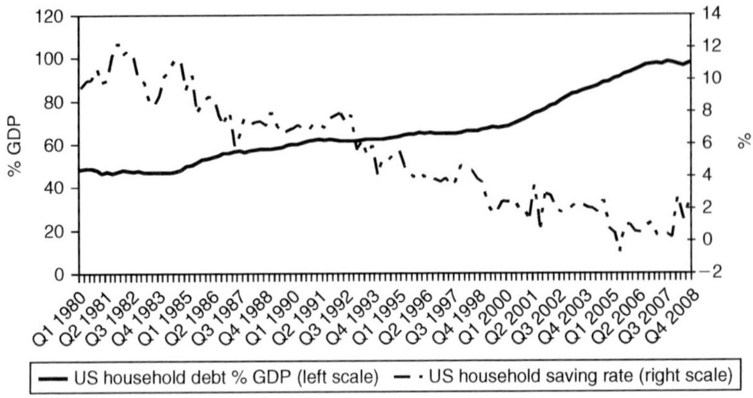

Figure 10.10 US household debt and saving rate
Source: Thomson Datastream

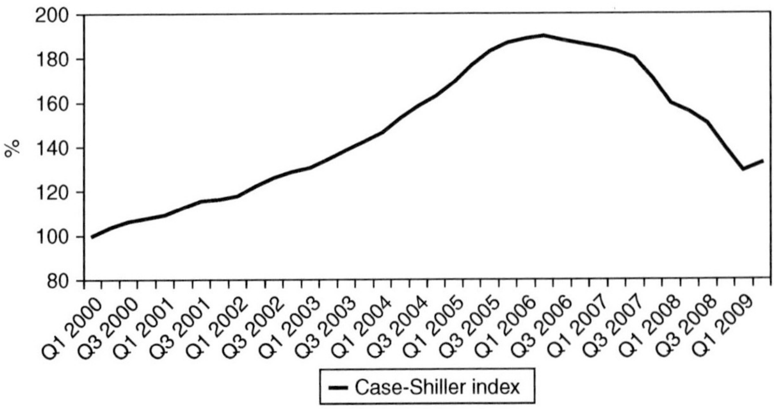

Figure 10.11 US home price index
Source: Thomson Datastream

and the loan value, by using different types of funding such as the home equity loans, allowed many American households to afford levels of consumption that would have otherwise been impossible. Thus, after the first half of 2004, the risk of deflation caused by the burst of the 'dotcom' bubble seemed a distant memory, and there were even signs of overheating. To keep inflation under control, the Fed raised the policy rate but, contrary to other phases of monetary tightening,

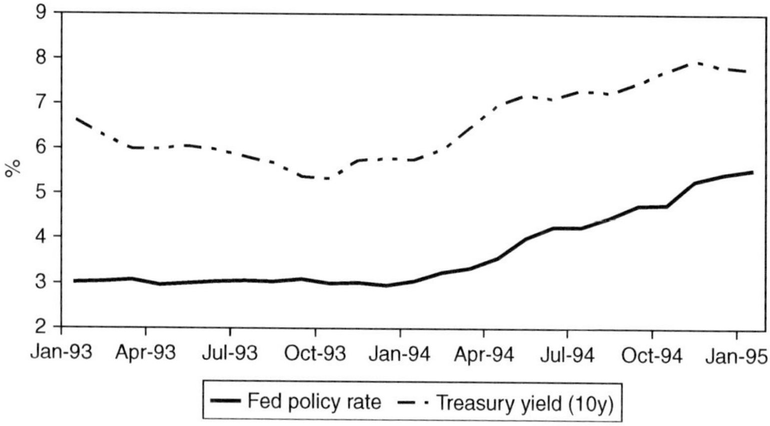

Figure 10.12 1994–95 Tightening
Source: Thomson Datastream

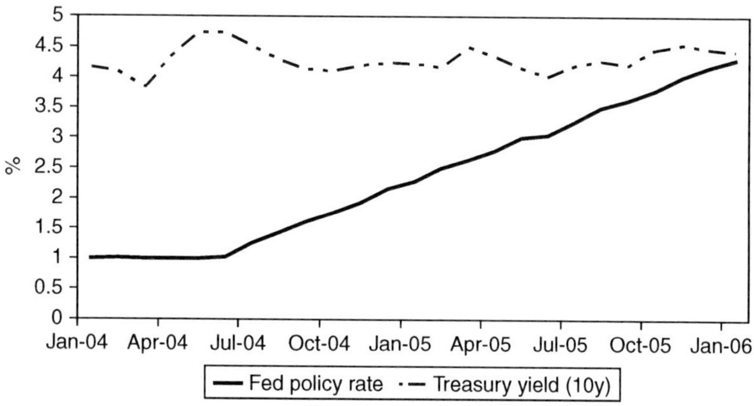

Figure 10.13 2004–06 Tightening
Source: Thomson Datastream

long-term rates remained low and, to a large extent, neutralized the effectiveness of monetary restriction (see Figures 10.12 and 10.13). Even then, the Chairman in charge of the Fed, Alan Greenspan, was taken by surprise and called the gap between the policy rates and the long-term rates a conundrum (Wu, 2006). As a result, the cost of fixed-rate loans remained substantially unchanged, the property boom continued and the speculative bubble kept inflating.

10.4.2 The role of the Fed's monetary policy

The overly easy monetary policy by the Fed is the other macroeconomic cause of the financial crisis (see Box 10.3). The policy rate was kept too low for too long by Alan Greenspan's Fed to ease the recessionary consequences following the burst of the 'dotcom' bubble.

But two feedback mechanisms amplified the negative effect of the overly easy monetary policy. The first circular mechanism – the balance-sheet channel described in section 4.2.1 above – is at work in the real estate market, where the supply of loans is closely related to the value of the collateral asset. Specifically, very low interest rates reduced the cost of debt and increased the demand for houses. As a consequence, real estate prices increased, allowing households to get more credit, thanks to the rise of the collateral value, which, in turn, inflated house prices even more (see Figure 10.17). This is because, in the short term, the rapid growth of the demand for houses collides with a limited supply. In fact, at the beginning of the year 2000, in spite of the increasing efficiency of the US building sector, the technical time to build new houses was still long and in some zones, especially in the coastal states such as Florida and California, there were no building areas left. The rules in force in the states even increased the time between the application for building authorization and the beginning of construction work. As a result, house prices ballooned, as shown by the Case-Shiller index that grew by more than 100 per cent between 2000 and 2006 (see Figure 10.11). The increasing employment rate following the 2001 recession, the low interest rates and the easier access to credit played a very important role, but are not enough to explain the huge house-price appreciation. The Yale economist Robert Shiller claims that it is a typical example of a speculative bubble in which property prices increase so much because households and investors expect them to increase even more in the future. In his famous book *Irrational Exuberance* (2000), Shiller describes a simplified model of bubble based on the interaction between prices and expectations. According to Shiller, with the supply of houses relatively inelastic, that is, hardly reactive to the short-term price, fundamental factors like the increasing rate of employment and the availability of credit increase demand and generate a remarkable growth in the market price. At this point, people searching high yield push up the demand for houses, because the gains grow very rapidly in the initial stages of the bubble. Thus, the demand grows more than the supply and paves the way for a period of steady price increases. Because of their irrational exuberance, some believe that the price of property will keep growing indefinitely. Hence, more people

Box 10.3 Monetary policy in the USA before the crisis

Fabrizio Venditti
Economist, Bank of Italy[a]

Some commentators have pointed out that the recent collapse of financial markets has been favoured, among other factors, by the excess liquidity generated by the loose monetary policy of the US Federal Reserve. In this Box we review John Taylor's argument and revisit the relationship between interest rates, unemployment and inflation in the past 20 years in the USA.

A commonly used tool for the historical evaluation of monetary policy is the so-called Taylor rule, a stylized description of monetary policy behaviour in which the main policy instrument (the deviation of the short-term nominal interest rate from its 'natural' rate) reacts linearly to the deviation of inflation and output from their desired levels.

Formally, the Taylor rule can be expressed as:

$$i - i^* = \theta_\pi (\pi - \pi^*) + \theta_q (q - q^*)$$

where i is the short-term nominal interest rate selected by the Fed (i.e. the federal funds rate), i^* is the natural rate of interest, π is the inflation rate and π^* its target level, q is the output and q^* is the output level at full employment, the weights θ_π and θ_q indicate the sensitivity of the federal funds rate to each of the two gaps – inflation and output.

The Taylor rule owes its name to the fact that a specific version of this rule was first proposed by John Taylor in 1993:[b]

$$i = 2 + \pi + 0.5 (\pi - 2) + 0.5 (q - q^*)$$

in this specification, Taylor set both i^* and π^* equal to 2, and both θ_π and θ_q equal to 0.5.

A number of authors have used this rule, either in its calibrated version put forward by Taylor or in estimated forms based on historical data, to evaluate monetary policy behaviour. Clarida et al. (2000), for example, estimate it on US data in different periods and conclude that a significant shift to a more anti-inflationary reaction function

(*continued*)

Box 10.3 Continued

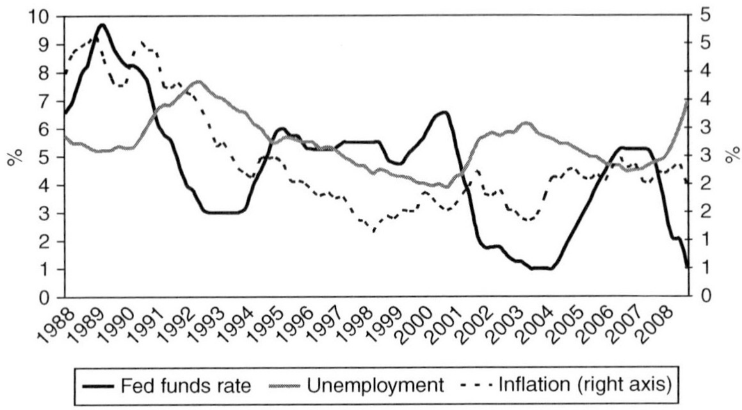

Figure 10.14 Federal funds, inflation (core) and unemployment rates in the USA
Source: Federal Reserve Bank of San Francisco

was behind the recent prolonged period of inflation and output stabilization, the so-called Great Moderation observed from the mid-1980s.[c] In the wake of the recent financial crisis, Taylor (2007) has blamed the Fed for having deviated from this rule after the 2001 recession, providing the market with an excess liquidity that led to the housing bubble.

Before dealing with this specific argument, it is useful to analyse briefly the Fed monetary policy in the past two decades. Figure 10.14 shows data on the inflation, unemployment and federal funds rates in the USA from 1988 to 2008. It is clear that the stance of the Fed has been strongly countercyclical: periods of low inflation and high unemployment are associated with low interest rates and vice versa.

Then, using the Taylor rule to evaluate the stance of the Fed monetary policy, Figure 10.15 shows the federal funds rates together with two theoretical paths of it. The first one is obtained with an estimated version of the Taylor rule. This estimate suggests an inflation parameter (θ_π) of around 1.3, but also a much stronger countercyclical behaviour than the one posited in the classic version of the rule. The parameter θ_q is in fact estimated to be close to 2, suggesting that over the considered sample the Fed has aggressively cut short-term

(continued)

Box 10.3 Continued

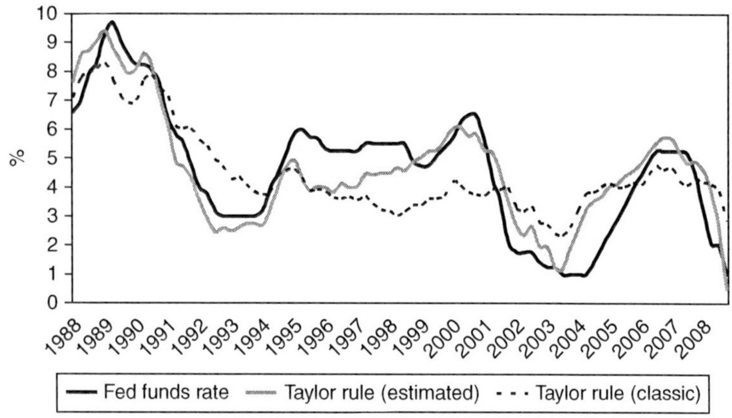

Figure 10.15 Actual and theoretical interest rates
Source: Federal Reserve Bank of San Francisco

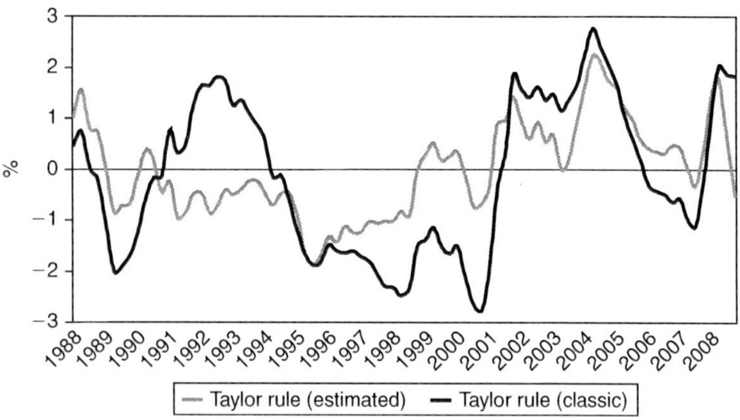

Figure 10.16 Excess monetary policy easing

rates by almost two percentage points for each percentage point increase of the output gap.[d] The second path is obtained through the classic rule calibrated using the parameters suggested by Taylor (1993). The difference between actual federal funds rates and the theoretical rates is plotted in Figure 10.16.

(*continued*)

Box 10.3 Continued

These differences provide a measure of the excess of monetary easing, being positive when actual rates were too low according to the Taylor rules and negative in the opposite case. The two measures of monetary slack behave quite differently. According to the estimated one, rates were relatively too high following the 1991 recession, but excessively low in the run up to the current crisis. Using the calibrated rule one still concludes that the Fed tightened far too late after the 2001 recession, in line with Taylor (2007). Two facts, however, stand out. First, a similar behaviour following the previous economic downturn (between 1991 and 1994) did not result in an asset bubble of the proportions experienced ten years later. Second, the excessively slack monetary policy since 2001 was preceded by a period of relatively tight monetary conditions. Using the simple Taylor framework it is therefore clear that while monetary policy has contributed to the financial crisis by providing markets with cheap liquidity, other factors that were specific to the past decade (like financial sophistication in the presence of loose regulation) were crucial in inflating the housing bubble from which the crisis originated.

Notes

[a] The views expressed in this article are those of the author and do not necessarily reflect those of the Bank of Italy.

[b] An important feature of the Taylor rule is that nominal interest rates respond more than one to one to the deviation of inflation from its target. This is because monetary policy needs to impact on the real interest rate in order to affect real activity and bring back output and inflation to their desired levels.

[c] Two caveats of these analyses are that Taylor rules should be assessed using real-time data (see Orphanides, 2008 for a concise summary) and that using an estimated rule as a guide for future actions causes past mistakes to repeat themselves (Taylor, 2009).

[d] See Rudebusch (2009) at http://www.frbsf.org/publications/economics/letter/2009/el2009-17.html. This is also the source of the data shown in Figures 10.14 and 10.15.

invest in real estate, the prices and appreciation expectations go up and the speculative bubble keeps inflating.

The second circular mechanism, the bank-lending channel described in section 4.2.2 above, is strictly linked to the spreading out of securitizations and is at work in the financial market: rising real estate prices increase the value of the financial assets originated via the securitization of mortgages, in turn allowing financial intermediaries to raise additional funds (thanks to the higher value of the collaterals) to be invested in acquiring more assets; usually, these new investments are in

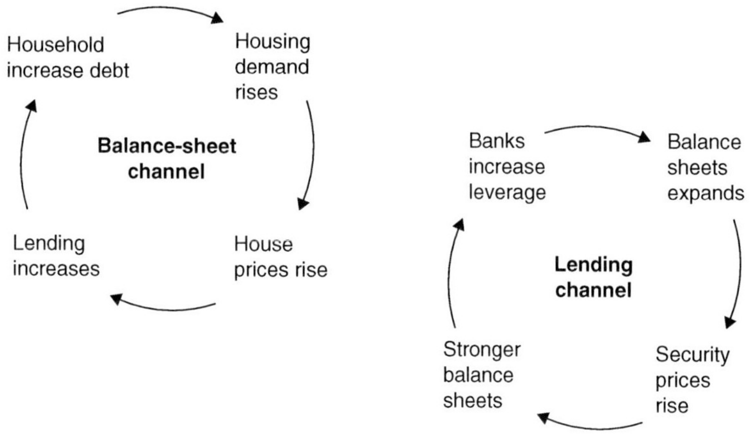

Figure 10.17 Balance-sheet and lending channel at work

mortgage-securitization-originated securities and, thus, contribute to increasing the funds for granting new mortgages on the **primary market**.

This mechanism is very important in the subprime crisis and the following example is very useful for understanding it (Adrian and Shin, 2008). Let us assume that a financial intermediary uses a **mark-to-market** accounting (whereby the value of a financial instrument reflects the current market value of that instrument) and wishes to keep a **leverage** (defined as the ratio of total assets to equity) of ten. For example, he might have assets worth €100 funded with €10 of equity and €90 of debt. Let us now have a look at the relationship between leverage and balance-sheet size. If, for example, the value of the securities (assets) grows by 1 per cent, from €100 to €101, keeping the value of the bonds unchanged, the value of the equity gets to €11 (10 + 1 per cent of 100 = 11), while the leverage drops to 9.18 (€101/€11). To keep the leverage unchanged, the bank has to get funds and issue bonds to buy more securities, so that: total assets/shares = (101 + new securities)/11 = 10. The equation shows that the bank has to issue €9 worth of bonds and use them to buy €9 of securities. Hence, the 1 per cent security price increase has allowed the bank to issue new bonds, which have increased the assets value by €9.

As the price of securities goes up, the demand for them increases, rather than going down as the law of supply and demand would say. The growing demand increases the security price even more, thus triggering a process that, by reducing the leverage, pushes the price of securities up. The bank's balance sheet is now as follows: assets €110 (securities), liabilities €110 (shares €11 and bonds €99). If the price of the securities drops to €109, keeping the value of the bonds unchanged, the equity makes up for the reduction in the assets' value and the bank's balance sheet is as follows: assets €109 (securities) and liabilities €109 (shares €10 and bonds €99). The leverage is now too high: (109/10) = 10.9 and, in order to get it back to 10, the bank has to sell securities that are worth €9 and use the funds to pay off some of the issued bonds (deleverage), so that the values of the balance sheet are as follows: assets €100 (securities) and liabilities €100 (shares €10 and bonds €90).

This mechanism is also not in line with the law of supply and demand, because the price of securities goes down but their supply increases. A negative sloped supply curve may trigger a circular process contrary to the one that was previously described: a drop in the security price increases the leverage level, pushes the supply up and brings their price further down. This is the reason why the leverage of some intermediaries, for instance the US investment banks, may cause pro-cyclical effects: during the periods of price growth, the increasing assets value pushes the demand for securities up thus amplifying the upward trend. On the contrary, when prices drop, the decreasing assets value pushes the supply of securities up amplifying the effect of the downward trend. Hence, the leverage can be significantly pro-cyclical and amplify the financial cycle. During the economic expansion between 2002 and 2006, low US interest rates increased the banks' assets value and generated a surplus that had to be invested somehow, possibly on high-rating and high-yield instruments, such as the senior tranches of CDOs (Collateralized Debt Obligations), obtained from the securitization of the real estate loans.

The strong demand for these instruments made enormous amounts of new funds available for investments on real estate, but it also increased the market value of these securities, thus swelling the financial operators' balance sheet. The availability of funds on the real estate market was so ample that the mortgage originators, seeking loans available for securitization, accepted significantly reducing their credit standards. As a consequence, rapid product and process innovation radically changed the US primary loan market. Before the beginning of the subprime crisis it had become very common to obtain loans covering 100 per cent (or more) of the real estate value, to have loans granted for property already mortgaged (second-line mortgage) and to obtain home equities loans. In particular, this last type of loan is quite usual at times of significant growth in the prices of real estate, as clients obtain funding – equal to the difference between the market value of the property and the value of the mortgage – to sustain their consumption.

From the loan-origination point of view, the main innovation was the Internet, which allowed many clients to bypass visiting a bank and to provide only limited documentation[4] (low doc loans) or, in some cases, even unreliable documentation (liar loans). The mortgage brokers were very active in this field: they were not subject to strict financial supervision and, at the end of 2006, they were accountable for nearly 80 per cent of the new loans, twice the figure in 1996. As they got their profits to a large extent from the commissions paid on the origination of loans, they did not have a long-term relation with their clients and were focused more on loan quantity than on loan quality. In addition, the possibility of grouping the loans and selling them to other brokers relieved them of the burden to select accurately the clients.

Without going into the details of all the products available on the US market, a differentiation should be made between prime mortgages, alternative-A mortgages and subprime mortgages. Prime mortgages are granted to clients with good payback features, while alternative-A mortgages are granted to those clients who declare high credit standards, but do not provide the needed documentation to prove it, so they might in effect be covert high-risk mortgages. Finally, subprime mortgages are given to clients with low payback features, that have poor credit standards, who are considered as very risky clients. According to the most accredited definition provided by the Interagency Expanded Guidance for Subprime Lending Programs, the typical **subprime borrower** generally displays a range of characteristics, including one or more of the following: a) two or more 30-day delinquencies in the past 12 months; b) one or more 60-day delinquencies in the past 24 months; c) judgment, foreclosure, repossession or charge-off in the prior 24 months; d) bankruptcy in the past five years; e) a **credit score** (FICO) of 660 or below; f) debt-service-to-income ratio of 50 per cent or greater. The growth of subprime and Alt-A mortgages, and related securities, was huge. For example, between 2001 and 2006, the value of the originations increased by 215 per cent for subprime mortgages and by 566 per cent for alternative-A mortgages; likewise the issuance/origination ratio went up from 46 to 75 per cent for subprime mortgages and from 19 to 91 per cent for alternative-A mortgages (Ashcraft and Schuermann, 2008). Therefore, the higher the number of originations the fewer the loans in the balance sheets of those who originated them.

10.5 Origin of the crisis: micro elements

The subprime crisis has also identified several microeconomic issues in the international financial system. The main problems are about the securitization processes, the financial regulations and the rating agencies.

10.5.1 The role of financial innovation

Securitization has drastically changed the banking industry. Many financial intermediaries shifted from the 'originate to hold' (OTH) to the 'originate to distribute' (OTD) business model (see Figure 10.18).

In the first model, the loan origination is a simple operation that involves just two subjects: the bank and the borrower. The bank gets the funds from the depositors and originates loans that it holds until their maturity. As the bank is exposed to the credit risk, it has strong incentives to accurately select borrowers (screening) and follow up their behaviour once the loan is originated (monitoring). On the contrary, in the second model the loan origination is a more complex operation, similar to a production process, which involves several subjects. Upstream of the production chain, the investors provide the funds that are needed to originate the loans; downstream the bank grants the

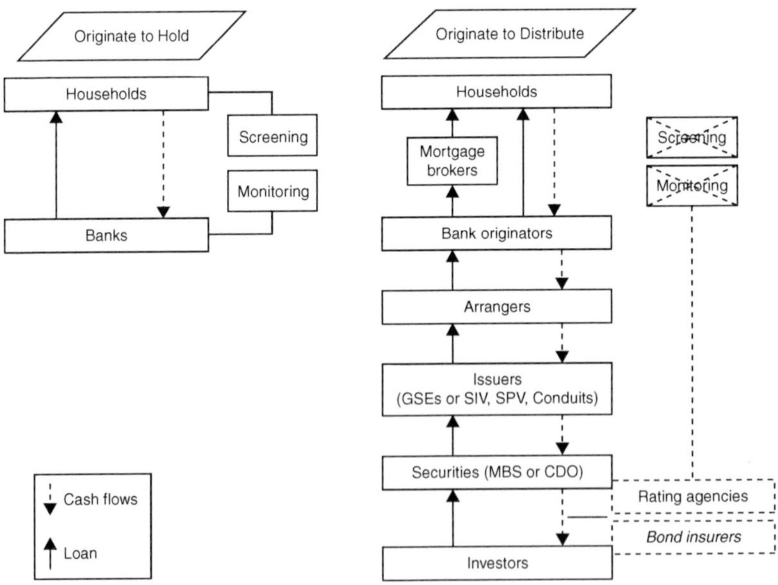

Figure 10.18 Banking business models

loans to the clients. Along this chain, many subjects – each of them specialized in a specific phase of the production process – use complex financial instruments to transfer the funds from the investors to the bank and the credit risk from the bank to the investors. The main advantages of this business model are specialization and risk distribution. On the one hand, specialization favours: a) a more efficient use of the bank's capital; b) a reduction of the loan's cost; c) a high degree of financial innovation; d) a widening of clients eligible for a loan. On the other hand, the fact that many financial instruments – with different risk/return combinations – are issued renders the financial system more stable and allows the investors to diversify their portfolios.

But the increase in efficiency has a cost, which sometimes can be very high. The transfer of the credit risk from the banks to the investors may distort the incentives of the 'originate to distribute' model and originates more low-quality loans. Moreover, due to their complexity, the risk of the financial instruments resulting from the securitizations is often very difficult to evaluate. The errors made by the rating agencies in estimating the default probability of these instruments – which were too complex even for them – and the investors' undue self-confidence in underwriting them have reduced the stability of the international financial system.

In this framework, the US financial deregulation has not only favoured the development of new loan types – questionable as they may be (e.g. the ninja mortgages granted to clients with no income, no job and no asset) – but also complicated the estimate of the potential credit losses and the identification of the most exposed subjects. Therefore, it is not surprising that the defaults of the last link in the complex US financial chain (subprime clients) have rapidly affected the whole sector. The lack of transparency of the instruments and players involved has hindered the reduction of the exposure to subprime mortgages and has also entangled those intermediaries and financial instruments that were not closely related to the real estate market. Hence, the crisis that started in a small segment of the US real estate credit market soon expanded to the whole US credit system, and the wind of globalization soon spread it to all the international markets.

10.5.1.1 Technical aspects of securitization

The securitization processes greatly exacerbated the effects of the US real estate bubble burst. Since the 1980s, this financial technique has been growing exponentially and expanded from real estate loans to many other sectors of the US financial system, such as credit card loans or loans to buy a car.

Securitization can be divided into three phases: a) identification of a group of homogeneous credits in the portfolio of the financial institution that – possibly through a broker – originated them (originator); b) sale of credits to an *ad hoc* vehicle (conduit, SIV or SPV); c) placement, by this vehicle, of asset-backed securities (ABS), whose interest-rate payment and repayment when due depend on the cash flow generated by the underlying credits. For instance, in the case of securitization of real estate loans, in phase 1 a bank (originator) issues the loans, which are then sold to another broker (arranger), who will also be entitled to get the cash flows of the loans and the collateral asset rights. During the second phase, the arranger groups the purchased loans and sells them to another subject (issuer), who has been specifically established to perform securitization operations. In the third phase, the issuer issues the bonds backed by the purchased loans, whose cash flows depend on the loan cash flows.

The bonds issued during the third phase are called structured bonds and can be classified as follows:

- Asset-backed commercial paper (ABCP);
- Mortgage-backed security (MBS) with residential mortgage-backed security (RMBS) or commercial mortgage-backed security (CMBS) depending on the collaterals type;
- Collateralized debt obligation (CDO) in which the ABS or MBS portfolios are securitized once again and are sliced into tranches. Depending on the type of collateral security, they can be classified as follows:
    - Collateralized mortgage obligation (CMO) guaranteed by residential mortgages;
    - Collateralized loans obligation (CLO) guaranteed by business loans;
    - CDO squared obligation, CDO guaranteed by CDO obligations;
    - CDO cubed obligation, CDO guaranteed by CDO squared obligation;
    - Synthetic CDO guaranteed by credit default swaps (CDS) portfolios. This instrument allows the special-purpose entity not to buy bonds, but rather to commit itself to paying back the nominal value of the MBS or CDO in case of a default, receiving in exchange a quarterly premium.

The issuers can meet the different investors' risk propensity by splitting the bond issue into multiple tranches, each one with its specific risk-return profile. The junior tranches get higher yields, but are first in line to absorb losses, should borrowers default. Mezzanine tranches get lower yields than the junior tranches, but are attacked only when the collateral security defaults exceed the junior tranche value. Finally, the senior tranches get the lowest yields, but losses are recorded only if the default exceeds the junior and mezzanine tranche values.

The tranching activity creates structured financial products whose risk is lower than that of the securitized assets average. This is the main justification for the significant growth in the issue of CDOs, whose senior tranches, also thanks to the triple-A granted to them by the rating agencies, were perceived by the investors as risk-free bonds, with yields higher than those of the corporate obligations with an equivalent rating.

Specifically, the risk class of each tranche depends on two variables: the degree of subordination and the credit enhancement. The degree of subordination of a tranche is given by the total value of the lowest seniority tranche, while the most common level of credit enhancement is over-collateralization. One common type of over-collateralization is the creation of a tranche equity that is not placed on the market, but remains in the vehicle and is the first one to get losses, in case of a collateral default. Another type of over-collateralization can be the creation of excess spread, resulting from the difference between the total yield of collateral securities and the yield of the obligations issued by the vehicle. In such a case, the first losses will be absorbed by this buffer and, should the losses be less than the excess spread, the difference will be assigned to the tranche equity; if the losses exceed the excess spread, the equity tranche does not get any premium and the other obligations will be attacked (according to their degree of subordination).

The possible relations between these instruments are shown in Figure 10.19. Initially a special-purpose entity buys the subprime mortgages (1) and issues the mortgage-backed securities. The MBSs are then bought by other entities, which use them as collateral securities to issue the CMOs. The high-quality tranches are used to issue high-grade CDOs (2), while the low-quality ones are used to issue mezzanine-grade CDOs (3). Finally, the low-quality tranches of the mezzanine CDOs are bought by another vehicle that uses them as collateral securities to issue the squared CDOs (4).

It should be kept in mind that the senior tranches are less risky than other tranche types only if the correlation between the collaterals default

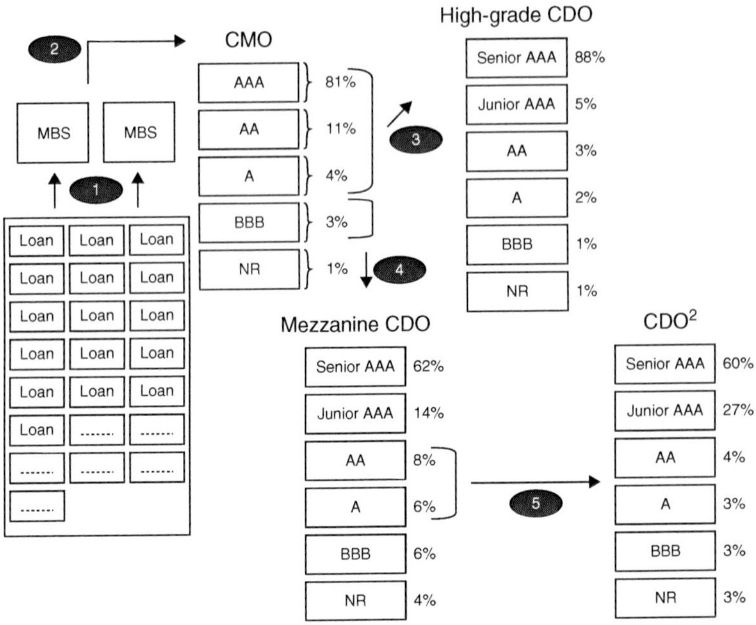

Figure 10.19 Structured finance

is low. For example, if the assets are 100 loans, all of them issued to very low-income households in the suburbs of New York, it is very likely that all the families will default at the same time should an economic slowdown occur. As a consequence, even the CDO senior tranches will probably get losses. On the contrary, should the 100 loans be issued to different clients, with very low to very high incomes in 100 different cities, the likelihood that all the clients default concurrently, should an economic slowdown occur, is much lower. In such a case the senior tranches are less risky than the others.

With regard to issuers, different categories of them can be identified depending on their financial structure. In most cases, the special-purpose vehicles (SPVs) buy credit pools from the brokers (e.g. loans), while the structured investment vehicles (SIVs) buy bond portfolios (e.g. CDOs). Instead, the conduits are characterized not only by the predominant short-term funding, resulting from the issue of the ABCP, but also by the possibility of taking advantage of a credit line granted by a bank and worth the value of the issued bonds. Formal obligations, such as the above-mentioned credit lines, or informal obligations, such as the need to maintain a good reputation, do not always relieve the banks from securitized loans' credit risk.

The Government-Sponsored Enterprises (GSEs) were the first issuers of mortgage-backed securities. These government companies, like Fannie Mae and Freddie Mac, buy loans from the originator banks and issue MBSs guaranteeing the cash flows on these instruments, in case of borrowers' default. For a long time this mechanism has granted liquidity to the banks on the primary market, and also developed a large secondary market of MBSs. Thanks to their crucial role, the GSEs have always benefited from the implicit guarantee of the US Treasury, which became explicit in July 2008, allowing them to collect funds by issuing bonds (agency debt) at a rate that is only slightly higher than the rate of the Treasury bonds. However, to minimize moral hazard behaviour, the US Treasury allows the GSE to buy only conforming loans, that is, good-quality loans which meet specific requirements, for instance in terms of size and loan-to-value ratio.

Until the mid-1990s, Fannie Mae and Freddie Mac controlled almost all the MBS market. However, later on a shadow banking system emerged, challenging GSEs. Non-banks' intermediaries like SIVs, SPVs, conduits, investment banks and hedge funds got into the business of securitization. Most of the intermediaries that operate in the shadow banking system use short-term funding to make long-term investments, such as structured bonds. They share with traditional banks many features, such as asset-maturity transformation, but operate in the shadow of financial regulation. Their low degree of capitalization gives them a powerful leverage effect, but also renders them very fragile. This explains why the liquidity crisis erupted in August 2007, precisely in the shadow banking system, and turned quickly into a solvency crisis with enormous systemic effects, amplified by the opacity of the instruments, the financial techniques and the operators involved.

Other important players in the securitization process are the servicers. They carry out the administrative, bureaucratic and legal activities that the loans require (e.g. get payments from borrowers, contact delinquent borrowers, undertake procedures when the borrower is insolvent, organize auctions and meet fiscal obligations) on behalf of the issuer. If the borrowers default, the servicer will pay the loan interest, not paid by the borrower, to the issuer, pay taxes on property and also the expenses for the sale by auction of the collateral property. Once the property has been sold, the servicer will get the funds that had been paid in advance. This is the reason why servicers also exercise a powerful effect on the issuer's efficiency on the structured bond rating.

10.5.1.2 Asymmetries of information in the securitization process

The crisis has highlighted at least seven critical elements of securitizations, mainly due to the effect of information asymmetries (see section 3.3 above) in the process (Ashcraft and Schuermann, 2008):

1. *Predatory lending or predatory borrowing*: the information asymmetry between the borrower and originator may cause predatory behaviour both by the bank and by the client: by offering a complex type of loan, the originator may sell to the client a mortgage that is well above his repayment possibility (predatory lending); by submitting incomplete or false documentation, the client may induce the originator to grant a mortgage that is well above his repayment possibility (predatory borrowing).
2. *Mortgage fraud*: by exploiting his knowledge about the mortgagor, the originator might induce the arranger, who does not perform a complete due diligence, to finance assets pools that are too risky for his portfolio strategies.
3. *Adverse selection*: the arranger might, in turn, exploit his information advantage, resulting from appropriate due diligence, to securitize the low-quality credits and keep the high-quality ones.
4. *Borrower's moral hazard*: the borrowers who are about to default might not undertake the activities that are needed to protect the value of the collateral assets (e.g. maintenance activities and paying property taxes).
5. *Servicer's moral hazard*: the servicer might decide to renegotiate the loans, rather than declaring them insolvent, because his commissions depend on the loan service.
6. *Principal–agent*: the investors (principals) evaluate the account (agent) performance by comparing it with the **benchmark** yield. However, before the crisis no differentiation was made between benchmarks for corporate bonds and benchmarks for structured bonds. Hence, as the yield on structured bonds was higher than that on corporate bonds with the same rating, the fund managers chose to invest in the former, even though, as suggested by the higher returns paid by the structured bonds, the underlying risks were higher than the level implied in the rating.
7. *Model error*: the rating agencies are paid by the arrangers, and not by the investors, to evaluate the bonds issued via the securitization of mortgage. Hence the difficulty in differentiating between errors caused due to an inaccurate statistical model and errors caused by conflicts of interest.

Shortly after the beginning of the crisis, empirical evidence on these critical elements was given. Keys et al. (forthcoming) demonstrate that among the loans with equivalent characteristics but incomplete documentation, the ones that will be most probably securitized (because their FICO is slightly above the minimum value of 620) are the ones that default most often. Mian and Sufi (2009) show that the rapid credit expansion in the areas with a high latent demand in 1996, that is, the areas with a high number of subprime clients who could not get a loan, caused a remarkable real estate price increase, but also a rapid growth of the default rates between 2005 and 2007. The authors argue that the increased supply of loans could not be justified by the improved economic conditions in these areas, because the income and rate of employment increased less than elsewhere between 1996 and 2005. Instead they claim that disintermediation, whereby the banks sold the originated loans to other intermediaries, was responsible for the rapid increase in new loan originations, house-price appreciation and the subsequent large increase in default rates. Moreover, the loans sold to the intermediaries who were not affiliated to the originator bank experienced higher default rates, thus confirming the moral hazard hypothesis. According to Mian and Sufi, the chance to completely transfer the credit risk led many banks to fund risky subjects, only to resell the loan shortly afterwards, to earn the commission fee. Dell'Ariccia et al. (2008) give more empirical evidence on this particular issue. They demonstrate that the areas with the highest default rates between 2004 and 2006 are the same where the origination of the subprime mortgages grew more between 2000 and 2004 because the credit standards were lower, fewer mortgage loan applications were rejected and the loan-to-value ratio increased.

10.5.2 The role of banking regulation

Basel I contributed to the growth of securitization by assigning lower capital charges to securitized assets (Demirgüç-Kunt and Servén, 2009). Hence, to reduce the regulatory capital in the years before the crisis, many banks established some special-purpose entities to which they could sell the originated loans through securitization (Acharya and Richardson, 2009). The special-purpose entities funded the procurement of the loans by using the ABCP guaranteed by the sponsoring bank. This guarantee has two important effects: first, the special-purpose entity can collect funds with low interest rates because the rating agencies give high rates to the ABCP thanks to the bank's guarantee. Second, no capital charge is expected from the bank if the guarantee refers to ABCP with a less than 12-month maturity (the most common on the market). Figure 10.4

Box 10.4 The origins of financial regulation

Bank rules are needed because, in the traditional model, the banks collect short-term deposits and make long-term investments, by exploiting their greater capacity to screen and monitor the borrowers. Their revenues are the result of the difference between long-term rates and short-term rates. As the different maturity of their assets and liabilities exposes them to liquidity crises, which might start a contagious bank run, deposit insurance is available in many countries. Such a mechanism guarantees repayment to the depositors should the bank go bankrupt. In exchange for this guarantee, the banks are asked to maintain a minimum capital to face unexpected losses on their loans. At international level, the criteria to determine this quota are given to the Basel Committee on Banking Supervision (BCBS), which is based in Basel and is part of the Bank of International Settlements. Although a revision process had started in 2004 to get to the implementation of a new agreement (Basel II), when the crisis started many countries still referred to the first international agreement published in 1988 (Basel I). According to this agreement, the banks are requested to maintain a regulatory capital that is at least 8 per cent of their risk-weighted assets.

shows the growth and collapse of the ABCP market. The issues peaked in the second quarter of 2007 but, when the crisis started, the special-purpose entities could not find any investors who were ready to underwrite these instruments. The sponsor banks had to support them since the many loans, previously securitized, went into default. However, the banks did not have enough capital to face the losses and the liquidity dried up from many financial markets.

Another way to reduce the capital charges was achieved by selling the loans originated and buying a triple-A CDO. In this case, under Basel I, triple-A tranches are characterized by provisions that are 50 per cent lower than those required for the loans to firms or households.

10.5.3 The role of the credit rating agencies

The financial-regulation reliance on ratings has given a significant contribution to the development of securitization and, as a consequence, to the activity of the rating agencies.

The capital charge of banks, insurance companies, broker-dealers and pension funds depends on the rating level of their assets: the higher

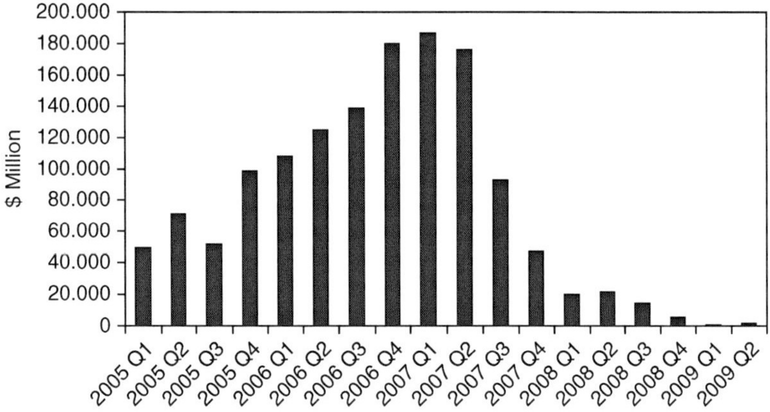

Figure 10.20 Global CDO market issuance
Source: SIFMA

the rating, the smaller the regulatory capital they need. The demand for high-rated and high-yield[5] instruments has encouraged the growth of structured bonds, because by creating different types of tranches it is possible to issue many bonds with a rating higher than that of the average pool of securitized assets. In 2007 the outstanding structured bonds amounted to almost $11,000 billion, approximately 35 per cent of the total US bond market; 60 per cent of them were triple-A. This is a very high value if one considers that less than 1 per cent of the corporate bonds had such a rating (Fitch Ratings, 2007).

However, since July 2007, the quality of structured bonds has rapidly decreased: in November of that year there were more than 2000 downgrades, with 500 tranches downgraded more than ten notches (e.g. since the one-notch downgrade is between two contiguous grades, from AAA to BB+). The downtrend continued in 2008, too, with more than 11,000 downgrades of structured bonds that had been given a triple-A (Benmelech and Dlugosz, 2009a). The CDOs were the most badly hit; in fact, they were the core cause of loss of the main international financial institutions involved in the crisis. Because of the numerous downgrades, the investors no longer trusted the rating system, and the demand for structured bonds, which was highly dependent on the rating, collapsed. In 2008 the private MBS, CDO and ABS issues decreased by 96 per cent, 88 per cent and 82 per cent, respectively (see Figure 10.20).

The main rating agencies have been harshly criticized for declaring some bonds nearly risk-free (triple-A), which then defaulted a few months later. The main cause of this debacle is probably the deep conflicts of interest in the rating industry. From the agencies' side, receiving the fees from the subjects who ask the rating can be an incentive to overestimate the quality of the bonds in order to meet the issuers', rather than the investors', needs (in literature this phenomenon is referred to as rating inflation). From the firms' side, the possibility of being rated by multiple agencies and communicating only the highest rating to the market is like going shopping for the agencies that are willing to grant the best ratings. Moreover, some agencies also provide consulting services on how to organize the issues and structure the tranches to get the highest possible rating. In fact, using the evaluation software made available by the agencies, the issuer can distribute the cash flow, thus allowing the tranche to get a given rating. Finally, using the iterative and interactive method, the details and evaluation of the operation can be finalized with the rating agency (Mason and Rosner, 2007).

Since the beginning of the crisis, an interesting field of research has been intensified to analyse the critical features of the rating market. Bolton et al. (2009) demonstrate that the rating-inflation probability grows as the number of naive investors in the market increases; that is, there are more people in the market who do not have a full understanding of the potential conflicts of interest in the agency ratings. On this issue, the agencies often state that conflicts of interest are eased by reputational costs, because if the ratings regularly overestimate the actual risk of the bonds, the agency's reliability would be unavoidably jeopardized. In line with this, Bolton et al. also show that the rating-inflation probability decreases as the reputational costs increase. However Mathis et al. (2008) argue that these costs are not enough to regulate the agencies when a significant portion of the revenues comes from the evaluation of complex bonds (e.g. structured bonds).

To thoroughly verify the role of securitization in the recent rating-system failure, a good point to start is to recognize that the rating agencies did relatively good work in the US securities market, even though conflicts of interest have characterized the rating industry since the 1970s,[6] at least until the beginning of the subprime mortgage crisis. This is the reason why Skreta and Veldkamp (2009) believe that the complexity of structured bonds is the root cause of the mistakes made by the rating agencies. They use a theoretical model to demonstrate that when the financial instruments are simple, the shopping incentives are weak because the variability of ratings across the agencies is low. On the contrary, when the financial instruments are complex, the shopping incentives are strong because the variability of ratings across the agencies is high. Benmelech and Dlugosz (2009b), analysing approximately 30,000 CDO tranches, test empirically this conjecture and find that the tranches evaluated by one agency have more chances to get downgraded.

The rating agencies have also been bitterly criticized for the methods they used in evaluating structured bonds. Benmelech and Dlugosz (2009a) analysed approximately 4000 CDO tranches and demonstrate that a B+ average-quality portfolio leads to approximately 70 per cent AAA tranches; the authors call this result 'the alchemy of ratings'. Among the possible explanations, there are: (a) very low default rates and very high recovery rates in the models used by the agencies; (b) optimistic hypotheses of a low correlation across the collateral assets defaults; (c) iterative and interactive software that allows the issuer to determine the minimum level of asset securities to get a triple 'A'.

Furthermore, because of the increasing complexity, the CDOs can only be evaluated by a selected group of highly qualified people; hence the need for the least qualified investors to resort to the rating as a synthetic evaluation instrument. Pagano and Volpin (2008) demonstrate that when very complex financial instruments are involved, giving much information to the market might induce the unsophisticated investors not to underwrite, thus reducing the demand on the primary market and the prices. This is the reason why, according to the authors, only rating-related information was given to the market when structured bonds were issued. Making the information conveyed to the market simpler, the primary market has attracted more investors; however, the stability and liquidity of the secondary market have been jeopardized. When the crisis started, the investors realized they did not have the necessary information to evaluate the risk of the bonds in the new financial scenario and trading activities stopped in many markets.

The crisis has shown several shortcomings in the international financial system, but it is unlikely that these problems will be resolved easily, if at all. In the last part of the book we analyse the recent proposals for reform.

11
Crisis in Academic Economics

In spite of some encouraging signals of recovery, the global economy still faces uncertainty about the consequences of the recession triggered by the Great Crisis of 2007–09. This uncertainty largely stems from the unprecedented disruption of the financial system as a whole brought about by the crisis. Thus, it is useful to analyse from an academic point of view what caused the financial excesses and rising leverage in the pre-crisis USA and elsewhere. The genesis of this is related to various underlying factors. Poor incentives were provided in a context of intense financial innovation accompanied by regulatory loopholes. On its part, an exceedingly lenient monetary policy underestimated the perils of inflation in asset prices. Furthermore, the set-up for the governance of globalization proved inadequate.

Thus, the issues we raise here go to the heart of the sustainability of the development model cast by the USA on a world scale. As globalization was to a large extent walking on the legs of the financial system, this global financial crisis is also a crisis of the way global relations were arranged.

Behind the accumulation of the excessive indebtedness leading to the crisis lay three main theoretical/policy errors: a) questionable risk-pricing models derived from the finance theory; b) fallacious evolutionary view subordinating banks to financial markets; c) improvident monetary policy conduct by the Fed. These are errors derived from theory that led to wrong business decisions and faulty regulation.

Two additional issues – the unsatisfactory set-up of regulation/supervision and the major conflicts of interest – though, need to be mentioned. While the stream of structured products was rapidly swelling, much of it was transacted in barely transparent, unregulated (OTC – over-the-counter) markets and hinged on the poorly regulated shadow banking system. This comprised the investment banks, that were greatly expanding their **leverage ratios**, the hedge funds and the structured investment vehicles (SIVs). Compensation schemes also favoured excessive risk-taking. Regulatory and supervisory loopholes were extensive also because inadequate global coordination opened up to massive international arbitrage, particularly to financial centres providing regulatory and tax havens. In turn, even within the USA, the multilayered set-up of regulation and supervision – involving the Fed, the SEC, the Comptroller of the Currency, the FDIC and individual states – made the environment less conducive to rein in excessive risk-taking at financial institutions.[1]

In addition, a key part of the pre-crisis easy finance impinged on the presence of conflicts of interest.[2] Nonetheless, as we will see, the three theoretical errors were *per se* enough to make stabilization interventions destabilizing. So, by bailing out the intermediaries that had made wrong choices and thus amplifying the moral hazard for financial intermediaries, the policies to overcome one crisis triggered by the explosion of a financial bubble were involuntarily intensifying systemic risk and consequently paving the way to a new – probably bigger – financial bubble.

11.1 Questionable risk-pricing models derived from the finance theory

The fact that risk-pricing models had problems had been known since at least 1998. The hedge fund Long-Term Capital Management (LTCM), technically bankrupt, was salvaged via the arrangement on the part of the Fed of a consortium of banks to bail it out. LTCM was no anonymous passer-by but the star of Wall Street (Lowenstein, 2000), with its trading models created by two Nobel-prize economists: Robert C. Merton and Myron S. Scholes. LTCM went bankrupt because those models underestimated the 'tail risk' (i.e. the occurrence of particularly devastating, though unlikely, events; Taleb, 2007) which materialized following the Asian crisis and the Russian sovereign default. Also, without due revision, those models thereafter became even more dominating – and even some pieces of regulation came to be based on them – up to the recent crisis (see Box 11.1).

What is more, the base models of finance hinge on the hypothesis that private risks and sovereign risk are uncorrelated (see Cuthbertson and Nitzsche, 2004 and Box 11.2).[3] However, such a hypothesis is untenable, as the recent crisis also reminded us when the unavoidable state interventions to salvage banks determined, at the same time, a reduction in the default risk of the banks (lower spreads on bank

Box 11.1 Value-at-Risk

Giovanni Tinella
Risk Manager at Pioneer Alternative Investments[a]

As risk is inherently a probabilistic or statistical concept, there are various notions and measures of it. In the past 20 years, the financial community has become more and more interested in Value-at-Risk (VaR) and, in the mid-1990s, this tool was adopted as the official risk measure by regulators as well.

Broadly speaking, VaR is a simple and summary statistical measure of possible portfolio losses due to market risk. Specifically, VaR measures the risk of an assets portfolio by estimating the probability that a given loss might occur in a specific time horizon. For example, the 'dollar VaR' of a particular portfolio can be expressed as: 'there is a 5% probability that this portfolio will lose more than $520 (VaR) over a specific holding period' (1 day, 1 week and so on).

Formally, the VaR can be expressed as:

$$P_t[V_t \leq \text{VaR}] = \alpha \text{ (where } \alpha \text{ is the specified probability)}$$

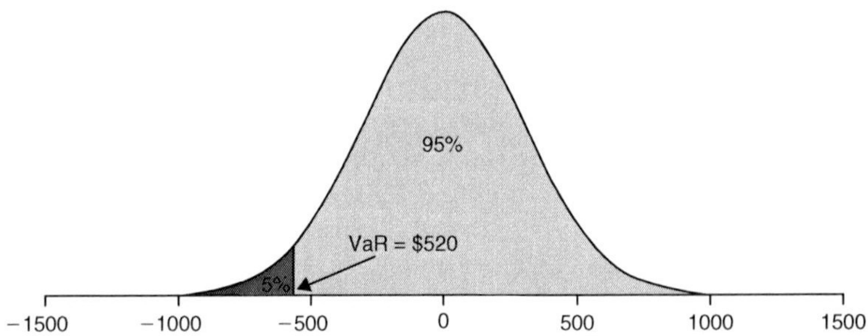

There are different approaches to estimating the VaR, which can be classified in two macro-groups:

- Parametric:
  - Asset Normal
  - Delta Normal
  - Delta – Gamma Normal
- Non-parametric:
  - Monte Carlo Simulation
  - Historical Simulation

(continued)

Box 11.1 Continued

The popularity of this risk measure comes from different factors:

- It is a forward-looking measure.
- It is equally applicable to different financial instruments.
- It focuses on the tails of the distribution.
- It is easy to communicate and understand.

Despite its popularity, the VaR has been criticized from the outset. The main criticisms are:

- It does not say anything about the magnitude of losses greater than the VaR.
- As it is calculated using past data, the history may not be a reasonable representation of what things will look like going forward.
- It is empirically verified that securities returns have fatter tails than those represented by the normal statistical distribution employed in the VaR model (if a parametric approach is used).
- As a consequence of the last point, the VaR is a coherent risk measure only if we assume that the returns are described by the normal distribution.

To overcome some of these drawbacks, and improve the description of the risk profile of the portfolio, in the risk-management community the VaR model has been used together with other risk measures and analyses, such as the Expected Shortfall and the Stress Tests.

However, even the most advanced risk-management tools proved deficient to predict what would happen after the outbreak of the subprime crisis. As the financial industry staggered on the verge of collapse, it became clear that many of the risk-management models used, mainly the VaR, were inadequate to estimate risk. This has led to justifiable, though sometimes overzealous and unwarranted, criticism of the VaR. Indeed, it is well known, especially after the LTCM collapse, that the VaR is imperfect, it is not a crystal ball and it cannot predict everything. However, being aware of its limitations, VaR can still be a good tool to monitor the day-to-day market risk during normal times.

To put it simply, the VaR is not constructed to deal with crisis risk. This is the main reason why, though used together with Stress Test

(*continued*)

Box 11.1 Continued

and other risk measures, it was unable to reflect the potential losses in the financial markets hit by the crisis.

As well pointed out by Richard Bookstaber:[b] 'when a crisis comes it starts with an exogenous shock and the resulting forced selling leads to a cascading cycle downward of the price'. And, it could be added that, the more leveraged is the market the more marked is the downturn. This vicious cycle breaks the historical relationships or, in other words, in time of crisis the correlation among different asset classes changes and it can even become positive for markets that, based on historical analysis, should not be linked. Therefore, this rules out one of the most important assumptions behind the VaR methodology, which is a stable correlation structure. As a result, the validity of the estimation of the risk is jeopardized.

If we analyse the recent financial crisis from a risk-estimation point of view, we can call it 'a perfect storm'. In fact, it started in highly leveraged markets which were trading highly illiquid and complex financial instruments. In some cases, like the CDOs and other more complex securities, these instruments were not always included in the risk analysis as they were held off-balance sheet. Moreover, that exclusion was not considered an immediate concern because they were believed to be low risk (thanks to the AAA rating assigned them by the credit rating agencies).

As reported by Richard Bookstaber, to improve the effectiveness of our risk analyses taking into account the crisis risk we have two options:

- Enhancing the VaR analysis with other risk measures helping to analyse the tail risk, like Stress Test, Expected Shortfall, CoVaR[c] and so on.
- Employing different tools which have few assumptions and which are not linked to the historical outcomes, such as leverage and liquidity ratios.

With regard to the first approach, the critical point for success is to believe that it is possible to model financial crises. Yet, it seems quite difficult to do this, as history teaches us; or, in other words,

(continued)

Box 11.1 Continued

we should suppose that the financial crises are not 'black swans'. Rather, the second approach seems easier, feasible and more reliable to manage and control.

Notes

[a] The views expressed are those of the author and do not necessarily reflect those of Pioneer Alternative Investments.

[b] R. Bookstaber (2009) 'The Risk of Financial Modelling: VaR and Economic Meltdown', Testimony Submitted to the US House of Representatives.

[c] The CoVaR is used to capture the marginal contribution of a particular financial institution to the overall systemic risk. For example, the CoVar for *i*'s institution is defined as the VaR of the whole financial sector conditional on institution *i*'s distress.

CDS – Credit Default Swaps) and an increase in the sovereign default risk (larger spreads on CDS).

11.2 Fallacious evolutionary view subordinating banks to financial markets

The banking business model based on 'relationship banking' appears to have been less affected by the deep financial instability of 2007–09. It is true that significant bank distress was experienced also in many countries of continental Europe, which normally rely more on banks than on financial markets in the international comparison. However, if we look at the individual intermediaries we notice that those suffering distress were generally the larger-sized banks and those banks that came to rely more on financial market-related non-interest operating income as a source of revenue. It is useful to observe that – in line with the findings of IMF economists Hesse and Čihák (2007) – more stability was enjoyed by the cooperative banks (with the exception of their central financial intermediation units, like Natixis in France). In fact, mutual and cooperative banks are everywhere champions of retail banking along the relationship banking model.

Indeed, the Anglo-American transformation of financial intermediaries in the past 20 years had at its centre the advent of the new banking model 'originate to distribute' (OTD) – whereby banks originated loans to be immediately securitized on the financial market – as opposed to the traditional 'originate to hold' (OTH). With the benefit of hindsight, we now know that the widespread recourse to OTD was one of the fundamental causes behind the generalized loss of responsible behaviour

Box 11.2 Efficient market hypothesis

Giovanni Walter Puopolo
Swiss Finance Institute and University of Lausanne

The efficient market hypothesis (EMH) is a cornerstone of modern financial economics. Eugene Fama first defined the term 'efficient market' as one in which security prices fully reflect all available information.[a] Therefore, the market is said to be efficient if the reaction of market prices to new information is instantaneous and, on average, unbiased. Nevertheless, some investors may overreact and some may underreact to new information. All that is required by the EMH is that, even if a person is wrong about the market price, indeed, everyone can be, the market as a whole has to be systematically right.

Three different versions of EMH have been proposed depending on the level of available information, each of which has different implications for how markets work.

The weak form EMH asserts that the current market price of a security reflects all the information contained in the past sequence of prices of that security. It implies that no one should be able to outperform the market using investment strategies based on historical prices or other historical data.

The semi-strong form EMH states that securities' current market prices reflect all publicly available information (historical data plus companies' financial statements, companies announcements, economic factors, etc.). It implies that no one should be able to outperform the market by trading on that information.

The strong form EMH affirms that all information, whether public of private, is fully reflected in the current market price. This means that even the company's managers (insiders) are not able to make gains from the inside information they hold.

One of the main drawbacks of the EMH, as underlined by Fama, is that 'the statement that in an efficient market prices fully reflect all the available information is so general that it has no empirically testable implications. Therefore, to make the model testable, the process of price formation must be specified in more detail.' In other words, from an empirical perspective, the analysis of EMH requires an asset-pricing model to provide the link from economic fundamentals to asset prices. In this way, empirical tests of market efficiency become

(*continued*)

Box 11.2 Continued

necessarily joint tests of market efficiency and of a particular asset-pricing model. When the joint hypothesis is rejected, as it often is, it is logically possible that this is a consequence of deficiencies in the particular pricing model chosen rather than in the efficient market hypothesis. This is the 'bad model' problem (Fama, 1991).

Most empirical tests of the EMH have often started with the following equation:

$$\tilde{r}_i = \bar{r}_i + \tilde{\varepsilon}_i \quad (1)$$

where $\tilde{r}_i$ is the realized return of security i, $\bar{r}_i$ is the risk-adjusted expected return from a pricing model (i.e. CAPM – Capital Asset Pricing Model – or APT – Arbitrage Pricing Theory) and $\tilde{\varepsilon}_i$ is the residual. More precisely, the econometrician assumed that returns followed a 'random walk', which is a term loosely used in the finance literature to characterize a price series where all subsequent price changes represent random departures from previous prices. The logic of the random-walk idea is that if the flow of information is unimpeded and information is immediately reflected in stock prices, then tomorrow's price change will reflect only tomorrow's news and will be independent of the price changes today. More formally, the random-walk EMH requires that the residual term $\tilde{\varepsilon}_i$ is zero on average (i.e. no systematic excess returns with respect to the benchmark model) and unpredictable, so that resulting price changes are purely random.

Almost at the same time, various researchers proposed several asset-pricing models to compute the risk-adjusted expected rate of return $\bar{r}_i$, focusing in particular on the CAPM. The CAPM shows the necessary equilibrium risk-return trade-off for all securities. It states that the risk premium (i.e. the expected return in excess of the risk-free rate) on any asset is equal to the risk premium of the market times the ratio of the covariance between the asset and the market portfolio over the variance of the market portfolio. This ratio is called beta and measures the systematic risk rewarded by the market.

Accordingly, the main pricing equation, called Security Market Line (SML) is:

$$E(\tilde{r}_i) = r_f + \beta_i[E(\tilde{r}_M) - r_f] \quad (2)$$

(continued)

Box 11.2 Continued

where $E(\tilde{r}_i)$ is the expected return on security i, r_f is the risk-free rate and $E(\tilde{r}_M)$ is the expected return on the (diversified) market portfolio. It is worthwhile to underline that the CAPM is a theoretical model, whose pricing relationship (the SML) exactly holds for all securities' expected returns. On the contrary, empirical tests of EMH require an econometric relationship based on realized returns. Thus, Markowitz suggested the following one-factor model (called the market model):

$$\tilde{r}_{i,t+1} = \alpha_i + \beta_i \tilde{r}_{M,t+1} + \tilde{\varepsilon}_{i,t+1} \quad (3)$$

where $\tilde{r}_{i,t+1}$ is the realized rate of return on security i in period t+1, $\tilde{r}_{M,t+1}$ is the realized return on the market portfolio at time t+1, $\tilde{\varepsilon}_{i,t+1}$ is a random noise and α_i and β_i are the parameters to be estimated. The returns $\tilde{r}_{i,t+1}$ and $\tilde{r}_{M,t+1}$ are often computed in excess of the risk-free rate r_f. Hence, the joint tests of EMH-CAPM require that:

- The estimated parameters $\hat{\alpha}_i$ and $\hat{\beta}_i$ remain fairly constant over time;
- $\tilde{r}_{M,t+1}$ and the estimated $\hat{\varepsilon}_i$ are close to serially independent;
- The estimated residual $\hat{\varepsilon}_i$ is independent of $\tilde{r}_{M,t+1}$;
- In case of excess returns, the estimated $\hat{\alpha}_i$ is not significant.

Notes
[a] E. Fama (1965) 'The Behavior of Stock Market Prices', *Journal of Business*, vol. 38, no. 1, 34–105.

on the part of the banks (Ashcraft and Schuermann, 2008; Dell'Ariccia et al., 2008; Mian and Sufi, 2009). Specifically, it is easy to understand that when the bank knows ex ante that – through securitization – it will sell at once those loans it is granting, the bank loses the appropriate incentives to duly perform its screening and monitoring on borrowers (see Figure 10.18). Thus, a generalized deterioration in lending standards is on the cards. And this is particularly worrisome in those contexts where the risk of borrowers' default is systematically high, such as in the subprime mortgage segment.

However, the crisis was compounded by deeper theoretical mistakes. The progress made by the theory of intermediation based on the asymmetric information approach (e.g. Stiglitz and Weiss, 1981; Diamond,

1984) was rather neglected. The evolution of information and communication technologies (ICT) had rooted the wrong perception that risk could be segmented and traded without major adjustment, a view which stood at the basis of securitization but also affected other segments of the credit market. This approach neglected the problem that if one unbundles complex financial relationships into segmented contracts this will, most likely, weaken the intermediaries' ability to assess and govern the overall dimension of that risk, thus amplifying systemic risk. When a borrower entrusts all his financial dealings on a single banking counterpart, in fact, that bank will have access to private (soft) information (Scott, 2006), which will instead be lost when that customer fragments his business among various counterparts, let alone if his debt is securitized on the financial market. At the same time, within a single banking relationship, the bank has the appropriate incentives to screen and monitor its borrowers, thereby acquiring private information on them. It is true that, as a consequence of the hold-up problem, the relationship bank might try to extract rents from its borrowers. Nevertheless, this might be a price worth paying to avoid falling into irresponsibility.

Eventually, in fact, through the advent of the OTD model, the responsibility of assessing the risk of the underlying loans was mostly transferred from the banks to the credit rating agencies. But the rating agencies were also part of the problem in four respects: a) they underestimated risks implicit in structured assets because they overlooked that systemic liquidity problems would impinge on the market valuation of these assets; b) they failed to see how the transformation of the banking model – from OTH to OTD – had undermined the incentives to screening and monitoring borrowers, thus lowering credit standards; c) they ventured into rating extremely complex structured finance products by 'marking them to model' on the basis of too rosy assumptions (Mason and Rosner, 2007); d) sometimes, the rating agencies underwent conflicts of interest problems whenever they acted as consultants in the structuring process of the products and then rated those products.

Theory and regulation contributed to spread the fallacious view that individual risks could be separated without appropriate system adjustment. On its part, regulation contributed to shape a less secure banking system, for example through the international accounting standards (IAS) and Basel II, which – adopting the mark-to-market approach – introduced a regulatory incentive to rely exclusively on the rating/scoring technologies. It may suffice to consider the pro-cyclical trends potentially induced by the diffusion of credit scoring and disseminated to the banks' minimum capital requirements through banks' internal rating models.[4] This may be labelled the 'dark side' of credit scoring (Ferri, 2001). Credit scoring is a substantially mechanical method to come up with the decision to grant credit on the basis of the collection of standardized information on applicants. This method relies on statistical models to assign the applicants to various ex ante risk classes and choose the threshold values to accept or reject the loan applications. As such, credit scoring is a potent instrument able to lower noticeably the administrative/management cost of the loans, to the point that, according to some authors, it could reduce asymmetric information and financial constraints (Petersen and Rajan, 2002). In our view, however, adopting credit scoring has shortcomings as well. It is a well-recognized fact that, in reality, the main role of the banks stems from their ability to develop relationship banking with their borrowers, a special situation facilitating the so-called Pareto-improving exchange of information between the borrower and the bank.[5] And relationship banking hinges in a critical way on the extraction by the bank of proprietary information on the borrowers, thanks to multiple interactions between financial intermediary and customer (Boot, 2000). In that, credit scoring lowers banks' ability to gather and process soft information on borrowers that are often crucial to overcome the asymmetries of information between the borrower and the lender. In truth, credit scoring implies totally trusting standardized data and automatic mechanisms, an approach which is the opposite of using soft information, which is, by nature, information that one cannot circumscribe in standard formats and that requires relationships rather than mechanical instruments. From this perspective, credit scoring – as it reflects the borrower's current situation rather than his future prospects – may induce pro-cyclical fluctuations in the cost and the availability of credit, something that could amplify the endogenous fluctuations in the loan supply (Rajan, 1994) and, thus, in economic activity. Analogous considerations apply to ratings and, so, also to Basel II.

The approach postulating the need for banks to evolve from the OTH to the OTD model (Bryan, 1988) implied a subordination of the banks to the financial markets, where their loans would now be priced as securities on the basis of statistical models rather than the bankers' *intuitus personae*. This subordination derived from the evolutionist view whereby multilateral financial markets would do a better job at allocating risks (Goldsmith, 1966, 1969). Alas this vision was based on a transactional view of the bank, which had been questioned by theory and evidence.

Perhaps, as Allen and Gale (2000) suggest, it is more fruitful to look at financial markets and banks as complements rather than substitutes.

The two actors can fruitfully play different functions in the financial system. Both are needed. In spite of that, we do observe that – even though some convergence took place over the past 20 years – differences exist across financial systems. Financial systems are often distinguished as financial 'market-based' (MB) – when they rely to a larger extent on financial market transactions – whereas they are labelled 'bank-based' (BB) – when bank intermediation has a larger weight. An interesting study by the IMF (2006) indicates that these underlying differences in financial structures may affect the response of households and firms to changes in the economic environment, and thus influence the cyclical behaviour of national economies. Specifically, the study reaches the following main findings.

First, within the common trend to bank disintermediation in favour of the financial markets, the pace has varied and important differences still persist across financial systems.

Second, in MB financial systems households seem to be able to smooth consumption more effectively in the face of unanticipated changes in their income, although they may be more sensitive to changes in asset prices.

Third, in BB financial systems firms appear to be better able to smooth investment during business-cycle downturns, as they are better positioned to access external financing based on their long-term relationships with financial intermediaries. However, when faced with more fundamental changes in the environment that require a reallocation of resources across sectors, MB financial systems seem to be better placed to shift resources to take advantage of new growth opportunities.

11.3 Improvident monetary policy conduct by the Fed

On its part, the Fed seemed at length overly hesitant to take action against the build-up of unsustainable US indebtedness. In truth, the Fed was comforted by mainstream academia, which mostly suggested that central banks should worry just about CPI (Consumer Price Index) inflation,[6] rather than financial imbalances and asset-price booms. Also, the gradual monetary policy tightening since mid-2004 affected only the short-term **Fed funds rate** and had little impact on long-term interest rates. This 'decoupling' of long-term rates – attributed in part to large capital inflows, mostly from surplus countries – implied that monetary policy tightening had only modest effects on aggregate demand (Wu, 2006). Nevertheless, it is clear by now that keeping short-term rates very low for so long helped increase maturity mismatches: before the crisis investment banks entrusted some 25 per cent of their funding to overnight repos and an additional 15 per cent to three-month asset-backed commercial paper, while holding assets with much longer maturities on their asset side. Therefore, too lenient monetary policy was certainly part of the problem.

In addition, the Fed's easy monetary policy contributed to creating global liquidity indirectly. The supplementary impact came from the many emerging market economies – some of them quite important – which have their currencies pegged to the dollar. To keep the peg, they had to follow the expansionary policies and this contributed to the expansion of world liquidity.

Moreover, perhaps the great 'moderation of inflation' of the past 15 years depends also on globalization (with production being relocated to lower cost-of-labour countries) besides the central banks' credibility and the rigour of their monetary policies (Benati and Mumtaz, 2005; Benati and Surico, 2009).[7] It is also useful to recall that: a) during the first globalization of the nineteenth century, developed countries experienced a drop in their price level – between 1870 and 1900, prices decreased by 1.2 per cent (0.8 per cent) per year in the USA (in the UK) – and not simply a lower increase in prices, that is, a moderation of inflation; b) at that time the international monetary system, based on the gold standard, ruled out discretionary monetary policy. If we consider a) and b) together we may actually doubt that, effectively, the discretionary monetary policies of the main central banks have been the only driver lowering inflation in the recent phase.

This takes us back to the mistakes made by the Fed, which kept too low interest rates for too long while the USA was accumulating its external imbalance. Furthermore, by salvaging the LTCM hedge fund (in 1998) and lowering rates decidedly after the burst of the new economy bubble (in 2000), the Fed had heightened the moral hazard for financial intermediaries, to the point that pundits described a kind of 'Greenspan put', that is, an option with which if things went well they cashed in the profits and if things went awry the Fed would come to their rescue lowering interest rates. All in all, the undesired fall-out of the stabilization policies to solve crises generated increasing moral hazard and exorbitant systemic risk and this is what explains how those stabilization policies became destabilizing. The crux of the problem, as we have tried to explain, was, however, that those policies were founded on theoretical mistakes.

For the future, as BIS (2009) argues convincingly, we need to enlarge the focus of monetary policy with central banks, not merely aiming at

CPI inflation while big imbalances grow at the macro level and, under the glitter of innovation, perilous fragilities undermine the financial system. However, even if leaning against asset-price inflation is embodied as an additional target, the problem will still exist of how to spot the bubbles early on, which normally become known only with the benefit of hindsight.

12
Conclusions and Perspectives

As we have largely argued, it seems inappropriate to look at this global financial crisis as an isolated crisis, as implied in a view à la 'Black Swan' (Taleb, 2007). On the contrary, as Reinhart and Rogoff (2008, 2009) argue convincingly, this crisis is similar to the financial instability crises that happened in past decades, such as the asset bubble followed by the debt-deflation crisis of Japan in the 1990s. To some extent, this crisis resembles also the systemic crises of the emerging economies across the 1990s and the beginning of the new millennium (Mexico 1994; East Asia 1997; Russia 1998; Argentina and Turkey 2001). Those crises were interpreted along the paradigm of the twin crises (Kaminsky and Reinhart, 1999). The chief difference with respect to those is that the Great Crisis of 2007–09 started at (and hit) the centre of the world's financial system, rather than its periphery, and excess debt was denominated in the domestic currency (the US$) rather than in a foreign hard currency. As such it seems to need re-regulation as a condition to finding a proper solution. According to various observers (e.g. Eichengreen, 2008a, 2008b, 2009; Wolf, 2008), the international financial system became increasingly inconsistent and instability-prone as it progressively abandoned the gold exchange standard (1971) and then, via deregulation and financial liberalization through much of the 1980s and 1990s, became weakly regulated/supervised at both the national and global levels.

In this book, we have proposed that it may be useful to cast the experiences of intensifying financial instability of the past decades within a political-economy cycle of finance. One could ask whether the recent crisis – which is the largest one since the 1930s – might bring this political-economy cycle of finance to a close.

The idea that crises may recur and strengthen over time until they reach an unsustainable intensity is found in the famous essay by Kindleberger

(1978) on 'manias, panics and crashes'. In a sense, Minsky's ideas may be viewed, in fact, as an attempt to formalize Kindleberger's vision. Indeed, Kindleberger takes the traditional belief that people are rational beings and introduces the fact that speculation leading to destabilization is very much present, and that many of history's crashes have come from this irrational behaviour, that is, manias, panics and ultimately crashes.[1] Kindleberger stretches his interpretation to encompass more than 300 years of financial crises. He also asks the important question of whether or not there was a lender of last resort acting to halt a run out of illiquid assets into money by making more money available, through a discount window. But Kindleberger warns that this is not the whole solution. Having a lender of last resort can pose its own problems. Many institutions, because there is someone to bail them out, partake in more risky practices. By simply bailing out these mismanaged firms, we are not giving them incentive to improve their operation. Thus, for Kindleberger, when the system runs from bubble to bubble and the subsequent panics and crashes are methodically cured with lender of last resort bailouts – as seems to have happened over the past 15 years in the USA – those stabilization interventions turn out increasingly destabilizing.[2]

The natural extension of Kindleberger's view is that at some point the financial system needs to be fixed again through in-depth re-regulation, in a way to regain a set-up coherent with financial stability. In fact, financial deregulation and liberalization have amplified the scope for speculation and the extent of speculation can no longer be cured with bailouts that soothe one crash only to intensify moral hazard and prepare for a larger bubble and crash in the near future. So, re-regulation is likely to happen when – after a sequence of crises at the periphery – a major financial crisis hits the centre of the financial system and, through contagion, hits the entire world unnerving public authorities and shaking the public's belief in the free market.

Have we reached that point? Perhaps, as implied by intense debate among the authorities on re-regulation potentially able to elicit restrictive actions across the board (a synthesis is provided in Box 12.1).

Overall, there seems to be much in common among the various reform proposals briefly sketched in Box 12.1. In each one of the proposals the main focus is on systemic risk and the consequent recommendation is recognizing the need for macro-prudential supervision. In turn, this calls for:

1 Empowering an institution with the appropriate authority and responsibility (the Fed in the USA, the ESRC in the EU, not clear for East Asia);

Box 12.1 The prospective financial reforms

This Box describes the essential approach and ingredients of the reform plans and/or policy discussions outlined by the G20, USA, EU and East Asian institutions.

G20

Important decisions towards financial reform were agreed by the G20 at its 2 April 2009 meeting in London and at its 25 September 2009 meeting in Pittsburgh.

The London meeting of the G20

Among the proposed measures the ones key to our discussion were:

1 Scaling up the resources available to the IMF for crisis prevention and assistance;
2 Establishing the Financial Stability Board (FSB) with the mandate of collaborating with the IMF to provide early warning of macroeconomic and financial risks and the actions needed to address them;
3 Reshaping regulatory systems to identify and take account of macro-prudential risks;
4 Extending regulation and oversight to all systemically important financial institutions, instruments and markets, for the first time including systemically important hedge funds;
5 Endorsing and implementing the tough new principles on pay and compensation mandated by the Financial Stability Forum (predecessor to the FSB) and supporting sustainable compensation schemes and the corporate social responsibility of all firms;
6 Taking action, once recovery is assured, to improve the quality, quantity and international consistency of banks' capital. In future, regulation should prevent excessive leverage and require buffers of resources to be built up in good times;
7 Taking action against non-cooperative jurisdictions, including tax havens, standing ready to deploy sanctions to protect members' public finances and financial systems;
8 Calling on the accounting standard setters to work urgently with supervisors and regulators to improve standards on valuation and provisioning and achieve a single set of high-quality global accounting standards;

(*continued*)

Box 12.1 Continued

9 Extending regulatory oversight and registration to credit rating agencies to ensure they meet the international code of good practice, particularly to prevent unacceptable conflicts of interest.

The Pittsburgh meeting of the G20

The outcome of the September 2009 meeting of the G20 suggested that the leaders' attention was still focused on restoring financial stability via sounder regulation/supervision. The communiqué at the end of the meeting stressed that 'where reckless behaviour and a lack of responsibility led to crisis, we will not allow a return to banking as usual'. It also committed to: raise capital standards; implement strong international compensation standards aimed at ending practices that lead to excessive risk-taking; improve the over-the-counter derivatives market; and create more powerful tools to hold large global firms to account for the risks they take, where the standards for large global financial firms should be commensurate with the cost of their failure. The G20 mandated the FSB to include major emerging economies and coordinate and monitor progress in strengthening financial regulation. More specific measures were designated to: building high-quality capital and mitigating procyclicality; reforming compensation practices to support financial stability; improving over-the-counter (OTC) derivatives markets; addressing cross-border resolutions and systemically important financial institutions. Regarding the controversial issue of the bonuses, it was agreed that more should be paid out in shares rather than cash, and more pay should be deferred. In particular, efforts should be made to tie remuneration more closely to long-term value creation – more paid in restricted shares, with employers able to claw back a portion if trades lead to big losses and multi-year bonus guarantees to be avoided.

It is also worth noting that, in the preamble, the world leaders admonished 'a sense of normalcy should not lead to complacency'.

The USA

In the USA, President Obama put forward his blueprint for reform on 17 June 2009.[a] In essence, this was a wide-range proposal that, if adopted, would greatly overhaul the financial system. It tackles

(*continued*)

Box 12.1 Continued

several issues with a macro-prudential approach under the authority and responsibility of the Fed:

1 Promoting robust supervision and regulation of financial firms: creating a Financial Services Oversight Council to facilitate information sharing and coordination, identify emerging risks and assist the Fed on the identification of firms whose failure could pose a threat to financial stability due to their combination of size, leverage and interconnectedness (Tier 1 FHCs); facilitating coordination among all the relevant agencies; implementing heightened consolidated supervision and regulation of all large, interconnected financial firms; strengthening capital and other prudential standards for all banks and BHCs; better aligning executive compensation practices of financial firms with long-term shareholder value and to prevent compensation practices from providing incentives that could threaten the safety and soundness of supervised institutions; adopting accounting standards to induce financial firms to employ more forward-looking loan loss provisioning practices that incorporate a broader range of available credit information; revise fair value accounting rules to provide users of financial reports with both fair value information and greater transparency regarding the cash flows management expects to receive by holding investments; strengthening firewalls between banks and their affiliates to protect the federal safety net that supports banks and to prevent spread of the subsidy inherent in the federal safety net to bank affiliates; close loopholes in bank regulation; requiring hedge funds and other private pools of capital to register; reducing the susceptibility of money market mutual funds to runs; enhancing oversight of the insurance sector;

2 Establishing comprehensive regulation of financial markets: strengthening supervision and regulation of securitization markets requiring originators to retain an economic interest in a material portion of the credit risk of securitized credit exposures, aligning compensation of market participants with longer-term performance of the underlying loans and increasing the transparency and standardization of securitization markets requiring robust reporting by issuers of ABS; strengthening the regulation

(*continued*)

Box 12.1 Continued

of credit rating agencies including robust policies/procedures to manage and disclose conflicts of interest, differentiate between structured and other products, and otherwise strengthen the integrity of the ratings process and reducing the use of credit ratings in regulations and supervisory practices; creating comprehensive regulation of all OTC derivatives, including CDS; harmonizing futures and securities regulation.

3 Protecting consumers and investors from financial abuse: creating a new Consumer Financial Protection Agency with the authority/responsibility to improve: a) transparency; b) simplicity; c) fairness; d) access; strengthening investor protection through the SEC.

4 Providing the government with the tools it needs to manage financial crises: creating a resolution regime for failing BHCs, including Tier 1 FHCs; amending the Fed's emergency lending authority so that it will not need prior written approval of the Secretary of the Treasury for any extensions of credit by the Fed to individuals, partnerships or corporations in 'unusual and exigent circumstances'.

5 Raising international regulatory standards and improving international cooperation: recommending the Basel Committee on Banking Supervision (BCBS) to improve Basel II by refining risk weights for trading book/securitized products, introducing supplemental leverage ratio and improving the definition of capital; urging BCBS to review the Basel II framework to mitigate its procyclical effects; improving the oversight of global financial markets urging national authorities to promote the standardization and improved oversight of credit derivative and other OTC derivative markets, in particular through the use of central counterparties, along the lines of the G20 commitment, and to advance these goals through international coordination and cooperation; enhancing supervision of internationally active financial firms with the involvement of the FSB; with the help of BCBS, BIS and FSB, reforming crisis-prevention and management authorities and procedures and set standards to develop macro-prudential tools; expanding the scope of regulation by setting the appropriate Tier 1 FHC definition and application of requirements for foreign financial firms, asking national authorities to

(*continued*)

Box 12.1 Continued

quickly implement the G20 commitment to require hedge funds to register and disclose the information necessary to assess the related systemic risk; introducing better compensation practices not providing incentives for excessive risk-taking; improving accounting standards by clarifying and making consistent the application of fair value and improving loan loss provisioning to make it more forward looking; tightening the oversight of the credit rating agencies.

The EU

In October 2008, Europe launched a High-Level Group on Financial Supervision in the EU chaired by J. de Larosière. The Group finalized its report by the end of February 2009.[b] Following a one-month consultation period, the European Commission's action in the area of supervision has been inspired by the findings and recommendations of this report. After examining in detail the numerous causes of the crisis, the report covers the issues of how to organize the supervision of financial institutions and markets in the EU; how to strengthen European cooperation on financial stability oversight, early warning and crisis mechanisms; and how EU supervisors should cooperate globally. The Group made a number of recommendations on regulation of financial markets. Regarding the new European financial supervisory framework, these recommendations are based on two pillars:

- a European System of Financial Supervisors (ESFS), for the supervision of individual financial institutions ('micro-prudential supervision') consisting of new European Supervisory Authorities working in tandem with the national financial supervisors, and
- a European Systemic Risk Council (ESRC) to oversee the stability of the financial system as a whole ('macro-prudential supervision') and provide early warning of systemic risks and recommendations where necessary.

The Spring European Council agreed on the need to improve both regulation and supervision of financial institutions in the EU and endorsed the de Larosière report as its basis for action. The key principles for the reform of financial market supervision were further

(*continued*)

Box 12.1 Continued

discussed by EU Finance Ministers and central bank Governors at the informal Ecofin Council in Prague on 4 April 2009. The Commission was then asked to prepare a document to evaluate the action plan.

To synthesize, the key points of the de Larosière approach are the following:[c]

1 Policy, regulatory and supervisory processes are intertwined but should be appropriately separated from an analytical and operational point of view. The interpretation of the main failures behind the crisis and the suggested course of repair hinge on this premise; the innovation of separating macro- and micro-prudential supervision allows to focus on the missing link of previous approaches: the need to identify and limit the distress of the financial system as a whole. Macro-prudential corrective action may require suggesting and bringing forth changes in economic policies.

2 The key underlying factors behind the crisis were: a) ample liquidity creation; b) low interest-rate conditions; c) global savings glut and excessive investment in housing notably in the USA; d) the financing of large US current account deficits by emerging countries who pegged their currencies to the dollar, imported US monetary policy and accumulated large reserves, which fuelled further global monetary expansion.

3 In this process, macro-prudential supervision was lacking, as well as multilateral surveillance on economic policies.

4 The lack of adequate macro-prudential oversight, on the one hand, resulted in inappropriate economic policies and ineffective identification of global risks, and, on the other, in regulatory weaknesses, and ineffective micro-prudential supervision. Key elements of regulation applied by microsupervisors thus played a negative role in fuelling the crisis. Official regulation in some cases aggravated things, generated perverse effects and contributed to the excesses of securitization.

5 The fundamental change implicit in the de Larosière Report is apparent. The traditional approach may be represented in terms of a 'ladder' scheme to the relationship between economic policy,

(*continued*)

Box 12.1 Continued

regulation and supervision. This top-down approach – abiding by the Lamfalussy process – puts economic policy at the tip, regulation follows and enforcement of regulation is delegated to relevant supervisors. Hence, national governments (parliaments) and the Ecofin decide economic policies, subject to European constraints.

6 The de Larosière model differs fundamentally. The innovation consists in macro-prudential oversight. Macro-prudential supervision is not confined to banks, but encompasses all sectors of finance, as well as the wider macroeconomic context. This oversight should also take account of global issues. Macro-prudential analysis addresses common or correlated shocks and shocks to those parts of the financial system that trigger contagious knock-on or feedback effects and stresses two main dynamic functions of oversight: a) identifying systemically important components of the financial system (intermediaries, markets, securities, products, derivatives) and sources of systemic risk; b) deciding which form of regulation/supervision is appropriate to which institution/market. Macro- and micro-prudential supervision are both necessary and important. Though they are intertwined, they should be clearly identified and kept logically separate. Macro-prudential supervision plays a key role, directly and in terms of interactions, not only with economic policy and micro-prudential action, but also with regulation. With specific reference to this last link, a clear lesson of the recent crisis is that better regulation can only be achieved in terms of a two-way relationship with adequate supervisory arrangements.

7 The Report suggests assigning the macro-prudential oversight to the newly created ESRC, under the auspices of the ECB, while conferring micro-prudential competences, according to a step-by-step plan, to the ESFS, based on independent 'Authorities' and on the network of national supervisors.

8 The ESFS should have the authority – with eventual override when needed – to settle the possible disputes between national supervisors should the case emerge of them being engaged with different views on the same intermediary operating cross-border.

(*continued*)

Box 12.1 Continued

East Asia

On its part, Emerging East Asia (EEA) also intensely debated actions to be taken to strengthen the set of finance through the region. The following considerations/guidelines were put forward by ADB:[d]

a) *Revamping regulatory structures*:
   - a.1 eliminating gaps and overlaps, avoiding regulatory arbitrage, increasing transparency and improving coordination among relevant authorities;
   - a.2 though there is no 'one-size-fits-all' regulatory structure, there is growing acceptance that an integrated approach to macro-prudential oversight and financial stability is needed.
   - a.3 reconsidering the supervisory role of central banks (e.g. lender of last resort role).

b) *Broadening regulatory parameters*:
   - b.1 extending supervision over a wider set of market segments and institutions – especially those deemed systemically important.
   - b.2 make effort to recognize what constitutes systemic importance and to identify or define these systemically critical institutions.
   - b.3 strengthening tests of systemic risk by assessing the financial institution's position and influence in the market, as well as its size.

c) *Strengthening prudential requirements*:
   - c.1 follow up on the broad agreement among financial regulators that existing capital adequacy requirements must be increased and supplemented by a forward-looking assessment of risks.
   - c.2 strengthening bank liquidity management and supervision at EEA authorities by determining whether banks could fall victim to problems encountered by institutions in advanced economies.
   - c.3 the riskiness of a bank's assets – as shown by the crisis – is intimately linked to a bank's funding source and its term structure.
   - c.4 capital adequacy requirement should also take into account the amount of leverage undertaken by a bank or non-bank financial institution.

(*continued*)

Box 12.1 Continued

c.5 the combination of these additional capital charges should be applied to the basic CAR, as in Tier 1 capital.

c.6 growing support for counteracting the pro-cyclicality of capital and liquidity requirements through the business cycle (e.g. anti-cyclical capital buffers).

c.7 such a dynamic provisioning helps recognize credit risks posed by the possibility of expected future losses – it can also limit excessive bank credit growth.

c.8 another more direct counter-cyclical mechanism is to add a capital charge linked to a measure of excessive credit growth.

d) *Formalizing macro-prudential supervision*:

d.1 system-wide macro-prudential supervision should complement extant micro-prudential regulation.

d.2 macro-prudential supervision (MPS) aims to ensure financial system stability by focusing on overall market trends or turning points – factors that can signal emerging systemic risks.

d.3 an effective MPS requires comprehensive supervision and analysis of how a failure in any segment of a financial system – whether bank or non-bank-related – affects the risks associated with any other segment or the system as a whole.

e) *Improving accounting standards and credit rating systems*:

e.1 in the run-up to the crisis, mark-to-market accounting, in combination with the pro-cyclical characteristics of asset prices, contributed to the delay in seeing rising risks and interdependencies.

e.2 the crisis identified several flaws in the design and function of credit rating agencies.

f) *Enhancing corporate governance*:

f.1 the crisis drew attention to flawed compensation incentives for financial managers and traders that rewarded imprudent short-term risk-taking.

g) *Promoting better cross-border cooperation*:

g.1 the crisis showed that the established framework for cross-border coordination and cooperation through memorandums of understanding and a College of Supervisors have limitations.

(*continued*)

Box 12.1 Continued

g.2 supervision of liquidity management of cross-border banks lacked consistency; an important issue as liquidity across domestic and international capital markets tightened.

g.3 a more effective cross-border bank resolution process needs to be established.

g.4 there are several models addressing cross-border issues, ranging at the extremes from establishing a global supranational authority to tightly regulating cross-border activities.

h) *The way forward*:

h.1 EEA must play its part in ensuring the new financial architecture meets both the challenges of globalized finance and the region's financial development agenda.

h.2 an important distinction should be made between the basic elements of capital market development and risky financial innovation.

h.3 the key challenge for the region's regulators is how to encourage and manage financial market development without stifling innovation.

h.4 EEA economies should reinforce cooperation on enhancing financial stability by accelerating regional initiatives.

h.5 EEA must play an appropriate role in shaping the new global financial architecture, with support from international financial institutions and multilateral development banks.

Notes

[a] US Department of the Treasury (2009).

[b] J. de Larosière (2009) *Report of the de Larosière Group*, Brussels: European Commission, 25 February.

[c] R. S. Masera (2009) Intervention, High-Level Conference 'Towards a New Supervisory Architecture in Europe', European Parliament, 7 May.

[d] ADB – Asian Development Bank (2009) *Asia Economic Monitor*, July.

2 Defining procedures to identify where serious systemic risks may build up (e.g. large/interconnected financial institutions; inadequately regulated shadow banking system; excessive leverage; unregulated OTC markets; cyclical accounting standards/capital regulation; excessive risk-taking incentives in compensation schemes; excessively optimistic expectations validated by external subjects like the credit rating agencies);

3 Proposing ways to tame and/or manage those risks (stricter regulation and supervision of systemic-threatening financial institutions

on a consolidated basis; prescribing maximum leverage ratios and building firewalls where needed; extending regulation/supervision to the hedge funds; regulating and providing oversight on OTC markets; selecting less cyclical accounting standards and anti-cyclical capital requirements; introducing longer-term-based compensation schemes; requiring originators to retain an economic interest in a material portion of the credit risk of securitized loans; prescribing regulation and oversight for the credit rating agencies).

A further important feature of the reform plans regards the direct links among the various dimensions they touch upon: macro-prudential supervision; micro-prudential supervision; regulation; macroeconomic policies. As represented in Table 12.1, all three proposals (USA, EU, East Asia) recognize the strong link between macro-prudential supervision and micro-prudential supervision. The same is true for the link between macro-prudential supervision and regulation as well as for that between micro-prudential supervision and regulation. Also, none of the plans features a direct link between micro-prudential supervision and regulation. However, the important difference among the three blueprints for financial reform concerns the links between macro-prudential supervision and macroeconomic policies, and that between regulation and macroeconomic policies. While these links are present for the EU and East Asia (i.e. adding a capital charge linked to a measure of excessive credit growth links regulation and macroeconomic policies) they are lacking in the US proposal.

This difference seems to stem from a different interpretation of the origin of the Great Crisis. While the EU and East Asia give great part of the responsibility for the crisis to the US global imbalance and its exceedingly lenient macroeconomic policies, the US proposal does not appear to acknowledge this explicitly.

Even though the experience of the Great Crisis of 2007–09 may lead one to doubt that this is always the case,[3] it is right to think that financial innovation is generally beneficial to the economy as it allows improving risk sharing and access to external financing. So it is important to ask whether the prospective reform would make financial innovation more sustainable.

Several of the prospective measures go in the right direction. The identification of the macro-prudential function, its assignment to a specific authority, and stricter regulation and supervision of systemic-threatening financial institutions on a consolidated basis should indeed contribute to rein in systemic risk overall. At the same time, extending

Table 12.1 Links among the various policy dimensions of the proposed financial reforms

	Macro-prudential supervision	**Micro-prudential supervision**	**Regulation**	**Macroeconomic policies**
Macro-prudential supervision	–	EU, East Asia, USA	EU, East Asia, USA	EU, East Asia
Micro-prudential supervision		–	EU, East Asia, USA	–
Regulation			–	EU, East Asia
Macroeconomic policies				–

regulation/supervision to the hedge funds as well as regulating and providing oversight on OTC markets should reduce the contribution to systemic risk of important segments of the financial system. In turn, introducing maximum leverage ratios and firewalls within financial conglomerates, selecting less cyclical accounting standards and anti-cyclical capital requirements, introducing longer-term-based compensation schemes, and requiring originators to retain an economic interest in a material portion of the credit risk of securitized loans should all play a part in lowering the generation of systemic risk at the individual intermediary's level. Finally, prescribing regulation and oversight for the credit rating agencies should reduce the contribution to systemic risk of individual financial products.

To make financial innovation sustainable we need to ensure that all the involved agents have the right incentives to responsible behaviour. The prospective new rules seem to take the financial system to a safer harbour. That appears to be the way to sustainable financial innovation. Perhaps, for the future, we should look more at the quality of financial innovation rather than at its quantity. Quite appropriately, the Asian Development Bank (ADB; 2009) suggests that an important distinction should be made between the basic elements of capital market development and risky financial innovation. Let us exemplify this with two cases: venture capital and securitization.

Many innovative firms in ICT (e.g. Google) and biotech as well as in other new sectors have greatly contributed to our wellbeing and even changed our lifestyles. Supporting the continuation of these innovations is paramount to improve living standards and wealth for the future. To be sure, venture capital was the fundamental engine that allowed these companies to emerge, moving swiftly from garage to global businesses. Venture capital was and is a sound financial innovation. In turn, we should make sure that venture capitalists are put in the best condition to accomplish their task. In terms of sourcing, this means helping them identify new promising business projects. Attentive bankers and/or business angels providing the initial external financing to those projects should be ingrained with the venture capitalists. As to exit strategies – where the venture capitalist finds its basic incentive via the listing of its successful intervened companies – we should ensure that venture capitalists find it easy to bring the worthy assisted companies to the Stock Exchange. To this end, it may be helpful to gear the venture capitalist within robust financial holdings endowed with the capitalization and the abilities to support such exit. In all, separating venture capital entities from bank-holding companies would probably damage this type of financial innovation.

Regarding securitization, as we have highlighted in the book, all too often the transformation from the OTH to the OTD banking model put many banks in a state of irresponsibility where their traditional screening and monitoring of borrowers were phased out. Naturally, that depended on the wrong incentives the intermediaries had. Now, if originators are required to retain an economic interest in a material portion of the credit risk of securitized loans, this will likely reinstate the right incentives for banks to screen and monitor borrowers. On the one hand, such retention could make it less palatable for the bank to securitize its loans and, thus, reduce – with respect to the past – the size of the securitized loan segment of the financial market. On the other hand, 'irresponsible' securitizations were unsustainable financial innovations and, with the crisis, investors flew away from those securities. To the contrary, the securities issued under the new prospective regulation would be sustainable innovations and investors should trust this class of securities again.

By and large, while venture capital seems to be a germane – welfare-increasing – financial innovation to be safely entrusted to small and large financial powerhouses, the same could not be said of securitization. In fact, the way securitization was put into practice often resembled circumventing innovation-building financial fragilities that by far outweighed the benefits it provided. In other words, the benefits of diversification obtained by taking to the multilateral markets previously bilaterally held financial assets were second order with respect to the damage caused by phasing out bank screening and monitoring of the borrowers. Yet securitization will provide net benefits if the appropriate incentives against opportunistic behaviour for the lenders and for the borrowers are preserved.

The gravity of the crisis has thus far induced an unusual degree of concerted action at the international level. Though we have to be patient and wait to see what the political process will eventually deliver, this is a good premise for the future. However, two considerations could doom the future. First, the signals of recovery from a severe recession and the recovery of financial markets leads us to question whether the political resolve behind reforming finance remains as strong (Cohen, 2009) when, at the same time, we see a postponing of the reform of finance in the political agenda (*The Economist*, 2009). Second, we highlighted that some of the proposals put forward might not be courageous enough. As we have seen, the debacle of finance came about because of the conjunction between the lack of a consistent international monetary order – at the root of the global imbalances – together with the spreading out of financial innovation that, de facto, made lenders less responsible – opening the Pandora's Box of ever increasing leverage. While great attention is devoted to addressing the latter problem via better regulation and supervision, not much is said on updating the international monetary order. So, the lingering question is whether better financial regulation/supervision and increased international cooperation can be entirely effective should inconsistent economic policies induce the persistence of major global imbalances.

To conclude with a look at the future, the most worrying concern is that the world does not seem to have the energy to tackle a new crisis of the same magnitude as that of 2007–09. With exhausted public finances in many developed countries, a failure to 'fix finance' could be fatal.

Appendix: Some Useful Definitions

The balance of payments

The balance of payments is the accounting scheme recording all economic transactions operated by the residents of the domestic economy with the residents of foreign economies, in a given period of time.

The balance of payments consists of two sections:

1 The current account, where real transactions (exchange of goods and services) and unilateral transfers are recorded.
2 The capital account, where purchases and sales of financial assets and properties as well as variations of official reserves are recorded.

In turn, the two sections include several subsections.

The current account is divided into:

- Exports and imports of goods. The difference between these two entries is often referred to as the trade balance.
- Exports and imports of services. This entry includes net incomes from work performed abroad by domestic residents; payments of services, such as purchase/sale of travels, insurance premiums, bank commissions; capital income (interest on foreign securities held by domestic residents, dividends paid by foreign companies to domestic residents, etc.).
- Unilateral transfers. This entry includes transactions such as donations and remittances.

The capital account is divided into:

- Direct investments: where net acquisitions of control shareholdings on foreign entities are recorded.
- Portfolio investments: where purchases and/or sales of foreign financial assets undertaken by domestic savers are recorded.
- Changes in official reserves: where transactions regarding foreign financial assets held by the central bank are recorded.
- Errors, omissions and statistical discrepancies.

The balance of payments is the sum of the current account balance and the capital account balance, including errors and omissions. By definition, it is as much as the net variation of official reserves.

The total balance of payments also includes the variation of reserves and shall always be equal to 0.

Exchange rates

- The *exchange rate* is defined as the amount (units) of a domestic currency required to buy one foreign currency unit.
- An *appreciation* of the exchange rate means that fewer domestic currency units are necessary to buy one foreign currency unit.
- A *depreciation* of the exchange rate means that more domestic currency units are necessary to buy one foreign currency unit.
- In a *flexible exchange-rate regime*, the exchange rate floats freely in order to offset the excess demand or supply of a currency with respect to any other currency.
- In a *fixed exchange-rate regime*, a country establishes the price of its currency in relation to another currency and the central bank takes on the role of offsetting the excess demand or supply of domestic or foreign currency, at the agreed-upon exchange rate, by using the country's official reserves.

Fundamental relations of international economics

- *Law of one price*: if the international markets are perfectly integrated, two identical goods must have the same price, even if they are sold in different countries.

  For any given good *i*, the Law of one price establishes that

  $$P_i = SP^*_i$$

  where P_i indicates the price of good *i* expressed in domestic currency, P^*_i indicates the price of the same good expressed in foreign currency and S indicates the exchange rate.
- The *Purchasing Power Parity* (PPP) is a generalization of the Law of one price in the case of *n* goods and establishes that two identical baskets of goods must have the same price, even if they are sold in different countries.

In formal terms:

$$P = SP^*$$

Therefore, the exchange rate between two countries can be expressed through the ratio between the relative price levels:

$$S = P/P^*$$

From the PPP, one can derive the real exchange rate, which is a very important competitiveness indicator of a country:

$$Q = (SP^*)/P$$

Q is defined as the real exchange rate and corresponds to the number of domestic baskets of goods and services required to purchase one unit of the foreign basket of goods and services. In this way, we take into consideration not only the variation of the nominal exchange rate, but also the price level variation of the two countries.

- The *Uncovered Interest Parity* (UIP) establishes that the interest rate on domestic assets equals the interest rate on similar foreign assets, plus (less) the expected appreciation (depreciation) rate of the domestic currency.
- The *Covered Interest Parity* uses forward markets to remove uncertainty on the future value of the exchange rate and establishes that the interest rate on domestic assets must equal the interest rate on similar foreign assets, plus (less) the forward discount (premium) on the exchange rate.

Notes

Chapter 1: Theories of financial crises

1 For a historical approach to the financial crises see Kindleberger (1978); for a technical approach see Allen and Gale (2007).
2 See Keynes (1936). Recently referred to by Akerlof and Shiller (2009).

Chapter 2: Macro models of financial crises

1 For a detailed analysis of the first-generation models, see Flood and Marion (1999).
2 For a detailed analysis of the second-generation models, see Jeanne (2000).

Chapter 8: Recent financial crises

1 For more details on the other two crises, see Nyberg and Vesa (1993) and Moe et al. (2004).
2 During the last quarter of 1992, at the height of the crisis, the bank losses on loans reached 7.5 per cent, that is, twice the value of the profits in this sector.
3 This mechanism is based on significant maturity mismatching between short-term liabilities and long-term lending and credit risk (which increases when the economy deteriorates as a result of interest-rate increase).
4 Treasury 'on-the-run' securities are newly issued and for this reason they are very liquid. On the other hand, Treasury 'off-the-run' securities are those issued a few months before the related 'on-the-run'. For example, a Treasury with 29 years and six-month term was 'on-the-run' six months ago, but it is now 'off-the-run', because a new 30-year security was issued. 'On-the-run' securities have more liquid markets as compared with 'off-the-run' securities and for this reason they are slightly more expensive.
5 Edwards (1999) reports that 33 per cent of hedge funds do not use any leverage, 54 per cent use a 1 to 1 leverage and just a few exceed the 10 to 1 ratio.
6 Statistical model indicating the worst potential loss, given a certain level of confidence, in a given timeframe.
7 The US financial legislation allows one party of the derivative contract to sell off assets in the case of default of the counterparty.
8 For example, in the case of the fragile democracy in Turkey, the opening of international capital flows would increase the recurrent 'populist cycles', with the subsequent inability to implement economic reforms: see Alper and Onis (2001).
9 Some observers note that the IMF would be more active towards Turkey than Argentina because of Turkey's particular strategic role, especially after 11 September 2001: see Beattie (2001).

Chapter 10: The Great Crisis of 2007–09

1 The CDS price can be considered as a proxy of the risk premium because these derivatives protect against the risk of default of a company or sovereign issue.
2 The data refer to the change in correlation between the local stock market and the US market. In this case the correlation in the daily change of the stock prices increased by 75 per cent, from 0.25 to 0.44.
3 Current account deficit means that a country consumes more than it produces, hence its foreign debt.
4 From 2000 to 2006 the percentage of the subprime mortgages with complete documentation went down from 73.4 to 57.7 (Ashcraft and Schuermann, 2009).
5 For example, in June 2006, the yield of the AAA CDO tranches was twice the yield of the corporate bonds with the same rating.
6 Since the 1970s the rating agencies have changed the business model by having the commissions paid for by the issuers, and not the investors.

Chapter 11: Crisis in academic economics

1 The US blueprint for financial reform recognizes this was a serious problem. Its Section D is devoted to 'Close Loopholes in Bank Regulation'. In it, it is said: 'One clear lesson learned from the recent crisis was that *competition among different government agencies* responsible for regulating similar financial firms *led to reduced regulation* in important parts of the financial system. The presence of multiple federal supervisors of firms that could easily change their charter *led to weaker regulation and became a serious structural problem within our supervisory system*' (US Treasury, 2009, p. 32; emphasis added).
2 US Treasury (2009): 'Securitization, by breaking down the traditional relationship between borrowers and lenders, created *conflicts of interest* that market discipline failed to correct. Loan originators failed to require sufficient documentation of income and ability to pay. Securitizers failed to set high standards for the loans they were willing to buy, encouraging underwriting standards to decline. Investors were overly reliant on credit rating agencies. Credit ratings often failed to accurately describe the risk of rated products. In each case, lack of transparency prevented market participants from understanding the full nature of the risks they were taking' (p. 6; emphasis added).
3 Only through this assumption that private risk and sovereign risk are uncorrelated is it possible to derive the CAPM (Capital Asset Pricing Model) fundamental formula: $ER_i = r + \beta_i(ER^m - r)$. Where ER_i is the equilibrium expected return on risky asset *i*, r is the risk-free rate (approximated by the return on government securities), ER^m is the equilibrium expected return on the diversified portfolio and $\beta_i = \text{cov}(R_i, R^m)/\text{var}(R^m)$.
4 Adrian and Shin (2008) show that in a continuous mark-to-market set-up, leverage is strongly pro-cyclical.
5 A Pareto-improving exchange is one in which at least one party is better off and no party is worse off.

6 Though some authors (e.g. Cecchetti et al., 2000; Borio and Lowe, 2002) argue that central banks should sometimes act against asset-price bubbles, other authors (e.g. Bernanke and Gertler 1999, 2001; Kontonikas and Ioannidis, 2005; Alexandre and Bação, 2005) show that monetary policy optimally stabilizing inflation (i.e. focusing on CPI and disregarding asset prices) is normally superior. It should be mentioned that both Bernanke and Gertler were, at that time, academics external to the Fed.
7 Pain et al. (2006) show that, in OECD countries: a) import prices have become a more important driver of domestic consumer prices since the mid-1990s; b) the sensitivity of inflation to domestic economic conditions has declined whereas the sensitivity to foreign economic conditions has risen, working through import prices; and c) the strong GDP growth in the non-OECD economies over the past five years has contributed to the growth of real oil and metals prices. Thus, they conclude that globalization has put upward pressure on inflation via higher commodity prices and downward pressure via lower non-commodity import prices with the latter effect having dominated in most OECD economies. On the contrary, Ihrig et al. (2007) find little support for the hypothesis that globalization dominates inflation dynamics. At the same time, they acknowledge that the fact that the volatility of real GDP growth has declined by more than the volatility of domestic demand suggests that net exports increasingly are acting to buffer output from fluctuations in domestic demand.

Chapter 12: Conclusions and perspectives

1 According to Kindleberger, a 'mania' (or bubble) is basically just excessive speculation in the market. Mania is movement from cash or money into illiquid real assets. It implies an upward price movement over an extended range that then implodes. In turn, 'panics' refer to the period after the mania has died down, and people begin speculating in the opposite direction. As the mania was the upswing, the panic is the downswing. Panics are movements away from illiquid assets to money or cash. Finally, 'crashes' – or extended negative bubbles – are sometimes thought to be the result of a prolonged period of panic.
2 For this reason, Stephen Roach (2009) recently criticized the reappointment of Bernanke as Chairman of the Fed. In his *Financial Times* op-ed he wrote: 'While America's head central banker deserves credit for being creative and courageous in orchestrating an unusually aggressive monetary easing programme, it is important to remember that his pre-crisis actions played an equally critical role in setting the stage for the most wrenching recession since the 1930s. It is as if a doctor guilty of malpractice is being given credit for inventing a miracle cure. Maybe the patient needs a new doctor.'
3 See the negative judgement by Posen and Hintershweiger (2009).

References

Abiad, A., Balakrishnan, R., Koeva Brooks, P., Leigh, D. and Tytell, I. (2009) 'What's the Damage? Medium-term Output Dynamics After Banking Crises', IMF Working Paper 09/245.

Acharya, V. V. and Richardson, M. (2009) 'Causes of the Financial Crisis', *Critical Review*, no. 21.

Adrian, T. and Shin, S. H. (2008) 'Liquidity and Financial Cycles', BIS Working Paper no. 256.

Aizenman, J. and Jinjarak, Y. (2008) 'Current Account Patterns and National Real Estate Markets', NBER Working Paper 13921.

Akerlof, G. A. and Shiller, R. J. (2009) *Animal Spirits: How Human Psychology Drives the Economy, and Why It Matters for Global Capitalism*, Princeton University Press.

Alexandre, F. and Bação, P. (2005) 'Monetary Policy, Asset Prices, and Uncertainty', *Economics Letters*, vol. 86, no. 1, 37–42.

Allen, F. and Gale, D. (2000) *Comparing Financial Systems*, Cambridge, MA: The MIT Press.

Allen, F. and Gale, D. (2007) *Understanding Financial Crises*, Oxford University Press.

Alper, C. E. and Onis, Z. (2001) 'Financial Globalization, the Democratic Deficit and Recurrent Crises in Emerging Markets: The Turkish Experience in the Aftermath of Capital Account Liberalization', Bogazici University ISS/EC Working Paper no. 01–14.

Ashcraft, A. B. and Schuermann, T. (2008) 'Understanding the Securitization of Subprime Mortgage Credit', Federal Reserve Bank of New York Staff Reports 318, Now Publishers.

Ashcraft, A. and Schuermann, T. (2009) '7 Deadly Frictions in Subprime Mortgage Securitization', International Financial Research Forum: 'Risk Management and the Financial Crisis', Europlace Institute of Finance Paris, 19 March.

Asian Development Bank (2009) 'Asia Economic Monitor', July.

Baba, N. and Hisada, T. (2002) 'Japan's Financial System: Its Perspective and the Authorities' Role in Redesigning and Administering the System', Institute for Monetary and Economic Studies, Bank of Japan, discussion paper no. 02-E-1.

Bagehot, W. (1873) *Lombard Street*, London: H. S. King.

Bank for International Settlements (2009) '79th Annual Report: 1 April 2008–31 March 2009', Basel, 29 June.

Barth, J. R., Bartholomew, P. F. and Bradley, M. G. (1990) 'Determinants of Thrift Institution Resolution Costs', *Journal of Finance*, vol. 45, no. 3, 731–54.

Barth, J. R. and Bradley, M. G. (1989) 'Thrift Deregulation and Federal Deposit Insurance', *Journal of Financial Services Research*, vol. 2, 231–59.

Barth, J. R. and Regalia, M. A. (1989) 'The Evolving Role of Regulation in the Savings and Loan Industry', in C. England and T. Huertas (eds) *The Financial Services Revolution: Policy Directions for the Future*, Boston: Kluwer Academic Publishers, 113–61.

Beattie, A. (2001) 'Turkey and Argentina Cause Headaches to the IMF', *Financial Times*, 28 November.
Benati, L. and Mumtaz, H. (2005) 'The "Great Stability" in the UK: Good Policy or Good Luck?', Bank of England, mimeo.
Benati, L. and Surico, P. (2009) 'VAR Analysis and the Great Moderation', *The American Economic Review*, vol. 99, no. 4, 1636–52.
Benhabib, J., Schmitt-Grohé, S. and Uribe, M. (2001) 'The Perils of Taylor Rules', *Journal of Economic Theory*, vol. 96, 40–69.
Benmelech, E. and Dlugosz, J. (2009a) 'The Alchemy of CDO Credit Ratings', *Journal of Monetary Economics*, Carnegie-Rochester Conference, vol. 56, no. 5.
Benmelech, E. and Dlugosz, J. (2009b) 'The Credit Rating Crisis', NBER Working Paper 15045.
Bernanke, B. S. (1983) 'Non-Monetary Effects of the Financial Crisis in the Propagation of the Great Depression', *American Economic Review*, vol. 73, 257–76.
Bernanke, B. S. (2002) 'On Milton Friedman's Ninetieth Birthday', Remarks by Governor Bernanke at the Conference to Honor Milton Friedman, University of Chicago, Chicago, 8 November.
Bernanke, B. S. (2004) 'The Great Moderation', Federal Reserve Board, Speech at the Meeting of the Eastern Economic Association, Washington, DC, USA.
Bernanke, B. S. (2005) 'The Global Saving Glut and the US Current Account Deficit', Remarks at the Sandridge Lecture, Virginia Association of Economics, Richmond, VA.
Bernanke, B. S. (2007) 'Global Imbalances: Recent Developments and Prospects', Federal Reserve Board, Speech at the Bundesbank Lecture, Berlin, Germany.
Bernanke, B. S. and Gertler, M. (1995) 'Inside the Black Box: The Credit Channel of Monetary Policy Transmission', *Journal of Economic Perspectives*, vol. 9, 27–48.
Bernanke, B. S. and Gertler, M. (1999) 'Monetary Policy and Asset Price Volatility', in Federal Reserve Bank of Kansas City, *New Challenges for Monetary Policy*, 77–128.
Bernanke, B. S. and Gertler, M. (2001) 'Should Central Banks Respond to Movements in Asset Prices?', *American Economic Review* (May), 253–7.
BIS (Bank for International Settlements) (2009) '79th Annual Report: 1 April 2008–31 March 2009', Basel, 29 June.
Blanchard, O. (2008) 'The Crisis, Basic Mechanism and Appropriate Policies', IMF Working Paper no. 09/80.
Bolton, P., Freixas, X. and Shapiro, J. (2009) 'The Credit Ratings Game', NBER Working Paper 14712.
Bongini, P., Chiarlone, S. and Ferri, G. (2009) *Emerging Banking Systems*, Basingstoke: Palgrave Macmillan.
Bongini, P., Claessens, C. and Ferri, G. (2001) 'The Political Economy of Bank Distress: Evidence from East Asia', *Journal of Financial Services Research*, vol. 19, no. 1, 5–25.
Bongini, P., Ferri, G. and Hahm, H. (2000) 'Corporate Bankruptcy in Korea: Only the Strong Survive?', *The Financial Review*, vol. 34, no. 4, 31–50.
Boot, A. W. A. (2000) 'Relationship Banking: What Do We Know?', *Journal of Financial Intermediation*, vol. 9, no. 1, 7–25.
Bordo, M., Eichengreen, B., Klingebiel, D. and Martinez-Peria, M. (2001) 'Is the Crisis Problem Growing More Severe?', *Economic Policy*, April, 53–82.

Borio, C. and Lowe, P. (2002) 'Asset Prices, Financial and Monetary Stability: Exploring the Nexus', BIS Working Paper 114 (July).

Bradley, M. G., Gabriel, S. A. and Wohar, M. E. (1995) 'The Thrift Crisis, Mortgage-Credit Intermediation, and Housing Activity', *Journal of Money, Credit, and Banking*, vol. 27, no. 2, 476–97.

Brunnermeier, M. K. (2008) 'Deciphering the 2007–08 Liquidity and Credit Crunch', *Journal of Economic Perspectives*, vol. 23, no. 1, 77–99.

Bryan, L. L. (1988) *Breaking up the Bank: Rethinking an Industry under Siege*, Homewood, IL: Dow Jones-Irwin.

Calvo, G. A. (1998) 'Capital Flows and Capital-Market Crises: The Simple Economics of Sudden Stops', *Journal of Applied Economics*, vol. 1, no. 1, 35–54.

Cecchetti, S., Genberg, H., Lipsky, J. and Wadhwani, S. (2000) 'Asset Prices and Central Bank Policy', Geneva Reports on the World Economy no. 2 (July), London: CEPR.

Chang, R. and Velasco, A. (1998) 'Financial Crises in Emerging Markets: a Canonical Model', NBER Working Paper 6606.

Chiodo, A. J. and Owyang, M. T. (2002) 'A Case Study of a Currency Crisis: The Russian Default of 1998', The Federal Reserve Bank of St. Louis Review (November).

Claessens, C., Djankov, S. and Ferri, G. (1999) 'Corporate Distress in East Asia: Assessing the Impact of Interest and Exchange Rate Shocks', *Emerging Markets Quarterly*, vol. 3, no. 2, 8–13.

Clarida, R., Gertler, M. and Galí, J. (2000) 'Monetary Policy Rules and Macroeconomic Stability: Theory and Some Evidence', *Quarterly Journal of Economics*, vol. 115, 147–80.

Cohen, N. (2009) 'Regulation: Doubts over Political Resolve for Reform', *Financial Times*, 5 October.

Cooke, D. and Foley, J. (1999) 'The Role of the Asset Management Entity: An East Asian Perspective', Special Report Asian Development Bank, Manila.

Corsetti, G., Pesenti, P. and Roubini, N. (1998) 'What Caused the Asian Currency and Financial Crisis?', *Japan and the World Economy*, vol. 11, no. 3, September, 305–73.

Corsetti, G., Pesenti, P. and Roubini, N. (1999) 'Paper Tigers? A Model of the Asian Crisis', *European Economic Review*, vol. 43, 1211–36.

Cuthbertson, K. and Nitzsche, D. (2004) *Quantitative Financial Economics: Stocks, Bonds and Foreign Exchange*, 2nd edn, Chichester: John Wiley & Sons.

Danske Bank (2009) 'Lessons from the Great Depression', Research Letter, 23 February.

de Cecco, M. (1974) *Money and Empire: The International Gold Standard 1890–1914*, Oxford: Basil Blackwell.

De Grauwe, P. (2009) 'Keynes Savings Paradox, Fisher's Debt Deflation and the Banking Crisis', www.eurointelligence.com, 6 April.

Dell'Ariccia, G., Igan, D. and Laeven, L. (2008) 'Credit Booms and Lending Standards: Evidence from the Subprime Mortgage Market', CERP Discussion Paper 6683.

Demirgüç-Kunt, A. and Servén, L. (2009) 'Are all the Sacred Cows Dead? Implications of the Financial Crisis for Macro and Financial Policies', World Bank Policy Research Working Paper Series.

Dewatripont, M. and Tirole, J. (1994) 'A Theory of Debt and Equity: Diversity of Securities and Manager-Shareholder Congruence', *Quarterly Journal of Economics*, vol. 109, 1027–54.
Diamond, D. W. (1984) 'Financial Intermediation and Delegated Monitoring', *The Review of Economic Studies*, vol. 51, no. 3, 393–414.
Dobson, W. D. (2004) 'Parmalat', Babcock Institute Discussion Paper no. 2004–4.
Domaç, I. and Ferri, G. (1999) 'Did Financial Shocks Disproportionately Hit Small Businesses in Korea?', *Economic Notes*, vol. 28, no. 3, 403–29.
Domaç, I., Ferri, G. and Kang, T. S. (1999) 'The Credit Crunch in Asia: Evidence from Field Findings on Bank Behavior and Policy Issues', Mimeo, World Bank.
Dooley, M. and Hutchison, M. (2009) 'Transmission of the US Subprime Crisis to Emerging Markets: Evidence on the Decoupling–Recoupling Hypothesis', NBER Working Paper 15120.
Durán, M. A. (2005) 'Norm-based Crisis and Deceitful Firms', Universidad de Granada, The Papers 05/12.
Economist, The (2009), 'Wobbling: Financial Reform in America: Barack Obama's Financial Reforms Meet Political Reality', 30 July.
Edwards, F. R. (1999) 'Hedge Funds and the Collapse of Long-Term Capital Management', *Journal of Economic Perspectives*, vol. 13, no. 12, 189–210.
Eichengreen, B. (2002) 'Crisis Prevention and Management: Any New Lessons from Argentina and Turkey?', Background paper for the World Bank's Global Development Finance.
Eichengreen, B. (2008a) *Globalizing Capital: A History of the International Monetary System*, Princeton University Press.
Eichengreen, B. (2008b) 'Thirteen Questions about the Subprime Crisis', Paper prepared for a conference on the Tobin Project, 'Toward a New Theory of Financial Regulation', White Oak Conference and Residency Center, Yulee, Florida, 1–3 February.
Eichengreen, B. (2009) 'Out of the Box Thoughts about the International Financial Architecture', IMF Working Paper 09/116.
Eichengreen, B. and Irwin, D. A. (2009) 'The Slide to Protectionism in the Great Depression: Who Succumbed and Why?', NBER Working Paper 15142.
Englund, P. (1999) 'The Swedish Banking Crisis Roots and Consequences', *Oxford Review of Economic Policy*, vol. 15, no. 3.
Fama, E. F. (1991) 'Efficient Capital Markets: II', *Journal of Finance*, vol. 46, no. 5, 1575–1617.
Ferri, G. (2001) Opening Remarks, as guest editor, of the special issue (no. 3/2001) *Economic Notes* on 'Capital Adequacy Requirements: Impact and Evolution'.
Ferri, G., Liu, L. and Stiglitz, J. E. (1999) 'The Procyclical Role of Rating Agencies: Evidence from the East Asian Crisis', *Economic Notes*, vol. 28, no. 3, 335–55.
FHLMC (1996) 'Financing America's Housing: The Vital Role of Freddie Mac', Federal Home Loan Mortgage Corporation, Washington, DC.
Ficarella, N. (2004) 'Enron and Parmalat: Two Twins Parables', BA dissertation, European School of Economics, Nottingham Trent University.
Fisher, I. (1933) 'The Debt-Deflation Theory of Great Depressions', *Econometrica*, vol. 1, 337–57.
Fitch Ratings (2007) 'Inside the Ratings: What Credit Ratings Mean'.

Flood, R. P. and Garber, P. M. (1984) 'Collapsing Exchange Rate Regimes: Some Linear Examples', *Journal of International Economics*, vol. 17, 1–13.

Flood, R. and Marion, N. (1999) 'Perspectives on the Recent Currency Crisis Literature', *International Journal of Finance and Economics*, vol. 4, 1–26.

Forester, T. (1993) *Silicon Samurai: How Japan Conquered the World's IT Industry*, Oxford: Blackwell.

Friedman, M. and Schwartz, A. (1963) *A Monetary History of the United States, 1867–1960*, Princeton University Press.

Furman, J. and Stiglitz, J. E. (1998) 'Economic Crisis: Evidence and Insights from East Asia', Brookings Papers on Economic Activity.

Gerlach, S. and Smets, F. (1996) 'Contagious Speculative Attacks', BIS Working Paper no. 22.

Goldsmith, R. W. (1966) *The Determinants of Financial Structure*, Paris: OECD.

Goldsmith, R. W. (1969) *Financial Structure and Development*, New Haven: Yale University Press.

Goldstein, M. (1998) *The Asian Financial Crisis*, Washington, DC: Institute for International Economics.

Greenwald, B., Stiglitz, J. E. and Weiss, A. (1984) 'Information Imperfections in the Capital Market and Macroeconomic Fluctuations', *American Economic Review*, vol. 74, 194–9.

Haugh, D., Ollivaud, P. and Turner, D. (2009) 'The Macroeconomic Consequences of Banking Crises in OECD Countries', OECD Economics Department Working Papers 683.

Hesse, H. and Čihák, M. (2007) 'Cooperative Banks and Financial Stability', IMF Working Paper 07/2 (January).

Hoshi, T. and Kashyap, A. (1999) 'The Japanese Banking Crisis: Where Did it Come from and How Will it End?', NBER Working Paper 7250.

Ihrig, J., Kamin, S. B., Lindner, D. and Marquez, J. (2007) 'Some Simple Tests of the Globalization and Inflation Hypothesis', Board of Governors of the Federal Reserve System, International Finance Discussion Papers no. 891 (April).

IMF (1999) 'Russian Federation: Recent Economic Development', IMF Staff Country Report no. 99/100.

IMF (2001) *IMF Survey*, vol. 30, no. 23 (10 December), 385–6.

IMF (2006) 'World Economic Outlook: Financial Systems and Economic Cycles' (September), IMF.

IMF (2009a) 'Country Report no. 09/247', IMF.

IMF (2009b) 'Sustaining the Recovery', World Economic Outlook (October), IMF.

Jeanne, O. (2000) 'Currency Crises: A Perspective on Recent Theoretical Developments', Special Papers in International Economics, no. 20, International Finance Section, Princeton University.

Jonung, L., Kiander, J. and Vartia, P. (2008) 'The Great Financial Crisis in Finland and Sweden: The Dynamics of Boom, Bust and Recovery', Economic Papers 350, European Commission.

Kaminsky, G. and Reinhart, C. (1999) 'The Twin Crises: The Causes of Banking and Balance-of-Payments Problems', *American Economic Review*, vol. 89, 473–500.

Kanaya, A. and Woo, D. (2000) 'The Japanese Banking Crisis of the 1990s: Sources and Lessons', IMF Working Paper 00/7.

Keynes, J. M. (1936) *The General Theory of Employment, Interest and Money*, London: Macmillan.

Keys, B., Mukherjee, T., Seru, A. and Vig, V. (forthcoming) 'Did Securitization Lead to Lax Screening? Evidence from Subprime Loans', *Quarterly Journal of Economics*, vol. 125, no. 1.

Kindleberger, C. P. (1978) *Manias, Panics and Crashes: A History of Financial Crises*, Basingstoke: Palgrave Macmillan.

Komulainen, T. (1999) 'Currency Crisis Theories: Some Explanations for the Russian Case', BOFIT Discussion Papers no. 1.

Kontonikas, A. and Ioannidis, C. (2005) 'Should Monetary Policy Respond to Asset Price Misalignments?', *Economic Modelling*, vol. 22, no. 6, 1105–21.

Kose, M. A., Otrok, C. and Prasad, E. S. (2008) 'Global Business Cycles: Convergence or Decoupling', NBER Working Paper 14292.

Krugman, P. (1979) 'A Model of Balance of Payments Crises', *Journal of Money, Credit, and Banking*, no. 11, 311–25.

Krugman, P. (1992) *The Age of Diminished Expectations: US Economic Policy in the 1990s*, Cambridge, MA: The MIT Press.

Krugman, P. (1998) 'What Happened to Asia?', Unpublished paper, MIT.

Krugman, P. (2000) *The Return of Depression Economics*, Harmondsworth: Penguin Books.

Leijonhufvud, A. (2009) 'Macroeconomics and the Crisis: A Personal Appraisal', CEPR Policy Insight 41.

Lowenstein, R. (2000) *When Genius Failed: The Rise and Fall of Long-Term Capital Management*, New York: Random House.

Mason, J. R. and Rosner, J. (2007) 'Where Did the Risk Go? How Misapplied Bond Ratings Cause Mortgage Backed Securities and Collateralized Debt Obligation Market Disruptions', Hudson Institute Working Paper.

Mathis, J., McAndrews, J. and J. C. Rochet (2009) 'Rating the Raters: Are Reputation Concerns Powerful enough to Discipline Rating Agencies?', *Journal of Monetary Economics*, vol. 56, no. 5, 657–74.

Mian, A. R. and Sufi, A. (2009) 'The Consequences of Mortgage Credit Expansion: Evidence from the US Mortgage Default Crisis', *Quarterly Journal of Economics*, vol. 124, no. 4 (November).

Miller, M. and Zhang, L. (2000) 'Sovereign Liquidity Crises: The Strategic Case for a Payments Standstill', *Economic Journal*, vol. 110, no. 1, 335–62.

Minsky, H. P. (1975) *John Maynard Keynes*, Cambridge University Press.

Mishkin, F. S. (1996) 'Understanding Financial Crises: A Developing Country Perspective', NBER Working Paper no. W5600.

Mishkin, F. S. (1999) 'Global Financial Instability: Framework, Events, Issues', *Journal of Economic Perspectives*, vol. 13, no. 4, 3–20.

Moe, T. G., Solheim, J. A. and Vale, B. (2004) 'The Norwegian Banking Crisis', Norges Bank Occasional Paper no. 33.

Nakamura, R. (2002) 'The Big Cleanse: The Japanese Response to the Financial Crisis of the 1990s Seen from a Nordic Perspective', Stockholm School of Economics, European Institute of Japanese Studies Working Paper 149.

Nurkse, R. (1944) *International Currency Experience: Lessons of the Interwar Period*, Geneva: League of Nations.

Nyberg, P. and Vesa, V. (1993) 'The Finnish Banking Crisis and its Handling', Bank of Finland Discussion Paper 8/1993.

Obstfeld, M. (1996) 'Models of Currency Crises with Self-fulfilling Features', *European Economic Review*, vol. 40, no. 3, 1037–47.

Obstfeld, M. (1998) 'The Global Capital Market: Benefactor or Menace?', *Journal of Economic Perspectives*, vol. 12, no. 4, 9–30.
Odgen Jr, W., Rangan, N. and Stanley, T. (1989) 'Risk Reduction in S&L Mortgage Loan Portfolios Through Geographic Diversification', *Journal of Financial Services Research*, vol. 2, 39–48.
Orphanides, A. (2008) 'Taylor Rules', in S. N. Durlauf and L. E. Blume (eds) *The New Palgrave Dictionary of Economics*, 2nd edn, Basingstoke: Macmillan, 200–4.
Pagano, M. and Volpin, P. (2008) 'Securitization, Transparency, and Liquidity', CEPR Discussion Papers 7105.
Pain, N., Koske, I. and Sollie, M. (2006) 'Globalisation and Inflation in the OECD Economies', OECD Economics Department Working Papers 524.
Petersen, M. A. and Rajan, R. G. (2002) 'Does Distance Still Matter? The Information Revolution in Small Business Lending', *Journal of Finance*, vol. 57, no. 6, 2533–70.
Posen, A. S. and Hintershweiger, M. (2009) 'How Useful were Recent Financial Innovations? There is Reason to be Skeptical', *Real Time Economic Issues Watch*, Peterson Institute for International Economics (7 May).
Prabhu, S. (2001) 'Long-Term Capital Management: The Dangers of Leverage', *Duke Journal of Economics*, no. 4, 24–41.
Radelet, S. and Sachs, J. (1998) 'The Onset of the East Asian Financial Crisis', NBER Working Paper 6680.
Rajan, R. G. (1994) 'Why Bank Credit Policies Fluctuate: A Theory and Some Evidence', *Quarterly Journal of Economics*, vol. 109, no. 2, 399–441.
Reinhart, C. M. and Rogoff, K. S. (2008) 'Is the 2007 US Sub-prime Financial Crisis So Different? An International Historical Comparison', *American Economic Review*, vol. 98, no. 2, 339–44.
Reinhart, C. M. and Rogoff, K. S. (2009) *This Time is Different: Eight Centuries of Financial Folly*, Princeton University Press.
Roach, S. (2009) 'The Case against Bernanke', *Financial Times*, 25 August.
Romer, C. D. (1993) 'The Nation in Depression', *Journal of Economic Perspectives*, vol. 7, no. 2, 19–39.
Romer, C. D. (2009) 'The Lessons of 1937', *The Economist* (Economics focus), 18 June.
Rosenberg, M. (1996) *Currency Forecasting: A Guide to Fundamental and Technical Models of Exchange Rate Determination*, Chicago: Irwin Professional Publishing.
Rudebusch, G. D. (2009) 'The Fed's Monetary Policy Response to the Current Crisis', FRBSF Economic Letter.
Scott, J. A. (2006) 'Loan Officer Turnover and Small Firm Credit Availability', *Journal of Small Business Management* (October).
Shiller, R. J. (2000) *Irrational Exuberance*, Princeton University Press.
Skreta, V. and Veldkamp, L. (2009) 'Rating Shopping and Asset Complexity: A Theory of Ratings Inflation', *Journal of Monetary Economics*, vol. 56, no. 5 (July), 678–95.
Sridharan, U. V., Dickes, L. and Caines, W. R. (2002) 'The Social Impact of Business Failure: Enron', *American Journal of Business*, vol. 17, no. 2, 11–21.
Stiglitz, J. E. (2002) *Globalization and its Discontents*, New York: W. W. Norton.
Stiglitz, J. E. and Weiss, A. M. (1981) 'Credit Rationing in Markets with Imperfect Information', *American Economic Review*, vol. 71, 393–410.

Summers, L. H. (2000) 'International Financial Crises: Causes, Prevention, and Cures', Richard T. Ely Lecture, *American Economic Association Papers and Proceedings*.
Suzuki, K. (2002) 'Organizational Learning Capacity of Policy-Making System for Financial System Recovery: The Case of Sweden with Some Suggestions to Japan', Stockholm School of Economics, European Institute of Japanese Studies Working Paper no. 148.
Taleb, N. N. (2007) *The Black Swan: The Impact of the Highly Improbable 2007*, New York: Random House.
Taylor, J. B. (1993) 'Discretion versus Policy Rules in Practice', *Carnegie-Rochester Conference Series on Public Policy*, vol. 39, 195–214.
Taylor, J. B. (2007) 'Housing and Monetary Policy', Paper presented at the 2007 Jackson Hole Conference, WY.
Taylor, J. B. (2009) 'To Prevent Bubbles, Don't Create Them', http://johnbtaylorsblog.blogspot.com, 11 October.
Thomson, J. B. (1993) 'The Cost of Buying Time: Lessons from the Thrift Debacle', Federal Reserve Bank of Cleveland.
US Department of the Treasury (2009) 'Financial Regulatory Reform: A New Foundation. Rebuilding Financial Supervision and Regulation' (June). www.financialstability.gov.
Vercelli, A. (2001) 'Minsky, Keynes and the Structural Instability of a Sophisticated Monetary Economy', in R. Bellofiore and P. Ferri (eds) *Financial Fragility and Investment in the Capitalist Economy*, Cheltenham: Edward Elgar.
Wälti, S. (2009) 'The Myth of Decoupling', manuscript, Swiss National Bank.
White, L. J. (1997) 'The Legacy of Deposit Insurance: The Growth, Spread and Cost of Insuring Financial Intermediaries', NBER Working Paper 6063.
Williams, M. A., De Silva, H., Koehn, M. F. and Ornstein, S. I. (1991) 'Why Did So Many S&L Go Bankrupt?', *Economic Letters*, vol. 36, 61–6.
Williamson, J. (1989) 'What Washington Means by Policy Reform', in J. Williamson (ed.) *Latin American Readjustment: How Much Has Happened*, Washington, DC: Institute for International Economics.
Winston, C. (1993) 'Economic Deregulation: Days of Reckoning for Microeconomists', *Journal of Economic Literature*, vol. 31, 1263–89.
Wolf, M. (2008) *Fixing Global Finance*, Baltimore: Johns Hopkins University Press.
World Bank (1996) *The East Asian Economic Miracle*, Washington, DC: World Bank.
Wu, T. (2006) 'Globalization's Effect on Interest Rates and the Yield Curve', Federal Reserve Bank of Dallas Economic Letter no. 9.

Index

adverse selection, 25, 27, 30, 69, 75, 164; *see also* asymmetric information; moral hazard
agency debt, 163
American International Group (AIG), 134
animal spirits, 11; *see also* Shiller, Robert
appreciation, 11, 19–20, 49, 64, 65, 70, 90, 101, 121, 144, 150, 154, 165, 202; *see also* exchange rate; *compare* depreciation
Arbitrage Pricing Theory (APT), 177; *see also* efficient market hypothesis
arranger, 158, 160, 164; *see also* special-purpose vehicle
Asian crisis, 24, 33, 35, 48, 68, 69–79, 82, 85, 88, 93, 98, 100, 171
asset-backed commercial paper (ABCP), 123, 131–2, 160, 165–7, 182
asset-backed security (ABS), 122, 131, 143, 160
asset-maturity transformation, 163
asymmetric information, 23, 25, 43, 68, 137, 164, 178, 180; *see also* adverse selection; moral hazard
auditing firm, 110–17; *see also* Enron; Parmalat

Bagehot, Walter, 14
balance-sheet channel, 30, 58, 76, 103, 143, 150; *see also* credit view
bank
  bad, 61, 63
  central, 14, 17, 18–20, 22, 39, 57, 60, 65, 76, 82, 85, 89, 105, 123, 134–7, 146, 182, 189, 191
  credit deflation, 12
  distress, 40, 42, 141, 175, 191
  holiday, 41
  lending channel, 30, 143, 154; *see also* credit view
  run, 28, 40, 42, 69, 92, 128, 144
Bank Support Authority, 61–2; *see also* Scandinavian crisis
banking
  crisis, 12, 18, 22–3, 64, 92, 138, 142
  rules, 45
  sector, 17, 22, 92, 104, 142
  system, 15, 18, 22, 23, 26, 40, 41, 42, 43, 45, 57, 66, 67, 69, 75, 76, 84, 91, 96, 100–1, 103, 107–8, 134, 163, 171, 179
bankruptcy, 4, 15, 18, 23, 28, 37, 42–3, 51, 61, 63, 67, 76, 84, 88, 104, 100–17,123, 133, 144, 157, 166, 171
  inefficient, 79
Basel Committee on Banking Supervision (BCBS), 166
Basel I, 165
Basel II, 166, 179
Bear Stearns, 89, 123, 133; *see also* investment banks
Black Monday, 40; *see also* Great Depression
Black and Scholes formula, 86, 88; *see also* Long-Term Capital Management
Black Swan, 184
Black Thursday, 40; *see also* Great Depression
Black Tuesday, 40; *see also* Great Depression
bond insurers, 130, 158
boom, 10–11, 15, 22, 39, 42, 57, 60, 64, 69, 79, 146, 149, 181
Brady Plan, 50
Bretton Woods, 34, 45
BRIC countries, 137, 145

Capital Asset Pricing Model (CAPM), 177–8; *see also* efficient market hypothesis
capitalism, 1–3, 79, 134
Case-Shiller index, 148, 150
CETES, 67; *see also* Mexican crisis
collateral, 27, 69, 150, 161
collateralized debt obligation (CDO), 122, 160, 166, 169
  cubed, 160
  high-grade, 161
  squared, 160
  tranche equity, 161
  tranche junior, 161
  tranche mezzanine, 161
  tranche senior, 162
collateralized loans obligation (CLO), 160; *see also* collateralized debt obligation
collateralized mortgage obligation (CMO), 160; *see also* collateralized debt obligation
Colosio, Luis, 67; *see also* Mexican crisis
conduit, 143, 158, 160–3; *see also* special-purpose vehicle
contagion, 23, 74, 79, 88, 139, 144, 185
cooperative banks, 175
cost-cutting deflation, 12
credit crunch, 12, 51, 76, 108
credit default swaps (CDS), 134, 144
credit easing, 136
credit enhancement, 55–6, 161
credit growth, 59, 66, 73
credit scoring, 179
credit view, 30
currency crisis, 18–23, 61, 72, 80, 89
currency mismatching, 22
currency reserve, 16, 17, 19, 49, 65, 67, 73, 83, 92, 110, 146
current account, 12, 15, 19, 22, 49, 53, 60, 64, 70, 73, 91, 96, 100, 146, 147, 191, 201

de Larosière report, 190–2
debt crisis, 18
decoupling, 136, 14–16
deflation, 12–14, 40, 44, 60–1, 79, 88, 104, 106, 129, 137, 148, 184
de-globalization, 2
deleverage, 12; *compare* leverage
deposit insurance, 43, 51, 52, 54, 61, 166
depositor, 23, 28, 40, 42, 66, 77, 84, 105, 128, 158, 166
depreciation, 13, 18, 19, 20, 39, 42, 62, 64, 65, 74, 75–6, 85, 92, 106, 144, 202; *see also* exchange rate; *compare* appreciation
depression, 12, 14, 35
  Japanese, 102, 105
  see also Great Depression
deregulation, 2–4, 10, 35, 47, 50, 52, 54, 57, 58–9, 64, 102, 108, 121, 159, 184, 185
destabilization, 3, 171, 182–5
devaluation, 11, 14, 17, 21, 23, 46, 50, 65, 67, 75–6, 84, 90, 100; *see also* exchange rate
disintermediation, 56, 165, 181

East Asia financial reform, 193
efficient market hypothesis (EMH), 176–8
Emergency Banking Act, 41
Enron, 4, 111–13, 115–16
enterprises, 13, 23, 25, 43, 68, 70, 76, 103; *see also* firms
eurodollar market, 49
European Central Bank (ECB), 123, 127, 129, 130, 134, 135, 136, 192
European financial system, 134
European System of Financial Supervisors (ESFS), 190
European Systemic Risk Council (ESRC), 190
excess demand crises, 48
excess spread, 161; *see also* securitization
exchange rate, 13–20, 35, 45, 57, 62–4, 74, 84
exchange risk, 57, 71, 73, 75
expectations, 1–3, 11, 14, 17, 21, 67, 75, 85, 89, 105, 111, 146, 150, 154
external finance premium, 30; *see also* credit view

Fama, Eugene, 176–9; *see also* efficient market hypothesis
Fannie Mae, 56, 124, 133, 163; *see also* Government-Sponsored Enterprise
fat tails, 88
Fed (Federal Reserve), 39, 42–4, 67, 86, 88, 89, 121, 126–7, 130–6, 144, 150–4, 170, 181–2, 185–9
Federal Deposit Insurance Corporation, 51
Federal Home Loan Bank Board, 51
Federal Savings and Loan Insurance Corporation, 51
financial crisis, 3, 9, 10, 14, 27, 28, 31, 35, 48, 57, 61, 64, 66, 74, 75, 76, 84, 93, 102, 119, 123, 135, 136, 137, 138–42, 144, 150, 152, 154, 170, 174, 184, 185
financial deregulation, 2, 4, 10, 35, 47, 48, 50, 52, 54, 57, 59, 102, 108, 121, 159, 184
financial fragility, 11, 16, 76, 100, 101, 107, 112
financial globalization, 45, 147
financial innovation, 2, 10, 11, 15, 31, 47, 51, 102, 113, 139, 156, 158–9, 170, 195, 198
financial instability, 1–5, 9, 14, 18, 21–2, 40, 70, 74, 83, 104, 175, 184; *see also* Minsky
financial instability hypothesis, 9; *see also* Minsky
financial liberalization, 66; *see also* liberalization
Financial Stability Board (FSB), 186
Financial Stability Forum (FSF), 186
firms, 26, 30, 32, 44, 61, 63, 70, 73, 76, 79, 103, 111, 116, 168, 181, 185; *see also* enterprise
first-generation models, 17–21, 48, 85
fiscal deficit, 50, 85
Fisher, Irving, 44
  debt deflation, 12, 60
flight to quality, 77, 87, 88, 137
foreign debt, 14–23, 49, 62–70, 81
Första Sparbanken, 60; *see also* Scandinavian crisis
Freddie Mac, 56, 124, 133, 163; *see also* Government-Sponsored Enterprise
free market economy, 1
free-riding, 27
Friedman, Milton, 43
funding liquidity, 143; *compare* market liquidity

G20, 136, 186
  London summit, 136, 186
  Pittsburgh meeting, 187
GDP growth, 18, 41, 62, 69, 74, 81, 93, 103, 136
Ginnie Mae, 56; *see also* Government-Sponsored Enterprise
GKO, 80; *see also* Russian crisis
Glass-Steagall Act, 45
global imbalances, 10, 11, 146, 147, 199, 200
globalization, 1–3, 35, 140, 159, 170, 182; *see also* financial globalization
gold exchange standard, 3, 4, 34, 45, 47, 49, 184
Gota Bank, 61; *see also* Scandinavian crisis
Government-Sponsored Enterprise (GSE), 158, 163; *see also* Fannie Mae; Freddie Mac; Ginnie Mae
Great Depression, 3, 5, 14, 37, 39–44, 45, 46, 51, 57, 102, 119, 135, 139, 144
Great Moderation, 10, 152
Greenspan, Alan, 86, 88, 105, 150
  Greenspan conundrum, 149
  Greenspan put, 89, 182

hedge fund, 86, 163; *see also* Long-Term Capital Management
households, 9, 11, 13, 14, 30, 40, 42, 44, 69, 121, 139, 147, 148, 150, 155, 158, 162, 165, 181

inflation, 10–19, 13–16, 17–19, 21, 50, 51, 52, 57, 59, 60, 61, 64, 67, 68, 72, 73, 75, 76, 80, 85, 90, 91, 92, 93, 99, 102, 106, 135, 148, 151, 152, 168, 170, 181, 182, 183

interest rate, 9–14, 18, 21, 23, 25, 26, 27, 29, 30, 31, 35, 39, 42, 44, 49, 51, 52, 53, 56, 57, 60, 61, 62, 67, 71, 75, 80, 85, 89, 90, 95, 100, 104, 123, 130, 135, 143, 146, 150, 160, 165, 181, 191
Interest Rate Control Act, 51
intermediaries, 3–4, 11, 14, 27, 30, 32, 54–5, 73, 76, 88, 107, 115, 121, 135, 143–4, 154, 158–9, 163, 171, 175, 180–2, 192, 199
international accounting standards (IAS), 179
International Monetary Fund (IMF), 15, 34–5, 46, 49, 50, 62, 79, 84, 90–2, 95, 97, 98, 100, 135, 137, 141, 175, 191, 186; *see also* Bretton Woods
investment banks, 45, 89, 114, 130, 133, 156, 163, 171, 182
investment grade security, 31, 56, 113, 116; *see also* rating agencies
investors, 2, 17, 18, 20, 21, 22, 23, 24, 30, 31, 32, 33, 40, 55, 65, 66, 67, 73, 75, 76, 80, 83, 85, 87, 88, 90, 92, 95, 100, 104, 110, 114, 116, 122, 133, 139, 143, 159, 176, 189, 199
irrational exuberance, 11, 105, 150; *see also* Shiller, Robert
IS-LM, 105
issuer, 31–3, 124, 158, 160, 162, 168, 188; *see also* special-purpose vehicle
iterative and interactive method, 168; *see also* rating agencies

Japan premium, 104
junk bond, 53
jusen company, 104

Keynesian savings paradox, 12
Kindleberger, Charles, 184; *see also* Minsky
Krueger doctrine, 96

Latin American crisis of the 1980s, 49
law of supply and demand, 155
Lehman Brothers, 133; *see also* investment banks
Lender of Last Resort (LOLR), 3, 185
leverage, 9, 39, 70, 73, 86, 89, 155, 163, 171, 174, 186, 188, 189, 193, 195, 198, 200; *compare* deleverage
liabilities, 16, 18, 22, 31, 52, 56, 60, 67, 75, 100, 115, 133, 156, 166
liberalization, 2, 11, 15–16, 22, 33, 35, 57, 64, 66, 69, 75, 79, 89, 102, 105, 146, 184; *see also* financial liberalization
liquidationist view, 43
liquidity crisis, 12, 14, 28, 65, 130, 136, 137, 143, 163
liquidity trap, 105
loans
  conforming, 163
  home equities, 156
  liar, 157
  low doc, 157
  non-performing, 53, 67, 108
Long-Term Capital Management (LTCM), 4, 85–9, 171, 173, 182
losses, 2–3, 12, 26, 28, 31, 42–3, 53, 60, 61, 63, 65, 69, 73, 75, 84, 87–8, 90, 98, 100, 110, 111, 112, 114, 123, 124, 128, 130, 134, 137, 138, 144, 159, 161, 166, 167, 172, 193–4

Madoff, Bernard, 110; *see also* Ponzi scheme
market liquidity, 143; *compare* funding liquidity
mark-to-market accounting, 155
McFadden Act, 45
Merrill Lynch, 134
Merton, Robert, 86, 88, 171; *see also* Long-Term Capital Management
Mexican crisis, 21, 64, 66, 70, 93
Minsky
  meltdown, 13
  model, 9–13, 185
  moment, 12
  see also Kindleberger, Charles

monetary policy, 14, 29, 41, 43, 51, 67, 90, 105, 121, 130, 134, 150–7, 170, 181–4, 191
  non-conventional, 136
money-market fund, 52, 124, 134
money view, 29; *compare* credit view
monitoring, 26, 117, 158, 178, 199; *compare* screening
moral hazard, 3, 22, 25–6, 30, 35, 54, 69, 75, 79, 89, 96, 98, 163, 171, 182, 185; *see also* asymmetric information
Morgan Stanley, 134
mortgage-backed security (MBS), 54, 56, 131–2, 136, 158, 160–3, 167
  commercial (CMBS), 160
  residential (RMBS), 160
mortgage brokers, 157, 158
mortgage fraud, 164
mortgages
  alternative-A, 157
  ninja, 159
  prime, 157
  second-line, 156
  subprime, 4, 11, 19, 33, 37, 51, 55, 57, 64, 119, 121–3, 128, 133, 135, 137–9, 144, 157, 161, 165, 168, 173

nationalization, 2, 14, 18, 60, 63, 113, 134
network risk, 144
New Deal, 41, 45; *see also* Great Depression
Nordbanken, 60; *see also* Scandinavian crisis
North American Free Trade Agreement (NAFTA), 64
Northern Rock, 127
Nyckeln, 60; *see also* Scandinavian crisis

originate to distribute (OTD), 158, 175, 179, 180, 199; *compare* originate to hold
originate to hold (OTH), 158, 175, 179, 180, 199; *compare* originate to distribute
originator, 55, 57, 156, 158, 160, 163, 164, 165, 188, 196, 198; *see also* special-purpose vehicle
over-the-counter (OTC), 170, 187–9, 195–6, 198

Parmalat, 113–17
Paulson, Henry, 134
Peronism, 93
petrodollars, 49
political-economy cycle of finance, 1–4, 184
Ponzi
  scheme, 110
  units 10, 11, 12
populist cycle, 89
predatory borrowing, 164
predatory lending, 164
Primary Dealer Credit Facility (PDCF), 130
principal–agent problem, 164
protectionism, 44
public debt, 18–19, 21, 44, 64, 67, 80, 81, 84, 85, 87, 90, 92, 95, 141, 142
public deficit, 15, 16, 17, 18–19, 22, 50, 52, 72, 80–1, 85, 90, 95, 96, 100, 140, 141
Purchasing Power Parity (PPP), 19

quantitative easing, 136

random walk, 177; *see also* efficient market hypothesis
rating, 31
  inflation, 168
  shopping, 168
  see also rating agencies
rating agencies, 31, 79, 113, 122, 161, 179
  Nationally Recognized Statistical Rating Organizations (NRSROs), 32
real estate, 10, 14, 18, 51, 53–6, 60, 73, 75, 102, 104, 107, 121, 125, 133, 137, 147, 150, 154, 156, 159, 160, 165

recession, 12–15, 21, 39, 40, 41, 42, 61, 69, 75, 90, 93, 102, 104, 123, 137, 138–42, 144, 150, 199
regulation, 1–5, 15, 32, 46, 52, 54, 56, 57, 58, 133, 146, 154, 158, 163, 165, 166, 170, 179, 186–200; *see also* regulatory framework; *compare* deregulation
Regulation Q, 45, 51, 53
regulatory
  capital, 63, 165, 166, 167
  forbearance, 108
  framework, 2–5, 15, 45, 51, 101, 193
  inconsistency crisis, 48
  loophole, 170
relationship banking, 175, 180
relative-value trading, 86
reputational cost, 168
re-regulation, 2–4, 54, 184–5
reset option, 122
Resolution Trust Corporation, 54
risk-pricing models, 170–5; *see also* Value-at-Risk
Roosevelt, Franklin Delano, 41
Roubini, Nouriel, 11
Russian crisis, 79, 85, 90

S&L crisis, 51
Sarbanes-Oxley Act, 117
saving glut, 146
Scandinavian crisis, 57
Scholes, Myron, 86; *see also* Long-Term Capital Management
Schwartz, Anna, 43
screening, 26, 158, 178; *compare* monitoring
second-generation models, 21, 24, 61, 65, 67, 85
securitization, 27, 33, 51, 55, 56, 121, 137, 146, 154, 155, 158–65, 165, 199; *see also* financial innovation
Security Market Line (SML), 177; *see also* Capital Asset Pricing Model
servicer, 163; *see also* special-purpose vehicle
shadow banking system, 89, 123, 163, 195
shadow exchange rate, 20
Shiller, Robert, 11, 105, 150; *see also* irrational exuberance
short-term debt, 14–22, 70, 81, 123, 133
soft information, 179; *see also* relationship banking
sovereign, 33, 97
  CDS, 144
  default, 171
  risk, 90, 171
  wealth fund, 128
special-purpose entity (SPE), 111
special-purpose vehicle (SPV), 55, 131, 158, 160–3
speculative attack, 62–7, 73–6, 84
speculative bubble, 1–4, 9, 22, 59, 75, 85, 89, 102, 105–8, 121, 148, 150, 152–4, 159, 171, 182, 184–5
  dotcom, 4, 89, 148, 150
  new economy, 10, 105, 121, 182
speculative grade securities, 31; *see also* rating agencies
speculators, 20, 21, 22
spill-over, 85; *see also* contagion
Stiglitz, Joseph, 4, 35, 79
stock market, 14, 39–40, 43, 57, 58, 62, 73, 74, 75, 84, 87, 102, 103, 107, 114, 117, 123, 134, 144
stress tests, 63
structured bond, 89, 160, 167, 168
structured investment vehicle (SIV), 143, 158, 160–3, 171
subordination, 161
supervisory
  authority, 53, 54, 63, 108
  framework, 2–3, 101, 190
  loophole, 171
systemic
  crisis, 1–4, 35, 48, 61, 70, 79, 97, 104, 107–9, 184
  risk, 3, 89, 163, 171, 179, 182, 190, 194–6, 198

tail risk, 171
Taylor rule, 105, 151
Ted spread, 123
Term Auction Facility (TAF), 130
Term Securities Lending Facility (TSLF), 130

Tesobonos, 67; *see also* Mexican crisis
third-generation models, 22–4, 75
traders, 20, 27, 86, 194
turmoil, 4–5, 61, 128
twin crises, 22, 75, 100; *see also* third-generation models

US financial reform, 187–90
US Treasury
  off-the-run, 86
  on-the-run, 86
  see also relative-value trading

Value-at-Risk (VaR), 87, 172
venture capital, 198
Volcker, Paul, 52

Washington Consensus, 34, 96
wealth, 10–13, 29, 40, 53, 60, 198
World Bank, 45, 49, 71, 84